ASSESSMENT AND INSTRUCTION OF CULTURALLY AND LINGUISTICALLY DIVERSE STUDENTS WITH OR AT-RISK OF LEARNING PROBLEMS

From Research to Practice

Virginia Gonzalez
The University of Arizona

Rita Brusca-Vega
Northeastern Illinois University

Thomas Yawkey
The Pennsylvania State University

Foreword by Leonard M. Baca
The University of Colorado at Boulder

Allyn and Bacon
Boston   London   Toronto   Sydney   Tokyo   Singapore

Senior Editor: Virginia Lanigan
Editorial Assistant: Nihad Farooq
Cover Administrator: Linda Knowles
Composition Buyer: Linda Cox
Manufacturing Buyer: Suzanne Lareau
Marketing Representative: Kathy Hunter
Production Coordinator: Deborah Brown
Editorial-Production Service: P.M. Gordon Associates
Cover Designer: Suzanne Harbison

Library of Congress Cataloging-in-Publication Data

Gonzalez, Virginia.
    Assessment and instruction of culturally and linguistically
diverse students with or at-risk of learning problems : from
research to practice / Virginia Gonzalez, Rita Brusca-Vega, Thomas
Yawkey ; foreword by Leonard M. Baca.
    p. cm.
    Includes bibliographical references and index.
    ISBN 0-205-15629-0
    1. Children of minorities—Education—United States. 2. Learning
disabled children—Education—United States. 3. Education,
Bilingual—United States. 4. Educational anthropology—United
States. I. Brusca-Vega, Rita. II. Yawkey, Thomas D. III. Title.
LC3731.G67 1996
371.97'00973—dc20   96-17473
                                                               CIP

Printed in the United States of America
10 9 8 7 6 5 4 3 2 1   01 00 99 98 97 96

To the memory of my father, Dr. Alfonso González Barrios,
and to my mother, Elvia de González,
for their unconditional support in nurturing
my developmental potential throughout my life;
and to my loving husband, Dr. Emmanuel Fernández,
for sharing the commitment to pursue our dreams.
V.G.

To my parents, Albert and Rose Brusca, for their lifelong support;
to my husband, Flavio Vega, for his unique insights about life in a diverse world;
to Janet Brusca, for sparking my interest in education and disability;
and to my students in the bilingual/English-as-a-second-language
special education program at Northeastern Illinois University
for providing a stimulating learning experience.
R.B.V.

To my wife, Dr. Margaret Louise Yawkey, for ongoing,
loving encouragement and support for my writing commitments;
to our sons, Shaun N. Yawkey and Brian M. Yawkey,
who are very happy to see "The Book" finally done;
to Dr. Mary T. Mahony, Coordinator, West Region, Office of Bilingual Education
Minority Languages' Affairs, U.S. Department of Education,
for her futuristic visions and leadership toward developing and disseminating
effective child and family programs and practices for culturally
and linguistically diverse populations;
to Mr. Gil Lopez (IN MEMORIAM), Former State Education Agency Director
of Bilingual Education, State of California, for his inspiration, dedication, planning,
and networking abilities for the good of bilingual children and parents;
and to teachers, administrators, children, and families who are using Title VII
Academic Excellence Project P.I.A.G.E.T. (Promoting Intellectual Adaptation for
Experiential Transforming) for child, family, and school development.
T.D.Y.

We also dedicate this book to the culturally and linguistically diverse (CLD)
students and the educators serving them, whose needs were our inspiration for
writing this book. We hope that our recommendations from research to practice will
have a positive impact on CLD students, and on their teachers and evaluators.
V.G., R.B.V., & T.D.Y.

CONTENTS

LIST OF FIGURES, TABLES, AND BOXES

Figures

Tables

Boxes

FOREWORD

It is a distinct pleasure and an honor for me to write a foreword for this important new text in the emerging field of bilingual special education. I am keenly aware of all the research and effort that have gone into this book. I remember vividly the early conversations and discussions I had with the authors relative to the design and direction it should take. It is thus rewarding to see the project come to closure and publication.

I was fortunate to have had the opportunity to review and critique the manuscript. This has allowed me to develop a sense of ownership as this work has evolved and been refined to the present fine text. The book addresses the most critical concerns in bilingual special education, which, in my view, are the improved assessment and instruction of these unique students. The authors have done an outstanding job synthesizing and organizing the latest research and best practices into a user friendly yet challenging text. The book is clearly written and will contribute to the professional development of teachers who will be helping to meet the needs of culturally and linguistically diverse (CLD) students.

The excellent introductory chapter sets the context for understanding the unique intersection of language, culture, and disability in our society and schools. The importance of providing a unified "one-system philosophy" rather than a separate and decoupled approach to special education is a very critical position the authors take in this chapter and throughout the book.

In later chapters, the authors present some of the latest thinking in the area of assessment paradigms and approaches for CLD students. They go on in subsequent chapters to show the critical and inseparable link between assessment and instruction, and give fine examples of how teachers can contribute to this process.

No text in this field would be complete without a strong emphasis on parent and community involvement. Fortunately, the authors have addressed this important dimension and have added some new insights in this area.

The text helps the reader to speculate about the future and encourages us to remain committed to lifelong learning and professional development. It provides a framework and sets the stage for improving our professional practice as society continues to change in this era of globalization and technological advancement. Teachers and all other professionals involved in the field will find this book to be a very helpful resource.

Leonard M. Baca

PREFACE

STATEMENT OF PURPOSE
AND PHILOSOPHY OF THE BOOK

Our purpose in writing this book is to assist educators working with culturally and linguistically diverse (CLD) students in the challenging task of delivering appropriate assessment and instructional services. We do this by offering some applied recommendations from the research developed by scholars who endorse the importance of a constructivistic and developmental perspective when working with CLD students. We refer to this approach as the "ethnic educator" perspective to emphasize how educators must be responsive to the needs of students and their families from backgrounds different than their own in order to provide effective assessment and instruction. However, in Chapter 4, on assessment models, we use the term "ethnic researcher." This term variation emphasizes the role of scholars who are departing from mainstream theories to develop cultural and linguistic models. Our goal is to present a text that integrates research and practice in the areas of bilingual and multicultural education, bilingual special education, and developmental and educational psychology.

We have divided the book into two parts. The first part is designed to promote an understanding of CLD students' idiosyncratic needs and characteristics by discussing the sociopolitical and legal aspects of serving them. Our goal is to build a context for understanding the unique cultural and linguistic backgrounds of minority students' educational needs. The second part of the book focuses on appropriate assessment and educational models and practices for CLD students by highlighting qualitative assessments and educational programs based on developmental, constructivistic, and "ethnic educator" perspectives. Our goal is to link assessment with instruction by using the findings of ethnic researchers to develop recommendations for improving the current state-of-the-art assessment, instructional, and administrative practices used with CLD students and their families. We conclude by generating a lively dialogue around some questions pertaining to current and future dilemmas facing educators when serving CLD students.

Throughout this book we define and examine our responsibilities to CLD students so that we can become better educators for a diverse society as well as better advocates for our students. We focus on CLD students suspected of or identified as having a disability because their needs especially have gone unmet.

The educational philosophy in this book advocates changing paradigms from the traditional "medical model" for assessment and the "transmission model" for instruction to the "ethnic educator" developmental model. As "ethnic educators," we advocate that practitioners endorse developmental principles for assessing and educating CLD students in a holistic manner. That is, educators need to stimulate CLD students to participate actively in learning by constructing critical meaning and thinking. We would like to model our own developmental constructivistic philosophy by initiating a dialogue with the reader across the chapters as we translate the contemporary findings of ethnic researchers into appropriate educational applications for CLD students. By linking research and practice, our aim is to give recommendations to improve current assessment and instructional practices with CLD students.

Given the present changes in educational and social paradigms in the school reform and restructuring movement, it is important for educators to realize that we know more than we can assess and instruct. It is imperative for educators to learn how to compensate for the gap between current technology (the "whats" and the "hows") and contemporary research findings (the "whys"). We encourage educators to assume an advocacy role for CLD students by acting as committed and empathic role models for improving the state-of-the-art of assessment and instructional practices. Given that we are in a transitional phase in the shift of paradigms, we believe that professionals need to undergo an awakening experience and realize that the most important tools for assessment and instruction are not the instruments and materials that they use but their own personalities.

This challenging transitional phase requires educators to assume personal responsibility by becoming committed advocates of CLD students in order to introduce change in the status quo of mainstream attitudes and beliefs in the educational and social system. That is, educators need to overcome their "shields" protecting old attitudes, myths, and misconceptions about traditional assessment and educational models. We believe that educators' and evaluators' cultural and linguistic identity, their attitudes as reflected in their values and beliefs, the particular schools of thought that they endorse, and their level of knowledge of how CLD students develop will influence the effectiveness of their assessment and instructional practices for CLD students.

We think that educators serving CLD students have both a privilege and a challenging imperative. We consider it a privilege to serve CLD students, because what we learn from them about language and culture challenges our thinking and enriches our lives personally and professionally. These students must be served because they are the future of our increasing multicultural nation. They are also the students most at-risk for failure in our schools. We think that our advocacy and intervention increase their potential for success in the adult world and benefit our individual communities as well as our national interests. We enlighten the state-of-the-art of current assessment and instructional practices with CLD students by offering recommendations for practitioners for improving the educational environment to develop further their learning potential.

THE AUTHORS' VISION OF THE CULTURALLY AND LINGUISTICALLY DIVERSE STUDENT

We have chosen the term "culturally and linguistically diverse" to describe these students in order to stress their distinctive characteristics and the intimate relationship between language and culture. Our vision of the purpose of educating CLD students relates to our "ethnic educator," constructivistic, and developmental philosophies that are portrayed across the chapters in this book. We explain our vision and our philosophy by referring to our beliefs regarding how CLD students develop and how educators need to assess and educate them.

We envision CLD students as individuals with idiosyncratic differences that are the product of the interaction between internal and external factors ranging from prenatal developmental conditions (e.g., health care, nutrition, age, socioeconomic status of the mother and family of origin) to the cultural and linguistic milieus in which students are immersed. That is, we consider development to be dynamically influenced by individuals' unlimited potentials for learning that are actualized and expressed differently across cultural and linguistic environments. We think that alternative qualitative assessments can more accurately represent the idiosyncratic differences of CLD students by portraying cultural and linguistic factors in the tasks and stimuli used. In addition, qualitative assessments can focus on the process CLD students use to solve problems and as a result measure their potential for learning in the form of problem-solving ability. In addition, qualitative assessments can also implement developmental ranges as diagnostic categories instead of using labels derived from the medical model.

We believe that both minority and majority students need to have equal access to an educational system that respects and values their idiosyncratic characteristics. Regardless of their cultural and linguistic background, all students are individuals, and their idiosyncratic educational needs ought to be honored, respected, and valued as sources of enrichment by educators. That is, educators need to realize that CLD students develop differently than majority students because they are immersed in bilingual and bicultural settings that influence their intelligence and overall personality development. We urge educators to use developmentally appropriate practices in relation to the particular needs of each student in order to honor their cultural and linguistic backgrounds.

We also believe that educators are presently confounding three fundamental concepts for honoring equal access to education to CLD students: race, ethnicity, and culture. We need to dispel the myth among educators who endorse the traditional medical model, which holds that CLD students are at-risk educationally due to internal factors such as race. First, ethnic groups such as Hispanics are not racially homogeneous. Individuals from different racial backgrounds can share the same cultural and linguistic environment and develop similar cultural and ethnic identities. Second, individuals belong to ethnic and social groups that have common cultural conceptualizations of the world (i.e., beliefs, ideas, and attitudes transmitted through cultural representational systems such as language, which in turn are considered cultural products). That is, heterogeneity is present in a culture due to the variety of ethnic groups that share the same cultural representations and products.

We also advocate educational practices that are soundly based on research stemming from a developmental, constructivistic, and "ethnic educator" perspective, because we believe that there is nothing more practical than a good theory. Educators serving CLD students need to become knowledgeable problem-solvers who can creatively transform mainstream practices into new assessment and instructional models and theories that take into consideration developmental and idiosyncratic differences between minority and majority students. Ethnic researchers need to depart from mainstream research paradigms by developing new models and theories that explain the idiosyncratic characteristics influencing the development of CLD students. We firmly acknowledge that practitioners need to be educated to become critical thinkers and problem-solvers who can model for CLD students how to learn and how to think. In fact, we are shifting paradigms in education because the needs of contemporary society have also changed. We no longer need to stimulate students to acquire massive amounts of information to be knowledgeable and productive. Instead, we must develop in students at every level (from preschoolers to educators in higher education institutions) their potential for learning in order to creatively construct new knowledge. We also need to restructure college curricula in response to the school reform movement by educating school personnel holistically through integrated curricula that cluster thematic and conceptual units with practical experiences. Professionals who advocate the "ethnic educator" model need to promote a higher conceptual level of understanding how CLD students develop by modeling culturally and linguistically relevant value systems in their assessment and educational practices.

We also endorse developmentally appropriate practices that can shed some light on linking assessment with instruction, given that the developmental perspective emphasizes the assessment of the potential for learning and the educational stimulation of higher level conceptual thinking processes to construct new knowledge. We consider that alternative assessment practices can provide important information and guidelines for improving educational practices with CLD students. We believe that qualitative assessment can integrate curriculum areas by providing students with holistic experiences that offer thematic units and conceptually interconnected activities that can stimulate transformational thinking in students. We think that multiple measurements across informants and contexts are needed, especially for including parents and teachers as valuable and knowledgeable informants in CLD students' development. Given the state-of-the-art of assessment and instructional practices, we advocate for the need to reach diagnostic decisions using a multidisciplinary assessment team that includes professionals with different perspectives, parents, administrators, and researchers. Furthermore, as stated, we also advocate a shift of focus in research and practice in the assessment and instruction of CLD students from a search for the panacea (the ultimate valid and reliable measurement and the most appropriate educational program) to an emphasis on the most important tool for assessment and instruction: the personality and actions of educators and evaluators. We firmly believe that the most important tool is not what measurements and educational programs are being used with CLD students, but who is responsible for their assessment and instruction.

THE AUDIENCE FOR THIS BOOK

This book has been written for professionals and pre-service educators serving culturally and linguistically diverse (CLD) students, as our recommendations use research findings to develop some possible cost-effective solutions for the needs and problems that both professionals and CLD students may encounter. These professionals include bilingual, bilingual special education, and special education teachers; educational diagnosticians; school psychologists; educational psychologists; counselors; speech pathologists; social workers; and school administrators. In addition, this book can also be used by graduate students taking courses in education and psychology as well as by professors researching, teaching, or serving in the areas of bilingual and multicultural education, bilingual special education, and educational psychology. It may be used, for example, in university courses on multicultural education, methods in bilingual education, bilingual special education, education for culturally diverse students, variations in learners, learning in the schools, schooling in the United States, and psychological testing and diagnosis.

ACKNOWLEDGMENTS

The authors want to acknowledge certain individuals who have provided valuable feedback in the realization of this project. First, we would like to thank Dr. Leonard M. Baca, Director of the BUENO Center for Multicultural Education, and Professor and Chair of Bilingual Education and Bilingual Special Education at the University of Colorado at Boulder, for his willingness to write the Foreword as well as for his important comments on previous manuscript versions of this book. Second, we are grateful to Julia de Valenzuela, a doctoral student working with Dr. Baca at the University of Colorado, for her help in revising the manuscript. Third, we would like to thank Dr. Myriam Assaf-Keller, Principal of Lloyd Elementary School in Chicago, Illinois, for her valuable contributions to the organization of this book. Fourth, we extend our appreciation to the two anonymous reviewers who offered helpful suggestions for improving the content and format of our book. Finally, we want to thank Lisa Sherill, a graduate student in the Department of Educational Psychology at the University of Arizona in Tucson, for her help in generating the Contents and Index.

1

UNDERSTANDING CULTURAL AND LINGUISTIC DIVERSITY AND DISABILITY

The goal of this initial chapter is to provide educators with a framework for understanding diversity in the schools and for conceptualizing their roles in promoting an inclusive educational environment. The chapter is divided into four sections that address topic areas that will be revisited throughout the text. In the first section, we discuss the controversial issues of diversity and discrimination, the changing demography of the school-age population, and the needs of students who are at-risk for failure. In the next three sections, we provide an overview of two human characteristics that account for much of the increased diversity in the schools—bilingualism and disability—and discuss how students with these characteristics are currently served in the educational system. We end the chapter with an appeal for the implementation of a holistic philosophy of service delivery in which the needs of culturally and linguistically diverse (CLD) students, especially those with or at-risk of learning problems, are carefully addressed in the context of the general education system.

DIVERSITY, DISCRIMINATION, AND EDUCATION

The term "diversity" has been omnipresent in recent discussions of educational issues and concerns and will doubtlessly remain so for some time to come. The term is widely used as a generic abbreviation for "racial diversity," "cultural diversity," or, even more holistically, "human diversity." Given its new-found popularity in education and in the society at large, one

1

would think that diversity was something new in the United States. But nothing could be further from the truth. Perhaps more so than any other country in the world, the history of our so-called nation of immigrants has been one of ethnic, racial, and cultural diversity. Unfortunately, it has also been one of bias, prejudice, and discrimination based on that same diversity.

The very roots of our nation are seeded with the struggles and conflicts of people seeking to escape some kind of oppression or discrimination. Our elementary school textbooks tell us, for example, that the founders of our country fled from Europe to escape religious persecution. Later, we learn that other religious groups, such as the Mormons and Quakers, then had to flee further west to escape the religious persecution of the earlier founders. American history also tells us that, while still a young nation, the United States developed one of the world's largest systems of black slavery, which it took nothing less than a civil war to abolish. Through the 1800s and 1900s, as the country expanded westward, European Americans came in contact with various other non-European peoples of color: American Indian groups in different areas of the country; Mexicans in the Southwest; and later, Chinese immigrants in the far West. That contact often led to open conflict, bloodshed, or wars that ultimately resulted in the oppression or domination of non-European peoples.

Thus, American history has not only been characterized by extensive diversity but also by a pattern of conflict relative to that diversity, especially as white Americans have come in contact with Native Americans, African Americans, Mexican Americans and other Latino Americans, and Asian Americans. From the latter's perspective, words such as "slavery," "conquest," "genocide," "oppression," "discrimination," and "racism" tend to be matter-of-fact descriptors of the racial minority experience in America. On the other hand, the response of the dominant culture to these realities of our history has often been characterized by denial, avoidance, rationalization, and controversy. Our discomfort with these issues seems so pervasive that we seek to escape them in every possible way: We commission study after study followed by little or no action; we focus on symptoms rather than causes; we pass legislation that is not enforced; and we continue to cultivate language, perhaps subconsciously, to soften the blow of the historic reality.

In keeping with the more favorable aspects of the American creed—equal rights, equal opportunity, and liberty and justice for all—we find it more comforting to focus on terms and concepts for improving "human relations," "intergroup relations," "cultural pluralism," "multiculturalism," and now "diversity," than to engage our problems directly. We find it easier to intellectualize and to add complex sociological concepts and abstract language to an already complex myriad of issues and concerns. The result has been that the concerns of individuals of color, individuals with disabilities, women, and other traditionally disenfranchised groups tend to be relegated to continuing controversy. Succeeding generations of Americans remain largely insensitive, unaware, and only grudgingly able to make progress beyond the negative stereotypes and conceptual generalizations we all tend to have of people outside our own social groups. We remain ignorant of the roles that we all play in the nature and functions of culturally induced bias, prejudice, and discrimination, not to mention the more complex systems of human discrimination we create, such as racism, sexism, ageism, and handicappism. That ignorance feeds the perpetuation of conflict based on human differences generation after generation.

What can we do as educators to deal with these complex issues in our schools? At a personal level, the first steps involve admitting our prejudices, exploring the reasons behind them, and identifying how they affect our behavior toward students. This process, although painful, is necessary as we evolve into being the educators required for the future. Only when we begin to deal honestly with our personal attitudes and actions can we move to addressing issues of diversity and discrimination at a societal level. At this level, we need to be aware that discrimination against certain groups is practiced on a systematic basis and be willing to oppose that discrimination when we see it occur in our schools. Using the field of mental retardation as an example, many educators have undergone a difficult personal transformation in the process of becoming effective advocates for their students. Having been prepared to teach in segregated settings, to "protect" their students, and to use age-inappropriate developmental models of instruction, educators were forced to reevaluate their positions in dramatic ways with the advent of inclusion, community-based vocational training, and functional curriculum models. Educators who were able to admit that their prejudices about mental retardation adversely affected their instruction to these students were eventually able to persuade others and advocate for change on a system-wide basis. This same lesson holds true with regard to students of color, students who do not speak English, students who live in poverty, students who are female, students who are gay, and so on. Ultimately, our ability to engage in self-reflection and to act on our resulting awareness is the best weapon we have to fight discrimination and to promote the acceptance of diversity. Understanding the characteristics and needs of the diverse students who constitute our schools is essential to this process.

The "New" Mainstream Student

The mainstream student in American public schools has been historically perceived as a monolingual, English-speaking Caucasian, who has no apparent physical or cognitive impairments to learning and was born to middle-class parents with similar characteristics. While a sizable segment of the school-age population fits this description, students of color, students who speak a language other than English, students who have significant difficulties learning, and students from low-income homes have always been present in the American educational system. How these students have been treated by the system over the years is in many ways a lamentable story. The segregation of students of color by states and school districts, the denial of educational services to students with disabilities, the tracking of certain ethnic and cultural groups into non-college-bound curricula, the lack of services to students learning English as a second language, inequitable state funding patterns for education, and curriculum written without regard to cultural diversity are all ways in which students outside the mainstream have been poorly served by American schools.

As long as students outside the mainstream "melted" into the system, primarily by looking, sounding, and behaving like the mainstream student, as long as their population was small and passive, and as long as the economy could absorb those who were not successful academically, there was no reason for schools to adjust the status quo. Over the past several decades, however, litigation and legislation on civil rights issues, the increasing growth of heretofore minority populations, changes in skills required for the job market, and the development of national values favorable to cultural pluralism have forced schools to reevaluate traditional curriculum and service delivery systems. As national reports have indicated, in a few short years fully one-third of our nation will be individuals of color and individuals for whom the English language and traditional Anglo-American ways will not be primary (Commission on Minority Participation in Education and American Life, 1988; Hodgkinson, 1992). We serve a large and growing proportion of students in general education settings who are younger, who have learning problems, and who come from homes with low levels of income, single parents, and/or little educational background (see Box 1.1). As such, students with these characteristics can no longer be perceived as outside the mainstream. These students constitute the school population we serve daily, and it is incumbent upon us to design and implement a suitable learning environment for them.

The CLD Student At-Risk

Virtually all students who have historically fallen outside of the mainstream in American schools are at-risk for poor treatment in a system that is only beginning to adapt to their needs. Strong relationships exist between certain characteristics of these students and indicators of school failure, including those between poverty and low reading and math scores, racial and ethnic minority status and high drop-out rates, and disability and under- or unemployment after graduation. Less attention, unfortunately, has been paid to

BOX 1.1 Who Are the New Mainstream Students?

The new mainstream students look, sound, learn, and live in ways that differ significantly from past populations.

Race and Ethnicity

Of the 45 million students enrolled in public and private elementary and secondary schools, over 30% are from groups designated as racial/ethnic minorities:

White, non-Hispanic	67%
Black, non-Hispanic	16%
Hispanic	12%
Asian/Pacific Islander	3%
American Indian/Alaskan Native	1%

This diversity will increase as the total U.S. population moves toward the 50% division between non-Hispanic whites and other groups that is expected by 2050.

Language and Culture

About 6.3 million, or 14%, of students in grades K–12 speak languages other than English at home, including 2.3 million, or 5%, who receive bilingual or ESL services. Of the latter group, the 20 most common languages are:

Spanish	72.9%	Creole (French)	0.9%
Vietnamese	3.9%	Arabic	0.9%
Hmong	1.8%	Portuguese	0.7%
Cantonese	1.7%	Japanese	0.6%
Cambodian	1.6%	Armenian	0.5%
Korean	1.6%	Chinese (unspecified)	0.5%
Laotian	1.3%	Mandarin	0.5%
Navajo	1.3%	Farsi	0.4%
Tagalog	1.1%	Hindi	0.3%
Russian	0.9%	Polish	0.3%

The number of students in bilingual or ESL programs has nearly doubled since 1984 and is expected to grow as the number of native-born and foreign-born home speakers of languages other than English increases into the next century.

Disability

About 4.5 million, or 10%, of students in grades K–12 receive special education services. This number increases to over 5 million if children under age 6 are included. The following disability categories account for over 90% of the K–12 population:

Learning disabilities	51%
Speech/language impairments	22%
Mental retardation	12%
Serious emotional disturbance	9%

In the future, more students with disabilities are expected to be educated at younger ages and in integrated settings.

Family and Economic Status

- 20% of all children live below the poverty threshold, including 43% of black and 34% of Hispanic children.
- 59% of all children born in 1983 will live with only one parent before reaching age 18.
- Several million children are either in foster care, live with extended family members, are homeless, or have been adopted.

analyzing relationships between characteristics of the learning environment itself and aspects of school failure. While a number of CLD students may have personal characteristics that contribute to a lack of academic progress (e.g., a genuine disability or an unstable home life), they may also be at-risk because characteristics of the school setting are detrimental to the learning process. In fact, our own inability (or perhaps unwillingness) as educators to distinguish between internal and external factors in the learning problems of CLD students may be the major contributor to their school failure.

Using principles of ecobehavioral psychology, the state of being at-risk for academic underachievement or failure is a function of the "goodness of fit" between the student and the learning environment. Let us examine the cases of Argentina and Shmeran, two bright Assyrian cousins about to enter the American school system with little formal education, no English skills, no awareness of peer customs regarding dress and music, and parents who can offer limited support. The school that Argentina enters is unaccustomed to immigrant families in the community and has no Assyrian staff. The school provides twice-weekly English as a second language (ESL) preparation and no direct instruction related to the acculturation process. The classroom teacher is angry that she is expected to teach a student without English skills, and peers either ignore or tease the girl. At the end of the first year, Argentina is speaking little English, does not complete assignments, and behaves sullenly in class. The school that Shmeran enters enrolls her full-time in an ESL program with social integration activities. As her conversational skills grow, she attends the general education classroom for longer periods of time and is paired with students who help to accustom her to the class routine. The school contracts with a community member who speaks Assyrian to translate during regularly scheduled parent-staff meetings. At the end of the year, Shmeran displays good beginning proficiency in English, has friends, and is eager for involvement in school activities.

When the concept of being at-risk is examined from an ecobehavioral perspective, we see that it is more accurate to describe at-risk situations rather than at-risk students. In the above example, Shmeran is considerably less at-risk than her cousin Argentina, despite having similar personal characteristics, because the school setting is better prepared to meet her needs. Working to increase the goodness of fit between learning environments and CLD students decreases the potential for academic failure and avoids the pitfall of attributing learning difficulties solely to the individual.

The CLD Student with Disabilities

CLD students are especially at-risk in relation to disability status, because most schools are not well prepared to deal with differences in learning, behavior, culture, and language either separately or in combination. On a level playing field, we would expect to find similar percentages of students from various racial/ethnic backgrounds receiving special education services. Data from the Office for Civil Rights ([OCR] 1990), however, indicate substantial differences by racial/ethnic status overall and across disability categories (see Table 1.1). For example, students of Asian/Pacific Island origin are about three times less likely to receive special education services than are students of other origins, yet they have the highest percentage of speech impairments of any group. Students of African origin are the most likely recipients of special education services, especially in the category of mild mental retardation, where the percentage is about double that of other groups. Bias and lack of understanding of cultural difference, not biology, account for these variations.

In general, CLD students are likely to be either overidentified, underidentified, or misidentified as having disabilities (see Box 1.2). In the case of overidentification, expectations for students with disabilities by educators and parents are often less than what is warranted, leading to inadequate educational experiences and a loss of human potential. CLD students with disabilities are especially vulnerable in this situation because they may be viewed as culturally and linguistically inferior as well as academically and socially incapable due to their disabling condition. In the case of underidentification, CLD students with genuine disabilities may drop out or be simply passed along without mastering basic literacy skills. These students also miss opportunities for legally mandated transition services to employment and independent living situations prior to graduation and for adult disability services later in life. In the case of misidentification, such as being diagnosed

TABLE 1.1   Percent of Students Receiving Special Education Services by Racial/Ethnic Group

Racial/Ethnic Group	% of Population	% of Identified Group by Disability*				
		LD	SI	MR (Mild)	MR (Moderate)	SED
African American	11.3	44.0	23.0	18.7	6.3	8.0
Asian/Pacific Islander	3.8	43.8	38.9	7.2	6.5	3.6
Hispanic	8.2	56.8	23.7	7.8	7.6	4.1
Native American	10.8	56.2	25.9	9.5	2.1	6.3
White	9.5	52.2	29.5	8.5	2.6	7.3

*LD (learning disabilities), SI (speech/language impairments), MR (mental retardation), and SED (serious emotional disturbance) are the only categories reported by OCR.

Note: From the Fall 1990 Elementary and Secondary School Civil Rights Survey by the Office of Civil Rights (1993).

BOX 1.2 Cases of Over- and Underidentification

Is a Discrepancy Always a Disability?

Eva, a 10-year-old girl who came from Poland at age 5, is being reevaluated after spending 2–3 years in a resource room program for students with learning disabilities. When Eva first entered school as a kindergartner, she was one of only a few children who did not speak English. This group was seen twice weekly by an ESL teacher, who terminated Eva's instruction after first grade because she showed good oral English proficiency. Eva was referred initially for an evaluation by her classroom teacher in the middle of second grade because she showed little progress in learning to read. The evaluation, which was conducted primarily in English by a bilingual Polish school psychologist, showed achievement at the K–1 grade levels on the Peabody Individual Achievement Test and low average scores on subtests involving memory on the Weschler Scales of Intelligence for Children—Revised. There were also reports of her poor attention and motivation in the classroom. At the time of the evaluation, Eva's younger brother was undergoing treatment for leukemia. Eva was being cared for by an elderly grandmother while her parents spent time at the hospital. At the multidisciplinary staffing, the district administrator and the psychologist felt that the data supported a diagnosis of learning disabilities because there was a discrepancy between potential and achievement, especially in light of the specialized language services that Eva had received. The special education coordinator believed that the evidence for a disability was weak but agreed to support the decision if Eva's parents had no objections. Eva's parents did not attend the staffing but agreed to the placement after speaking to the psychologist on the phone.

Ms. Winslow, the special education teacher, noted from the very first semester in the resource program that Eva did not have the type of processing difficulties typical of students with learning disabilities. Eva learned easily in the small group and individual tutoring sessions, and even helped other students in the class. Her weakest area was vocabulary, which improved considerably when Ms. Winslow supplemented the general education basal reading series with a selection of children's literature. After about a year in the resource program, the school's enrollment of Polish-speaking children increased to the number required for a bilingual teacher. Since Eva was excited about learning to read in Polish, Ms. Winslow began to mainstream Eva on an informal basis in the bilingual classroom. The bilingual district coordinator objected at first, because Eva was progressing well in English, but later relented when Ms. Winslow and Eva's parents insisted that the special education placement had been wrong from the start. A staffing was called to reexamine Eva's program. Her parents, however, would not agree to another evaluation until she had received bilingual services for at least a year, because they were afraid that she would be put back in the English-only class on a full-time basis.

As the time for the reevaluation approaches, Eva's performance in English appears to be nearly at grade level across the subject areas, while her reading and writing skills in Polish are improving rapidly. Ms. Winslow feels confident that the new evaluation will not support a diagnosis of disability and is working with other special education teachers in the district to develop a referral policy for CLD students.

BOX 1.2 *Continued*

Do Nice Kids Finish Last?

Margarito is a 13-year-old boy in eighth grade who moved to a large city in the Midwest from rural Mexico about 4 years ago. His mother, father, older sister, and younger brother share a rented house in the city's largest Mexican community. His parents are employed at a local factory. Margarito and his siblings had little formal education before their arrival in this country. The brothers attend the same elementary school, where instruction is conducted bilingually throughout the grade levels. The junior high classes at the school are departmentalized, and Margarito has three teachers he sees regularly. Ms. Ortiz, his math teacher, noticed from the beginning of the semester that he understood little more than simple addition and subtraction concepts and had great difficulty grasping the beginning algebra skills that other students in class were learning. She assigned Margarito a partner to work with and adapted his written assignments to incorporate work on basic math skills while she investigated his school history.

First, Ms. Ortiz looked at previous assessment data and spoke with Margarito's former teachers. On the Language Assessment Scales, given a year ago, Margarito scored at the second-grade level in reading and writing in both Spanish and English. Performance on the Metropolitan Achievement Test, given two years ago, ranged from below first- to the second-grade level. Margarito's teachers all agreed that he learned slowly but tried hard and was one of the most polite students in class. One teacher felt that his poor achievement came from his lack of schooling in Mexico; another teacher had wanted to retain Margarito in fifth grade, but the principal at the time would not hear of it, citing district policy to keep students with their same-age peers; a third teacher had considered making a referral to special education but abandoned the idea when he heard that Margarito might be sent to another school. Second, Ms. Ortiz spoke with Margarito and his mother. Margarito said that he liked school very much but that the work was hard. He hoped that he could graduate from high school and become an auto mechanic like his cousin. Margarito's mother said that her son had always been a little slow to learn but that the teachers had never mentioned a problem to her. Finally, to confirm her suspicions before making a referral, Ms. Ortiz administered the Test of Nonverbal Intelligence to Margarito. He scored at the first percentile with a quotient of 65 ($M = 100$, $SD = 15$).

A full case study evaluation was initiated, and Margarito was assessed for cognitive functioning, academic skills, and adaptive behavior. The Bateria Woodcock Psico-Educativa en Espanol, cognitive portion, indicated scores between 2 and 3 standard deviations below the mean. The academic portion of the Bateria confirmed previous findings of skills at the primary level. On the Vineland Adaptive Behavior Scales, Interview Edition, Spanish version, Margarito's adaptive behavior composite score was 66 ($M = 100$, $SD = 15$). At the multidisciplinary staffing, which included Margarito, his mother, and a parent advocate along with the school staff, all agreed that Margarito should continue in his typical classes with one period of special education resource services. The special educator would also provide consultative assistance to the classroom teachers. After graduation, Margarito would be enrolled in the program for students with cognitive disabilities at the local high school, with a focus on building functional academics and vocational skills. Margarito's mother left the staffing feeling optimistic about her son's future but wondering why no one had offered help earlier.

with mild mental retardation instead of learning disabilities, CLD students may suffer the consequences of an inappropriate curriculum and lowered expectations for employment and life in the community.

CLD students who have been appropriately identified may still be at a disadvantage if their individualized education programs (IEPs) make no provision for services relevant to language and cultural differences. These students, unlike their peers, may be unable to communicate adequately in their native language with family members and may be unfamiliar with their cultural heritage because their IEPs do not call for native language instruction or culturally relevant curriculum. They may also not learn English as quickly or as adequately as their peers if they do not receive ESL services in the special education program by qualified specialists.

Building Shared Concerns

Besides addressing the educational problems caused by personal and institutional prejudice and discrimination, a critical aspect to resolving the poor treatment of CLD students in the schools is the mutual effort of educators across specialty areas. As educators, we share a common bond in the dynamics of the teaching and learning process and in our quest to help students reach their potential. Yet, we are often isolated academically and socially in our own circle of expertise. Our isolation results from differences including our subject matter (e.g., whether we are teachers of history or math); our assigned positions in the school (e.g., whether we are administrators or counselors); the grade level of our students (e.g., whether we are in early childhood or secondary settings); and the type of service we provide (e.g., whether we teach gifted classes or provide speech and language services). Special educators lament that general educators know little (and may care less) about the field of disabilities, including characteristics of the students, teaching methodologies, and program structure. Bilingual educators tire of explaining to monolingual educators why the native language is used so often in the classroom when students are supposed to be learning English. General educators are certain that specialized support staff have no concept of curriculum development and instruction of large groups. And, of course, administrators and psychologists feel grossly misunderstood. This lack of mutual understanding, which is fostered in university training programs and in school settings, undermines our comprehensive service delivery to students as well as inhibits our development as professionals.

Baca and Payan (1989), in their discussion of the bilingual special education interface, call for the connection of programs at the ideological and operational levels. Only when the theories, philosophies, strategies, and problems of the programs and disciplines involved are mutually understood can the concept of the interface move from abstraction to implementation. In the education of CLD students, especially those with or at-risk of learning problems, building a successful interface is particularly difficult because of the multiple areas of service involved. From prereferral activities to formal evaluation to coordinated services, a shared knowledge base is essential among administrators, special and general education teachers, psychologists, and other support staff to design organizational structures appropriate for CLD students; to make differential diagnoses between problems related to language and culture and problems related to disability, and to enhance and adapt curriculum and instruction. We present the following sections on bilingualism and disability as a foundation for this mutual understanding.

BILINGUALISM AND EDUCATION

Despite the language and cultural diversity of the United States, Americans cannot seem to agree on whether bilingualism is a valued asset, an unnecessary skill, or downright un-American. On one hand, we admire individuals who speak two languages well, we profess to see the social and economic benefits of a multilingual society, and we have laws against discrimination based on language and national origin. On the other hand, we provide minimal bilingual instruction to CLD students, we have never committed sufficient resources to foreign language instruction to build a competent multilingual work force, and we elect state politicians who enact English-as-the-official-language legislation. Taking a strictly pragmatic viewpoint, bilingualism in the United States is a natural outcome of the country's changing demographics and economic base. While English will continue as the common language in which residents of the United States communicate, competence in languages other than English will be actively promoted by CLD groups and the business community. Schools will be expected to develop and maintain the native language of students learning English while teaching foreign languages to high levels of proficiency to students who speak only English. Educators can prepare for this occurrence by becoming aware of language-related demographic trends across the country and within their communities, by learning about the language acquisition process; and by learning from past and present experiences in delivering services.

Language Diversity in the United States

The development of language diversity in the United States is strikingly presented by Waggoner (1993), who compares data from the 1980 and 1990 Census reports (see Table 1.2). These data show a substantial increase in the number and percentage of individuals who speak languages other than English at home, while speakers of English only have increased only slightly since 1980. Today, approximately one individual in seven age five and older speaks a language other than English at home, compared to one individual in nine in 1980. Contrary to what many Americans might guess to be true, slightly more than half (52%) of the 31.8 million in this group are native born. Of the foreign-born group, slightly less than half (48%) immigrated within the past ten years. Data from the 1990 Census also reveal that of the five languages other than English spoken by at least one million people, Spanish is dominant in thirty-nine states across the geographic regions of the country and in the District of Columbia. Italian and German are spoken most frequently in the Northeast and the Midwest, while French and Chinese are more popular in the South and West. In the future, the Asian languages are expected to show the greatest proportional increase, but Spanish will continue to be the most represented language besides English. What data bases do not clarify, however, is the extent to which individuals who are familiar with two languages are proficient users of those languages. This knowledge will become more important as we move toward multilingualism and a global economy, as will information about how individuals develop bilingual abilities and how bilingualism can be fostered.

An Overview of Bilingualism

Bilingualism refers to the ability to communicate in two languages and is more accurately conceptualized as a process than as an ultimate state. Individuals who are more advanced in the bilingual process have native or near-native competency in both languages in the abilities of listening, speaking, reading, and writing that is appropriate for their age, ability, and educational background. Five-year-old Marcos, for example, who grew up in a multigenerational bilingual household and entered kindergarten with well-developed vocabulary and prereading skills in both English and Spanish, is well along in the bilingual process, provided of course that his educational program continues to facilitate both languages. Julie, a monolingual English speaker until age fifteen, just passed the dreaded state certification test for French teachers but knows that she will need to continue work on her pronunciation and understanding of French literature to provide near-native instruction for her students. Individuals who are less advanced in the bilingual process have limited proficiency in one language, and may exhibit various levels of competence in oral and written skills in the other language. A typical example of someone in the beginning stages of the bilingual process is Zakia, a thirteen-year-old girl from India who speaks, reads, and writes well in her native language, Hindi, and who is beginning to use conversational English

TABLE 1.2   Bilingualism in the United States

Overall Growth of English Only and Other Language Groups

Home Language	Number of U.S. Residents		
	1980	1990	% Change
English only	187,187,000	198,601,000	+6.1
Other language	23,060,000	31,845,000	+38.1
Total	210,247,000	236,446,000	+9.6

Languages Spoken by at Least 1 Million People

Home Language	Number of U.S. Residents		
	1980	1990	% Change
Spanish	11,116,000	17,340,000	+56.0
French	1,551,000	1,702,000	+9.8
German	1,587,000	1,547,000	−2.4
Chinese languages	631,000	1,319,000	+109.2
Italian	1,618,000	1,309,000	−19.1

Selected Languages with Increases of at Least 50% Since 1980

Home Language	Number of U.S. Residents		
	1980	1990	% Change
Asian Indian languages	243,000	644,000	+164.8
Vietnamese	195,000	507,000	+160.6
Thai and Laotian	85,000	206,000	+142.8
Korean	266,000	626,000	+135.3
Chinese languages	631,000	1,319,000	+109.2
Filipino languages	474,000	899,000	+89.5
Farsi	107,000	202,000	+88.7
Arabic	218,000	355,000	+63.3
Spanish	11,116,000	17,340,000	+56.0

States with at Least 300,000 Home Speakers of Languages Other Than English

California	8,619,000	Michigan	570,000
Texas	3,970,000	Ohio	546,000
New York	3,909,000	New Mexico	494,000
Florida	2,098,000	Connecticut	466,000
Illinois	1,499,000	Virginia	419,000
New Jersey	1,406,000	Washington	403,000
Massachusetts	852,000	Maryland	395,000
Pennsylvania	807,000	Louisiana	392,000
Arizona	700,000	Colorado	321,000

Note: From "The Growth of Multilingualism and the Need for Bilingual Education: What Do We Know So Far?" by D. Waggoner, 1993, *Bilingual Research Journal, 17,* 1–12.

on the school playground. But there are also cases like eight-year-old Juan. Born to Spanish-speaking parents and given over to foster care at an early age, Juan has alternated between Spanish-only and English-only homes and school programs. He has yet to learn to read in either language and has a sparse oral vocabulary in both languages.

A popular theory of language development that has practical educational implications is the linguistic interdependence theory (Cummins, 1981). According to this theory, individuals appear to use their two languages as though they were unrelated; in reality, however, there is a common operating system or underlying proficiency beneath the surface aspects of the languages. Appropriate input in either language helps the entire system to develop, but if a student is forced to operate in the less developed language without adequate support, academic functioning is likely to suffer across all areas. This prediction of failure is also true for students who have poorly developed proficiency in both their languages. To understand how this theory applies to educational programs, let us return to the examples of Zakia and Juan. Zakia has well-developed skills in her first language (L1) and is beginning to learn English as her second language (L2). Since she has a strong base in L1 upon which to integrate new knowledge in L2, she is likely to do well in one of several bilingual or ESL models in which instruction is carefully implemented. However, if she is placed in learning situations where the linguistic demands consistently exceed her mastery of English, her academic progress across the content areas will be jeopardized. Juan, who has poorly developed language skills in L1 and L2, will be at even greater risk for school failure unless consistent, language-rich instruction in a bilingual program is implemented across basic skills and content areas.

A fundamental question to be answered when educating CLD students is, "How can we provide instruction that enhances cognitive development and maximizes academic achievement?" The answer to this question begins with a statement borrowed from the Hippocratic oath, "First, do no harm." In the rush to make students proficient in English, one of the greatest downfalls of bilingual education in the United States is the failure to distinguish surface or conversational proficiency from deep or cognitive/academic proficiency (Cummins, 1989). As a result, students who display conversational skills in English are assumed to be ready for instruction designed for monolingual English-speaking students, when in fact they may not have the language to support the concepts to be learned. Based on a review of relevant studies, Cummins (1989) estimates that conversational proficiency can be developed adequately in about two years, while the development of cognitive/academic proficiency takes from five to seven years. In a model that is helpful to educators in understanding the language learning and teaching process, Cummins (1984) explains that basic interpersonal communication skills (BICS) develop in situations where physical cues help to promote understanding and where events are relatively undemanding cognitively. In school, BICS are developed in situations such as playing games in the gym, ordering food in the cafeteria, or deciding where to go after class with a group of friends. Cognitive/academic language proficiency skills (CALPS), on the other hand, tend to occur in situations where obvious cues to promote understanding are absent and where the demand for cognitive skills is high. Following a science lecture, answering questions independently from a social studies reading, and reviewing math vocabulary for the upcoming test all require language and cognition beyond what are needed to function at a social level. Educators can work to enhance CALPS by providing learning environments that are rich in context cues prior to moving to decontextualized instructional situations.

A Glimpse at the State of Bilingual Education

In the United States, bilingual education is associated almost exclusively with students who speak languages other than English at home and who enter the school system with less than native proficiency in English. The use of the term "bilingual" conveys the impression that both languages are given equal consideration during instruction and that the long-term outcome of such instruction for students is advanced proficiency in L1 and L2. In practice, however, the vast majority of bilingual education programs are transitional, designed with the goal of improving students' proficiency in English with support in their native language only until the students are able to benefit from monolingual English instruction. In fact, many programs referred to under the rubric of bilingual education use English as the only language of instruction. A more ideal situation would involve the melding of foreign language instruction and bilingual education to meet the goal of producing a multilingual society, but that is a topic for another text. For the present, bilingual education is primarily a program for students who do not fit the traditional mainstream because of their unique language and cultural needs. As we discuss in greater detail in Chapter 2, bilingual education per se, unlike special education, is not mandated at the federal level. However, federal civil rights legislation does require schools to take some type of appropriate action when students have language needs that impede their progress in educational programs. We need to understand bilingual education in its current context to facilitate its development and to clarify the role it plays in the delivery of services to CLD students with or at-risk of learning problems.

Definition of Students with Limited English Proficiency

Of the 6.3 million students in grades K–12 who speak languages other than English at home, 2.3 million, or approximately one-third, have been identified by school districts as having limited English proficiency (LEP). While administrative definitions of the term vary across states and districts, current federal legislation defines LEP to include:

1. Students who were not born in the United States or whose native language is a language other than English;
2. Students who come from environments where a language other than English is dominant;
3. Students who are American Indian and Alaska natives and who come from environments where a language other than English has had a significant impact on their level of language proficiency; and
4. Students who, by reason thereof, have sufficient difficulty speaking, reading, writing, or understanding the English language to deny them the opportunity to learn successfully in classrooms where the language of instruction is English or to participate fully in our society (Bilingual Education Act, 1994).

This definition includes a range of students who differ widely across age and language proficiency continuums. For example, a school district might serve a kindergartner like Alba, a girl born in the United States to Mexican American parents who has age-appropriate oral and written skills in Spanish and beginning oral skills in English; a junior high student like John, a boy with Down's syndrome who lives on the Navajo reservation and is beginning to read simple words in English and Navajo; or a seventeen-year-old student like Rasho, a recent immigrant from Serbia who is several years below grade level in his native Serbo-Croatian and knows only a few English phrases.

Evaluation Procedures

A national study of services to students with LEP commissioned by the U.S. Department of Education found that schools employ a wide range of criteria and evaluation procedures for initial identification, for assignment to specific services, and for termination of services (see Table 1.3; see also Fleischman & Hopstock, 1993). Oral proficiency tests in English and home language surveys are the most common methods for identifying students, while teacher judgment is the most common method used to reclassify students. The majority of schools report using more than one assessment strategy or instrument. More objective methods of evaluation tend to be used by districts serving a large population of students with LEP, while more subjec-

TABLE 1.3   Types of Data Used by School Districts to Assess LEP[a]

Data Used to Determine LEP Status	% of Districts[b]
Oral proficiency tests in English	83.1
Home language survey	76.6
Teacher judgment	69.4
Achievement tests in English	52.3
Teacher ratings of oral proficiency	49.2
Writing samples in English	45.5
Oral proficiency tests in native language	34.4
Literacy tests in English	33.9
Achievement tests in native language	11.6
Other	7.8

Data Used to Reclassify Students	% of Districts[b]
Teacher judgment	78.6
Achievement tests in English	75.0
Oral proficiency tests in English	74.4
Teacher ratings of English proficiency	57.0
Writing samples in English	52.8
Literacy tests in English	29.8
Other	10.3

[a]Based on a sample of approximately 700 districts. Results weighted to be nationally representative.
[b]Totals exceed 100% because of multiple responses.
Note: From *Descriptive Study of Services to Limited English Proficient Students* (pp. 17, 19) by H. L. Fleischman and P. L. Hopstock, 1993, Arlington, VA. Development Associates.

tive methods tend to be used by districts serving smaller numbers of students. In addition, districts with a greater percentage of students with LEP served under the federally funded Bilingual Education Act (BEA) (1994) and/or state-funded programs tend to use more information to determine LEP status than districts with smaller percentages of such students, presumably due to funding and reporting requirements. Overall, the study reported: (1) a lack of standardized assessment procedures nationally; (2) differences in the types of assessment methods used based on the number of students with LEP in the district; and (3) differences in the amount of assessment information gathered by districts based on the percentage of students with LEP who are in programs supported by federal and state funding.

Student Characteristics
Data from the same study show that the vast majority of the 2.3 million students with LEP have Spanish as their native language, with next largest group having Asian language backgrounds (see Box 1.1). Students with

Native American language backgrounds account for 2.5 percent of all students with LEP. Of Hispanic students with LEP, 40 percent were born in Mexico, 39 percent in the United States, 7 percent in Puerto Rico, and the remaining 14 percent in other countries. Overall, 33 percent of students with LEP are native born. Higher concentrations of students with LEP are found in lower grades than in higher ones. Of the total public school population, students with LEP account for 8 percent of enrollment in kindergarten but for only 3 percent of enrollment in grade twelve. The socioeconomic level of students with LEP, as measured by eligibility for free or reduced lunch, is lower than that of the general school population. Of the schools reported in the study, 77 percent of students with LEP met criteria for eligibility, compared to 38 percent of all students. Nearly 15 percent of students with LEP have missed more than two years of school since age six, and 12 percent are enrolled in grade levels at least two years lower than the national average. These figures increase to 20 percent and 27 percent, respectively, for high school students.

Instructional Services

Once identified, nearly 90 percent of students with LEP receive some type of service designed to meet their language needs for periods up to approximately 3.5 years (see Table 1.4; see also Fleischman & Hopstock, 1993). Of these students, about 30 percent receive services in instructional contexts that are not specific to students with LEP, such as the monolingual English classroom, while about 70 percent receive services in contexts that are focused on such students, such as an ESL or a bilingual classroom. Nearly 34 percent of students who receive special services are instructed only in English, while the remaining 66 percent are instructed using at least some native language. When this information is examined by grade level, some notable differences appear. High school students with LEP are more likely not to receive services than are elementary students, 0.9 percent and 4.8 percent, respectively. Elementary students are most likely to receive intensive services with significant native language (Type 8) and next most likely to receive some services in English only (Type 3), while high school students are most likely to receive any of the intensive services (Type 6, 7, or 8). Instruction in native language is more likely when schools have a high concentration of students with LEP who speak the same language and have teachers who also speak the language. Intensive services are more likely when schools have a high concentration of students with LEP and students who are foreign born. Of the teachers responsible for students with LEP across all service types, approximately 40 percent share the native language of their students, while less than 20 percent hold certification in either bilingual or ESL instruction.

TABLE 1.4 Types of Services Received by Students with LEP Nationally[a]

Type of Service	% of Students Receiving Services	Mean Years in Elementary Program Prior to Exit
Type 1: No special or additional services Students receive no specialized instruction and may or may not be specially monitored.	1.9	2.9
Type 2: Additional services nonspecific to LEP needs Students receive services that are not designed for LEP needs, such as in-class aids, tutoring, and special education.	1.3	2.6
Type 3: Some services, English only Students receive services designed for LEP needs but delivered in English in special settings not designed for such students. Services include special aids, teachers, or ESL instruction provided less than 10 hours per week.	17.4	2.8
Type 4: Some services, some native language[b] Students receive services similar to Type 3 but with some native language instruction.	6.4	3.4
Type 5: Some services, significant native language[c] Students receive services similar to Types 3 and 4 but with significant native language instruction.	2.8	2.5
Type 6: Intensive services, English only Students receive services designed for LEP needs in English in settings focused on such students. Services include ESL instruction for less than 10 hours per week and content instruction.	13.3	2.6
Type 7: Intensive services, some native language Students receive services similar to Type 6 but with some native language instruction.	14.4	3.4
Type 8: Intensive services, significant native language Students receive services similar to Types 6 and 7 but with significant native language instruction.	33.7	3.3
Unknown: Type of services could not be determined	9.0	

[a]Based on a sample of 1,677 schools reporting on 2,307,444 students.
[b]"Some native language" is defined as <50% in one academic subject or <25% in math, science, and social studies combined.
[c]"Significant native language" is defined as >50% in one academic subject or >25% in math, science, and social studies combined.
Note: From *Descriptive Study of Services to Limited English Proficient Students* (pp. 34, 37) by H. L. Fleischman and P. L. Hopstock, 1993, Arlington, VA. Development Associates.

Program Effectiveness
The effectiveness of our current delivery of services to students with LEP is a topic that is hotly debated in educational and political circles. The prevailing issue is the relative effectiveness of ESL-only instruction; "early exit," or short-term transitional bilingual programs; and "late exit," or long-term transitional bilingual programs. Collier (1992), in a synthesis of studies that examined achievement over periods of at least four years, decides in favor of longer term bilingual programs: "the greater the amount of L1 instructional support for language-minority students, combined with balanced L2 support, the higher they are able to achieve academically in L2 in each succeeding academic year, in comparison to matched groups being schooled monolingually in L2" (p. 205).

This conclusion supports popular theoretical models of bilingualism and raises serious questions about our current service delivery practices. If we are reasonably certain that longer term bilingual instruction enhances achievement while also producing students who can operate effectively in two languages and two cultural systems, why are nearly two-thirds of students with LEP being instructed in English only or with limited use of native language, and why are students being exited from specialized programs after a few short years? We will need to address the gap between best practice and current practice, including the lack of standard state policies, assessment procedures, and teaching credentials, to provide better long-term outcomes for CLD students.

DISABILITY AND EDUCATION

In general, public support for the education of students with disabilities has been more consistent, stronger, and less controversial than for the education of CLD students. The reason for this support is related to the fact that disability has no racial, ethnic, cultural, language, or socioeconomic barriers. Disability is a potential state of existence for all of us, whether it occurs by accident or as a result of disease, aging, or a traumatic emotional event. Disability as either an acquired or hereditary condition may also occur in those close to us. While our capacity to deal effectively with disability is certainly influenced by the resources we have or are able to access, disability is a human condition that engages us all. Societal responses to disability, therefore, tend to reflect our personal concerns. For example, we are more likely to support education for students with mental retardation when our own grandchildren may be born with Down's syndrome or to favor the funding of mandatory lifts on buses when we may someday be in need of such services.

In many ways, the progress of individuals with disabilities in this country is a model of what we as Americans think should happen when there are wrongs that need to be set right. Finding little recourse in the educational and welfare systems, disability advocates began to argue successfully for equal opportunities in the courts. Civil rights legislation and the establishment of public funding sources soon followed, with the most recent federal developments being the Individuals with Disabilities Education Act (IDEA), (1990), formerly known as the Education for All Handicapped Children Act (EAHCA) (1975) which mandates free appropriate public education to all students with disabilities, and the Americans with Disabilities Act (ADA) (1990), which mandates against the discrimination of individuals with disabilities in employment, transportation, public accommodations and services, and telecommunications. Based on this history, we have every reason to believe that the lives of students with disabilities will continue to improve. However, the field of special education continues to grapple with unsettled issues: How do we identify learning and behavior problems without labeling? How do we provide early intervention in times of reduced funding? How do we provide service in the context of the general education setting? How can we support the transition of students into productive adult lives?

Disability Awareness

A major obstacle to improving the quality of life for individuals with disabilities is the lack of public knowledge about the nature of disability. A "disability" is a physical and/or cognitive impairment that significantly limits the ability of an individual to participate in one or more of the major activities of life, including working, learning, and caring for one's self. A chronic heart condition, multiple dystrophy, manic depression, and dyslexia are all examples of disabilities that may occur in adults or children. A disability may be obvious, as in the case of an individual who is in a wheelchair, or it may be often inconspicuous, as in the case of an individual who has trouble with math calculations due to a learning disability. While always serious, each of the major categories of disability range from mild to severe. In the case of hearing impairments, for example, an individual may experience a loss that results in missing only certain sounds or a loss that results in having virtually no sound perception. Historically, the most obvious disabilities have received the most attention, leading to both positive and negative outcomes. However, the most obvious disabilities are not always the ones that are most severe. An individual who cannot read or write due to a learning disability, for example, may be more limited in her capacity to earn a decent salary than someone with a prosthetic arm.

As educators, we are often aware of disabilities only to the extent that we have to make certain minimum adaptations for students with these disabilities in our schools. We remain largely unaware of the educational, psychological, and social implications of growing up with a disability and consequently impede the development of these students in our classrooms. Many of us believe, for example, that a disability is largely under the control of the individual. We think that if eight-year-old Erica would just pay attention long enough, she could learn her numbers, when in fact it is her very inability to attend consistently and to remember stimuli, especially in sequence, that qualifies her for learning disabilities services. We also think that certain disabilities, such as mental retardation, are beyond intervention. So, despite evidence to the contrary, we see basic reading instruction in English—let alone in two languages—for thirteen-year-old Jorge as unproductive. In the area of social relationships, we see students with disabilities as outcasts. Miranda is ready to graduate and will stay at home, won't date, and certainly won't marry, so why should we be bothered with silly ideas about inclusive sex education classes for her? On a more positive note, educators are increasingly recognizing that former ideas about disability are no longer valid and have begun to reformulate their notions about disability based on personal experience with students in their classrooms.

A Glimpse at the State of Special Education

Students with disabilities are served in special education programs under the auspices of the IDEA. As we explain in detail in Chapter 2, all states are required to provide educational services to students with disabilities under specific nondiscriminatory guidelines. While many states had special education programs in place prior to the 1970s, special education as we know it today began in 1975 with the passage of the EAHCA. Since that time, there have been changes in service delivery patterns and in the age, number, and characteristics of students. The following sections will describe the students currently served by the IDEA, their educational placements, and the program outcomes.

Definition of Students with Disabilities

The IDEA defines students with disabilities, ages three through twenty-one, as those who have autism, deaf-blindness, hearing impairments including deafness, mental retardation, multiple disabilities, orthopedic impairments, other health impairments, speech or language impairments, serious emotional disturbance, specific learning disabilities, traumatic brain injury, or visual impairments including blindness, and who require special education and related services as a result of these impairments (see Box 1.3). In the case of students ages three through five, states may also include those who need special education and related services because they are experiencing developmental delays in physical development, cognitive development, communication development, social or emotional development, and/or adaptive development.

BOX 1.3   Disabilities as Defined by the IDEA

Autism: Developmental disability significantly affecting verbal and nonverbal communication and social interaction, generally evident before age 3, that adversely affects a child's educational performance. Other characteristics often associated with autism are engagement in repetitive activities and stereotyped movements, resistance to environmental change or change in daily routines, and unusual responses to sensory experiences. The term does not apply if the child's educational performance is adversely affected primarily because the child has a serious emotional disturbance.

Deaf-blindness: Concomitant hearing and visual impairments, the combination of which causes such severe communication and other developmental and educational problems that they cannot be accommodated in special education programs solely for children with deafness or children with blindness.

Deafness: Hearing impairment that is so severe that the child is impaired in processing linguistic information through hearing, with or without amplification, that adversely affects educational performance.

Hearing impairment: An impairment in hearing, whether permanent or fluctuating, that adversely affects a child's educational performance but that is not included under the definition of deafness in this section.

Mental retardation: Significantly subaverage general intellectual functioning existing concurrently with deficits in adaptive behavior and manifested during the developmental period, which adversely affects a child's educational performance.

Multiple disabilities: Concomitant impairments (such as mental retardation–blindness, mental retardation–orthopedic impairment, etc.), the combination of which causes such severe educational problems that they cannot be accommodated for in special education programs solely for one of the impairments. The term does not include deaf-blindness.

Orthopedic impairment: A severe orthopedic impairment that adversely affects a child's educational performance. The term includes impairments caused by congenital anomaly (e.g., clubfoot, absence of some member, etc.), impairments caused by disease (e.g., poliomyelitis, bone tuberculosis, etc.), and impairments from other causes (e.g., cerebral palsy, amputations, and fractures or burns, which cause contractures).

Serious emotional disturbance: A condition exhibiting one or more of the following characteristics over a long period of time and to a marked degree that adversely affects educational performance:

- An inability to learn that cannot be explained by intellectual, sensory, or health factors;
- An inability to build or maintain satisfactory interpersonal relationships with peers and teachers;

Continued

23

BOX 1.3 *Continued*

- Inappropriate types of behavior or feelings under normal circumstances;
- A general pervasive mood of unhappiness or depression; or
- A tendency to develop physical symptoms or fears associated with personal or school problems.

The term includes schizophrenia. The term does not include children who are socially maladjusted, unless it is determined that they have a serious emotional disturbance.

Specific learning disability: A disorder in one or more of the basic psychological processes involved in understanding or using language, spoken or written, which may manifest itself as an imperfect ability to listen, think, speak, read, write, spell, or do mathematical calculations. The term includes such conditions as perceptual disabilities, brain injury, brain dysfunction, dyslexia, and developmental aphasia. The term does not apply to children who have learning problems that are primarily the result of visual, hearing, or motor handicaps, of mental retardation, of emotional disturbance, or of environmental, cultural, or economic disadvantage.

Speech or language impairment: A communication disorder such as stuttering, impaired articulation, a language impairment, or a voice impairment, that adversely affects a child's educational performance.

Traumatic brain injury: An acquired injury to the head caused by an external physical force, resulting in total or partial functional disability or psychosocial impairment, or both, that adversely affects a child's educational performance. The term applies to open and closed head injuries resulting in impairments in one or more areas, such as cognition; language; memory; attention; reasoning; abstract thinking; judgment, problem solving; sensory, perceptual, and motor abilities; psychosocial behavior; physical functions; information processing; and speech. The term does not apply to brain injuries that are congenital or degenerative, or brain injuries induced by birth trauma.

Visual impairment including blindness: An impairment in vision that, even with correction, adversely affects a child's educational performance. The term includes both partial sight and blindness.

Number and Disability of Students Served

According to the *Sixteenth Annual Report to Congress on the Implementation of the Individuals with Disabilities Educuation Act,* over five million children and youth with disabilities receive special education services (U.S. Department of Education, 1994 [see also Box 1.1]). This number represents approximately 6.4 percent of all children from birth through age twenty-one in the nation, an increase of about 2 percent since the inception of the IDEA. The report suggests that poverty, prenatal exposure to drugs and alcohol, and improved identification due to fiscal incentives may be factors responsible for the increase. Over 90 percent of the students receiving services fall in the categories of specific learning disabilities, speech/language impairments, serious emotional disturbance, and mental retardation (see Box 1.1). Specific learning disabilities is the largest and fastest growing category. Students with multiple disabilities, hearing impairments, orthopedic impairments, and other health impairments each account for approximately 1 percent to 2 percent of the group served. Students with visual impairments, deaf-blindness, autism, and traumatic brain injury account for the remainder of the group.

Educational Placement

Data from the same report show that the vast majority, or approximately 94 percent, of students with disabilities receive services in general education settings, including the general class, the resource room, and the separate class. The remaining students are served in either separate schools, residential facilities, at home, or in hospital settings.

- General class placement includes students who receive the majority of education in the general class and their special education services for less than 21 percent of the school day either in or outside of the general class. Approximately 35 percent of students are served in this placement type.
- Resource room placement includes students who receive special education services outside the general class for at least 21 percent but no more than 60 percent of the school day. Approximately 36 percent of students are served in this placement type.
- Separate class placement includes students who receive special education services outside of the general class for more than 60 percent of the school day. Approximately 24 percent of students are served in this placement type.

Placement patterns vary considerably by state, with some states having much higher segregated placements than others. Placement also varies by age group and disability. Younger students are more likely to be served in the general class compared to secondary students. Overall, students with disabilities traditionally perceived as mild (e.g., speech/language impairments, learning disabilities) are more likely to be served in less restrictive settings than students with disabilities traditionally perceived as more severe (e.g., multiple disabilities, deaf-blindness). Students with speech or language impairments are most likely to be served in the general class. For students with learning disabilities, a resource room is most typical, while for students with mental retardation, a separate class placement is most typical.

Program Effectiveness

Although the IDEA has been in existence for two decades, the long-term effectiveness of special education programs has not been well researched.

Reports from the National Center on Educational Outcomes indicate that this lack of information is due largely to the exclusion and/or poor accommodation of students with disabilities in state and national assessments (McGrew, Thurlow, Shriner, & Spiegel, 1992; Ysseldyke & Thurlow, 1993). There is also difficulty in defining and measuring appropriate indicators of the success and quality of life for individuals with disabilities. Initial data from the National Longitudinal Transition Study of Special Education Students, which is one of the few longer-term studies to document qualitative aspects of successful transition, indicate that the majority of students with disabilities are able to function independently as adults in at least two of three important life domains—employment, residential, and social (Wagner, D'Amico, Marder, Newman, & Blackorby, 1992). However, even among these individuals, employment opportunities tend to consist of low-skill, low-wage jobs that are often part-time, and the quality of their residential situations and social lives may also not be comparable to those of people without disabilities. Clearly, the IDEA has expanded the opportunity for individuals with disabilities to pursue academic and vocational options, but developing programs that will maximize these options, particularly in relation to the needs of CLD students, remains a challenge in special education.

SERVING STUDENTS WITH DUAL NEEDS

National reports on bilingual and special education have yet to document fully the status of services to students with dual needs. Concerning identification issues, we know that there are disparities in the percentages of students receiving special education services by racial/ethnic origins (see Table 1.1), but we have much to uncover about the specific parameters of the population served, including procedures for diagnosis, native language background, pertinent cultural issues, proficiency levels in L1 and L2, and socioeconomic status. We also have much to learn about the parameters of the population that is unserved, including geographic location, unique needs, and the structure and staffing of agencies responsible for the outreach and coordination of services. Concerning programmatic issues, we presume that students with LEP and disabilities receive the same types of services as other students with LEP (see Table 1.4), ranging from no services (Type 1), to some services, English only (Type 3), to intensive services, significant native language (Type 8), in the same types of settings as other students with disabilities, ranging from the general education class (bilingual or monolingual English) to a resource class to a separate school. However, there is little information about how culturally and linguistically appropriate instruction is actually addressed in the individualized education program (IEP), including whether students receive native language or ESL services, the context in which these services are delivered, and the qualifications of those responsible for the instruction.

In general, the goals and problems of bilingual and special education are remarkably similar. Both fields are concerned with the inclusion of previously excluded groups; with working collaboratively with peers, parents, and community members; with developing relevant curriculum and related strategies of assessment and instruction; with selecting appropriate methods of delivering services; and with assuring improved long-term academic, vocational, and social outcomes for students. Both fields are also concerned with developing experimental and descriptive data bases that help translate theory into successful practice. Relatedly, students served by each field share similar struggles. They are often socially and physically isolated in separate environments for all or part of the day and academically isolated by curricular decisions that place them in remedial and vocational tracks. As a result, many are unable to break through the glass ceiling to higher education to fulfill their academic potential or to participate fully in life's major domains. In addition, the concerns and values of the family are often excluded from the educational process.

When students have dual needs, these goals and problems are intensified. Let us take the case of a young Hispanic boy who has good receptive and expressive oral language in English and Spanish, but who also has a learning disability that has significantly impeded the development of his reading and writing skills. From a bilingual education perspective, biliteracy is valued, and a case could be made for teaching reading in the language most often used at home (i.e., Spanish) before introducing English. From a special education perspective, we have a bright child who is capable of learning orally in both languages but who will need to spend considerable time and energy to build written language skills. Do we promote English or Spanish reading and writing? Do we attempt both? Do we minimize emphasis on written skills in favor of bilingual oral instruction and responding? And once a path is chosen, who will be responsible for providing instruction, and where and how will the instruction take place? If we conceptualize learning problems as belonging solely to the student, we would place the boy in a self-contained class for students with severe learning disabilities, work primarily on his deficit areas, conduct the instruction in English, and hope that he would one day "catch up" with his peers. But if we conceptualize the origin of learning problems more holistically, however, we would keep him in the general education setting, provide an enriching bilingual curriculum through oral means, and work to improve his written skills without sacrificing the development of his knowledge in content areas. This approach includes rather than excludes students and presents an opportunity for educators from both fields to do what they do best—provide specialized instruction to meet unique learning needs.

AN "ALL-ONE-SYSTEM" PHILOSOPHY

Meeting the needs of CLD students with or at-risk of learning problems will require a major transformation of our perceptions of the educational process. Hodgkinson (1985) argues that the major source of difficulty in schools is the perception of the educational system as a set of isolated institutions rather than as a single entity through which individuals move. From day care centers to elementary schools to universities, the system operates as discrete units based restrictively on age. Educators behave as though there is no relation among these units, and students consequently experience poor transition and follow through from one unit to the next. To improve the quality of American education, Hodgkinson (1985) encourages us to view the educational system as a continuum much like an ecological food chain, in which any alteration in the chain has the potential to affect organisms at all points on the chain. It is only when the system is perceived in terms of the individuals who move through it will we be able to make substantial positive changes.

A related source of difficulties in schools is the failure of the educational system and other community systems to recognize that they serve essentially the same clients and to provide coordinated services (Hodgkinson, 1989). Providers of education, correction, transportation, health, and housing often operate as though there is no relation between factors such as dropout rates and incarceration or poverty and achievement levels. But as Hodgkinson (1989) vividly points out, a homeless, sick, or hungry student is obviously a poor learner, yet schools have limited interaction with the very systems that could provide crucial support for such a person.

Building on this holistic perspective, we suggest a student-centered collaborative model among the systems of service delivery within schools. Currently, services to students are often delivered as though there is no connection between the goals of general education and specialized support areas. Concerning CLD students, this lack of interaction often results in segregated placement in remedial bilingual or special education programs. These students are put in the position of having to "earn" their way back to general education, as though there is something wrong with them that has to be fixed. In a student-centered collaborative model, however, the general education environment is a function of the students it serves. Students and their families are viewed within the context of a responsive general education environment where curriculum in the humanities, the sciences, and the arts that is appropriate for the community is offered. Specialized curriculum or services in areas including bilingual/ESL, gifted/talented, vocational, counseling, academic development, and special education are planned for and delivered in ways that support general education goals. Community systems are easily accessible for personal and school performance-related concerns. The practical application of an all-one-system philosophy for CLD students with or at-risk of learning problems would be highly favorable to the delivery of services in general education and community settings; the linkage of assessment and instructional methods to meet idiosyncratic learning needs; the development of skills needed for a multicultural world, including bilingualism; and the involvement of family and community members in addressing academic and vocational outcomes.

Three beliefs are critical to an all-one-system philosophy and its practical application to CLD students. First is the belief that our educational programs are no better than the long-term outcomes for our students. Second is the belief that we need to reach beyond our own disciplines and areas of service in order to comprehend the full impact of the education system on students. Third is the belief that these disciplines and service areas form an interdependent network that contributes to the failure and success of students in their adult lives. Acting on these beliefs, we are more likely to design and implement programs that suit the needs of CLD students rather than the structure of our particular setting; we are less likely to make uninformed and prejudicial decisions in our instructional planning; and we are apt to work across disciplines and service areas. For students who belong to the new mainstream, an all-one-system philosophy holds the promise of an improved quality of life. For society, an all-one-system philosophy holds the promise of streamlined and more effective educational and social services with lowered national costs and an increasing number of productive citizens.

In summary, we have attempted to relate the fields of bilingual education and special education to the broader concepts of diversity and discrimination and to identify concerns common to CLD students and students with disabilities. We have also attempted to frame a role for educators that demands a critical analysis of their value systems, self-education and collaboration across disciplines in education, and advocacy on behalf of CLD students and their families. We believe that the many problems faced by students who have been historically discriminated against in the schools, especially CLD students with or at-risk of learning problems, can be significantly reduced by the adoption of an all-one-system philosophy of service delivery. We also believe that educators can be more effective advocates for their students when working in a system that demands collaboration and constant attention to long-term outcomes.

REFERENCES

Americans with Disabilities Act of 1990, P.L. 101–336, 104 Stat. 327.

Baca, L. M., & Payan, R. M. (1989). Development of the bilingual special education interface. In L. M. Baca & H. T. Cervantes (Eds.), *The bilingual special education interface* (pp. 79–99). Columbus, OH: Merrill.

Baker, C. (1993). *Foundations of bilingual education and bilingualism.* Clevedon, England: Multilingual Matters.

Bilingual Education Act of 1994 (Title VII of Improving America's Schools Act, P.L. 103–382), 108 Stat. 3716.

Collier, V. P. (1992). A synthesis of studies examining long-term language minority student data on academic achievement. *Bilingual Research Journal, 16,* 187–212.

Commission on Minority Participation in Education and American Life. (1988). *One-third of a nation.* Washington, DC: American Council on Education, Education Commission of the States.

Cummins, J. (1981). The role of primary language development in promoting educational success for language minority students. In California State Department of Education (Ed.), *Schooling and language minority students: A theoretical framework.* Evaluation, Dissemination and Assessment Center, California State University, Los Angeles.

Cummins, J. (1984). *Bilingualism and special education: Issues in assessment and pedagogy.* Clevedon, England: Multilingual Matters.

Cummins, J. (1989). *Empowering minority students.* Sacramento: California Association for Bilingual Education.

Education for All Handicapped Children Act of 1975, P.L. 94–142, 89 Stat. 773.

Fleischman, H. L., & Hopstock, P. J. (1993). *Descriptive study of services to limited English proficient students.* Arlington, VA: Development Associates.

Hodgkinson, H. H. (1985). *All one system.* Washington, DC: Institute for Education Research.

Hodgkinson, H. H. (1989). *The same client: The demographics of education and service delivery systems.* Washington, DC: Institute for Education Research.

Hodgkinson, H. H. (1992). *A demographic look at tomorrow.* Washington, DC: Institute for Education Research.

Individuals with Disabilities Education Act of 1990, P.L. 101–476, 104 Stat. 1103.

McGrew, K. S., Thurlow, M. L., Shriner, J. G., & Spiegel, A. N. (1992). *Inclusion of students with disabilities in national and state data collection programs* (Technical Report 2). Minneapolis: University of Minnesota, National Center on Educational Outcomes.

Office for Civil Rights, U.S. Department of Education (1993). The Fall 1990 Elementary and Secondary School Civil Rights Survey. Washington, DC: Author.

U.S. Department of Education, Office of Special Education Programs. (1994). *Sixteenth annual report to Congress on the implementation of the Individuals with Disabilities Education Act.* Washington, DC: Author.

Waggoner, D. (1993). The growth of multilingualism and the need for bilingual education: What do we know so far? *Bilingual Research Journal, 17,* 1–12.

Wagner, M., D'Amico, R., Marder, C., Newman, L., Blackorby, J. *What happens next? Trends in the postschool outcomes of youth with disabilities.* Menlo Park, CA: SRI International.

Ysseldyke, J., & Thurlow, M. (1993). *Developing a model of educational outcomes* (NCEO Outcomes & Indicators Report 1). Minneapolis: University of Minnesota, National Center on Educational Outcomes.

2

LEGAL ASPECTS OF BILINGUAL
AND SPECIAL EDUCATION

This chapter provides a foundation for educators seeking to expand their roles as policy-makers and advocates for CLD students, especially those suspected of or identified as having disabilities. We begin the chapter with the concept of achieving educational equity and then present overviews of various legal developments related to serving CLD students and students with disabilities. These sections include a summary of major civil rights legislation, the Bilingual Education Act, the Individuals with Disabilities Education Act, and related case law. We close the chapter by examining the implications of the legal issues for CLD students suspected of or identified as having disabilities in the areas of assessment and instruction and presenting an example of advocacy at the state level that has the potential for significantly improving services to this group.

ACHIEVING EDUCATIONAL EQUITY

Providing appropriate education to CLD students, especially those with or at-risk of learning problems, is part of the larger, historical effort in the United States to improve educational equity across groups that have been historically discriminated against on the basis of characteristics including race, national origin, gender, disability, and economic status. The African American community provided the major impetus for change in this struggle when attorneys from the National Association for the Advancement of Colored People (NAACP) successfully argued against racial segregation in the schools in *Brown v. the Board of Education of Topeka* (1954). The U.S. Supreme Court declared that "in the field of public education the doctrine of 'separate but equal' has no place." Following this landmark decision, a national study of the lack of equal educational opportunity was mandated by civil rights legislation in the 1960s. Known commonly as the Coleman Report (Coleman, et al., 1966), this document began what continues to be a heated debate over the concept of educational equity and how this concept might be realized. In general, the legislative and court systems have moved away from the notion of equal educational opportunity as a means of simply providing equal treatment and services across different groups to a more sophisticated analysis of the fairness of educational outcomes. Obviously, the opportunities and support that students receive in school have a tremendous impact on their ability to contribute to society economically and to participate socially in later years. Since students begin school with different needs, these opportunities and support should be designed accordingly. Attempts to improve educational equity for CLD students suspected of or identified as having disabilities have been especially trying because of the unique needs of this population and because patterns of discrimination related to language, culture, poverty, and disability persist.

Legal developments in providing services to CLD students and to students with disabilities have taken somewhat different paths. In general, we operate under fairly straightforward mandates in disability-related areas, but we do not operate consistently or under firm regulations when dealing with areas of cultural and linguistic diversity. For example, in special education, states are directly mandated to follow specific guidelines in both the identification and education of students with disabilities under penalty of the withdrawal of federal funds. In fact, federal legislation actually encourages parents to sue for noncompliance by requiring the losing education agency to pay attorneys' fees and/or money damages. No comparable legislation exists in relation to bilingual education, although civil rights laws clearly ban discrimination against CLD students. This lack of uniformity adds to the complexity of providing appropriate services to CLD students with disabilities. In addition, few legislative actions and court decisions specifically mention these students or comprehensively address their needs. As advocates, therefore, we often face the difficult task of synthesizing federal, state, and local policies and procedures related to bilingual/ESL education and special education while attempting to provide the best possible program for the individual. These next sections are presented to assist educators in this task.

THE STRUGGLE FOR THE RIGHT TO CULTURALLY AND LINGUISTICALLY APPROPRIATE EDUCATION

Although the United States prides itself on the cultural diversity of its society, the establishment of curriculum that meets the needs of CLD students in

American schools has been a difficult endeavor. Chronicles of bilingual education depict a saga of accomplishments and setbacks (Ambert & Melendez, 1985; Andersson & Boyer, 1978; August & Garcia, 1988; Crawford, 1991). In colonial and early national times, acceptance of the cultural and linguistic differences among European groups was typical as settlers from these various nations entered the country. The German community, for example, established many private schools for the purpose of retaining their language and culture and the Continental Congresses of 1774–89 regularly published documents in German and French. Favorable public attitudes toward bilingualism changed, however, as a distinct American culture began to form and as English continued to dominate as the obvious although unofficial language of the country. Beginning in the late 1800s, public and private bilingual education programs were terminated in many states, and by the early 1900s, there was a federally sanctioned national trend to suppress Native American and immigrant languages and cultures. Fear over possible disloyalty by German Americans during World War I virtually destroyed the German school network. Native American children were often taken from their families and forced to attend English-only schools as a way of destroying ties to their native culture. In the Southwest, Mexican American children and their teachers were restricted from using Spanish on school grounds, in some cases well past the mid-1900s.

Hope for culturally and linguistically appropriate education was not revitalized until after World War I. Several factors helped to set the stage for the establishment of bilingual education programs, including the *Brown* decision of 1954 and subsequent discussions of the meaning of educational equity, a national interest in upgrading the quality of American education in response to the Soviet launching of the *Sputnik* satellite in 1957, and research on the development and treatment of children in poverty who were often from CLD backgrounds. During this time, specialized instruction in ESL began to emerge as a way to remediate what was seen as "deficiencies" of language and culture. The ESL approach, however, did not erase problems of underachievement or deal with growing social concern over the retention of native language and culture in the American mainstream. The reemergence of bilingual education came in the early 1960s, largely as a result of the influx of Cuban refugees to Dade County, Florida. Unlike other immigrant groups or indigenous peoples of the time, the Cuban community was largely professional and politically favored. In a relatively short time, they established a pilot two-way bilingual education program, in which Spanish-speakers learned English and English-speakers learned Spanish, that received national attention for the outstanding achievement of its students. The success of this project and the passage of civil rights legislation helped to persuade politicians and school districts to establish programs for students with LEP in which the use of native language and culture was included. Unfortunately, as Crawford (1991) stresses, these programs were established and perceived largely as programs for "disadvantaged" students rather than as programs of enrichment, thus setting the stage for future negative public opinion about bilingual services.

Fitzgerald (1993) suggests that we view our past experience with bilingual education as a series of history lessons that help us to analyze current trends. The first history lesson involves the change in American values from colonial times to the present. In the colonies, personal freedom and individual expression were high priorities and major reasons for settlement. In current times, however, practical concerns over issues such as economics, health, and crime often take precedence over idealized principles. Hence, bilingual education is viewed as a luxury that the country cannot afford. The second history lesson is that times of peak immigration are associated with declines in support for bilingualism. Large numbers of immigrants, such as exist currently, appear to make the American public uneasy. Insisting that immigrants learn and use English is one way of settling fears about demographic and social change. The third history lesson is that public sentiment leans toward nationalism, and even isolationism, when the country is involved in offshore conflicts. Our increasing global involvement may be associated with the overall lack of support for bilingualism in the country. On a more positive note, history suggests that, just as the Anglo-Saxon language and culture grew to dominate the country in earlier times, increasing numbers of individuals from CLD backgrounds will slowly rise to positions of authority. As this happens, and as the global economy grows, culturally and linguistically appropriate education may become the norm rather than the exception.

Legislative Actions

Federal legislation has played a major role in framing the development of culturally and linguistically appropriate education by dealing with civil rights issues and by establishing sources of funding (see Ambert & Melendez, 1985; Andersson & Boyer, 1978; August & Garcia, 1988; Baca & Cervantes, 1989; Crawford, 1991). Civil rights legislation has established a legal basis for specialized educational services for students with LEP, while the creation of discretionary funding programs has helped to shape the content and delivery of these services in the field. In relation to students with disabilities, civil rights legislation prohibits discrimination against CLD students regardless of disability, while discretionary funding programs include and sometimes focus spending on students with LEP and disabilities.

Civil Rights Legislation

The Civil Rights Act of 1964 prohibits discrimination on the basis of race, color, sex, and national origin by any program or activity receiving federal funding. In related guidelines issued in 1968 by the U.S. Department of Health, Education, and Welfare (HEW), students of a particular race or national origin may not be denied the opportunity to receive curricula, classes, and activities available to other pupils. HEW expanded these guidelines in 1970, in a document referred to as the May 25 Memorandum, by requiring districts to (1) rectify the language deficiencies of students from national origin minority groups; (2) refrain from assigning pupils to special education on the basis of criteria that reflected English skills; (3) insure that ability grouping based on language skills did not result in permanent tracking; and (4) notify parents of school activities in a language that they understood. The Equal Educational Opportunities and Transportation of Students Act of 1974 further strengthened the civil rights basis for culturally and linguistically appropriate education. This act states that the failure of school districts to take action to overcome language barriers that impede equal participation in instructional programs is an unlawful denial of equal educational opportunity. While neither piece of legislation directly mentions students with LEP and disabilities, the acts and related guidelines make it clear that schools must address the needs of all students with LEP. Schools are given broad latitude, however, in deciding the nature and delivery of such services.

Discretionary Funding: The Bilingual Education Act

The Bilingual Education Act (BEA), also known as Title VII of the Elementary and Secondary Education Act (ESEA), was added to the ESEA in 1968. The BEA has been reauthorized at four-year intervals since that time, with the latest reauthorization occurring in 1994 as part of the Improving America's Schools Act (IASA). Over the years, the BEA has greatly influenced the delivery of services to students with LEP at the local and state levels. Originally, the BEA was designed to serve only students with limited English speaking ability (LESA). However, this narrow focus was expanded in the 1978 reauthorization to include students with limited written as well as oral abilities in English, and the terminology was changed from LESA to limited english proficient, or LEP. (See Chapter 1 for the definition of LEP contained in the BEA.) The BEA does not directly address disabilities in its definition of LEP, but students with LEP and disabilities are subsumed under the broader category. Unlike the Individuals with Disabilities Education Act of 1990 (IDEA), which guarantees the provision of services to students in addition to discretionary funding, the BEA does not compel school districts to offer specialized programs. However, the BEA presents a strong rationale to states and local districts for providing culturally and linguistically appropriate education and encourages the development of such programs through discretionary funding. The BEA also presents ideas and options for the creation and evaluation of services by describing the characteristics of programs eligible for federal funding.

Rationale for Bilingual Programs

The BEA provides an extensive list of the reasons why it should be the policy of the United States to encourage the development of appropriate programs for students with LEP. In general, the BEA officially recognizes the need to provide specialized instruction to students with LEP, affirming instruction in students' native language and culture and citing the problems of doing so, including the lack of qualified educational personnel and poor assessment techniques. The new BEA also directly recognizes the importance of bilingualism as a long-term outcome. The inclusion of this concept is viewed by the National Association for Bilingual Education (NABE) as the most significant recent change in the law, especially in light of the political challenges to bilingual education during the entire ESEA reauthorization process (Lyons, 1994).

The points in the federal policy most germane to advocates seeking culturally and linguistically appropriate services for students with LEP include the following:

- The federal government has a special and continuing obligation to ensure that state education agencies (SEAs) and local education agencies (LEAs) take appropriate action to provide equal educational opportunities to students with LEP.
- Multilingual skills constitute an important national resource that deserves protection and development.
- Quality bilingual programs enable students to learn English and meet high academic standards, including proficiency in more than one language.
- The use of a student's native language and culture in classroom instruction can (1) promote self-esteem and contribute to academic achievement; (2) benefit English-proficient students who participate in such programs; and (3) develop our national language resources, thus promoting our competitiveness in the global economy.
- Students with LEP face educational challenges, including segregated programs, disproportionate and improper placement in special education and other special programs due to the use of inappropriate evaluation procedures, and a shortage of teachers and other staff qualified to meet their needs.
- Parent and community participation in bilingual education programs contributes to program effectiveness.

Instructional Programs Eligible for Funding

Part A, Subpart 1, of the BEA—Bilingual Education Capacity and Demonstration Grants—provides competitive funding in four program categories: development and implementation grants, enhancement grants, comprehensive school grants, and systemwide improvement grants. Each category supports projects in which either a "bilingual education program" or a "special alternative instructional program" for students with LEP is utilized. A bilingual education program uses both English and the student's native language in instruction. The bilingual program may also develop the student's native language, including the ancestral languages of American Indians, Alaskan natives, and native Hawaiians, although this is not required. Students who are English proficient may participate in a bilingual education program provided that its goal is to enable all enrolled students to become proficient in English and a second language. A special alternative instructional program uses specially designed English language curricula and services, without instruction in the student's native language. The BEA states that this approach is particularly appropriate in situations where either the diversity of languages spoken or the small number of students with LEP makes bilingual education impractical and in situations where the shortage of bilingual teachers is critical. However, priority is given to applications that provide for the development of bilingual proficiency in English and another language. Meeting standards in concert with the National Education Goals (Goals 2000: Educate America Act of 1994—see discussion in Chapter 9), including academic mastery of subject area content and age-appropriate grade promotion and graduation, are requirements of both types of instructional programs.

Other Features of the BEA
The BEA also provides funds for activities under other related categories. These categories deal with (1) research, evaluation, and dissemination, including the National Clearinghouse for Bilingual Education (NCBE), technical assistance centers, and grants to SEAs for data collection and evaluation; (2) professional development, including career ladder programs and training for all teachers about assessment and instruction to students with LEP; (3) foreign language assistance to promote the study of foreign languages in elementary and high schools; and (4) emergency immigrant education to assist LEAs with large increases in the number of immigrant students.

Litigative Actions
Litigation concerning the specific responsibilities of school districts in educating students with LEP began following the passage of civil rights legislation (see Ambert & Melendez, 1985; Andersson & Boyer, 1978; August & Garcia, 1988; Baca & Cervantes, 1989; Crawford, 1991; Fernandez, 1992). The most notable of these cases was *Lau v. Nichols* (1974), which originated in San Francisco and was decided by the U.S. Supreme Court. In this case, Chinese students who did not speak English charged that the district was denying them equal educational opportunity by not providing them with some type of appropriate instruction. Approximately 1,800 of these pupils were not receiving the district's limited ESL services at the time of the lawsuit. The

school district argued that it provided the same instruction to all students and was not responsible if some students did not speak English. Although the court side-stepped the issue of equal protection under the Fourteenth Amendment, a decision was made in favor of the plaintiffs based on the Civil Rights Act of 1964 and related regulations. The Court stated that "there is no equality of treatment merely by providing students with the same facilities, text books, teachers, and curriculum; for students who do not understand English are effectively foreclosed from any meaningful education." The district was ordered to implement appropriate assessment and instruction to students with LEP. The court did not, however, specify what the content of that appropriate instruction was to be, that is, bilingual instruction, ESL services, or some other method.

Subsequent cases have further defined the responsibilities of school districts. For example, in *Aspira of New York v. Board of Education of the City of New York* (1975), the court required the New York school district to implement a language proficiency testing program for Hispanic students and to provide bilingual education, not simply ESL instruction, for students who tested as Spanish dominant. In *Castañeda v. Pickard* (1981), the court ruled that school districts must provide CLD students with programs that are (1) based on sound educational theory; (2) implemented in an effective manner that includes adequate training and funding; and (3) produce positive results over a reasonable time. In *Keyes v. Denver School District No. 1* (1983), the court applied the *Castañeda* standards and found that the district had not directed adequate resources to its language program. The court issued a comprehensive opinion on language programming in the schools, and, as a result, the Denver public schools began several initiatives, including setting standards for bilingual teachers and establishing programs for Asian students.

In what can be considered a "primer" for school district administrators in bilingual/ESL and bilingual special education, Fernandez (1992) discusses eight areas of program requirements that are supported by civil rights legislation and related case law: (1) the provision of appropriate instruction; (2) the selection of programs based on sound theory; (3) the implementation of effective programs; (4) the development of program evaluation procedures; (5) the setting of program standards and monitoring practices; (6) the identification and assessment of students; (7) the monitoring of student progress; and (8) the recruitment and training of personnel. These requirements may be translated as four major obligations that schools have to students with LEP. First, schools have an obligation to identify students with LEP and to monitor their progress once placed in appropriate programs. Identification procedures may include the assessment of English and native language proficiency, English proficiency only, and oral and written proficiency. Evaluations to monitor progress should be closely linked to program assessment and ensure that students do not exit programs prematurely. Second, schools have an obligation to provide appropriate instruction to students with LEP to meet their language needs. Appropriate instruction may include native language instruction and bicultural education, ESL-only instruction, or other beneficial methods. Third, schools have an obligation to offer programs to students with LEP that are based on sound theory, have been adequately implemented, and are evaluated for effectiveness. Programs based on sound theory may or may not include native language instruction, but should ensure that students do not lose ground in academic areas while learning English. Requirements for adequate implementation of programs include the sufficient assignment of resources such as curriculum and teacher training. Evaluations of programs should be designed to ascertain whether satisfactory gains in language and other areas of achievement are being made. Finally, states and school districts have an obligation to establish standards for the education of students with LEP and to monitor programs to ascertain whether standards are being meet.

State Policies

Despite the combined message of civil rights legislation, court decisions, and discretionary funding programs to provide specialized services to students with LEP, only twenty-five of fifty-one SEAs actually require their LEAs to do so (Fleischman & Hopstock, 1993). Most of these SEAs require native language instruction in content areas in addition to ESL services. Of the twenty-six SEAs that do not require specialized services, sixteen promote or encourage such services. Nearly all of these sixteen SEAs encourage ESL services, while about half also encourage native language instruction. In addition, only twenty-two states provide LEAs with funds specifically for instructional programs for students with LEP. Given such varied state policy, and in many cases *weak* state policy, we can easily see how the delivery of services to students with LEP may often be less than adequate. We can also easily see how an inadequate educational program for students with LEP at the local school level may translate into difficulties for students with LEP and disabilities. Even typically well-run special education programs may be hard pressed to provide culturally and linguistically appropriate instruction when there is no comprehensive base of services to students with LEP on which to build.

THE STRUGGLE FOR THE RIGHT TO A FREE, APPROPRIATE PUBLIC EDUCATION FOR STUDENTS WITH DISABILITIES

The history of the treatment of individuals with disabilities shows the best and the worst of societal values and behavior (see Scheerenberger, 1983; Winzer, 1993). The best are examples of community acceptance, such as the story of Shanadar I, a man with physical disabilities who could not hunt but who contributed to his ancient community by cooking and was buried with artifacts signifying respect (Solecki as cited in Scheerenberger, 1983), and of public support for educational programs such as the Perkins Institute and Massachusetts School of the Blind in the 1830s. The worst are examples of cultures practicing infanticide, illustrated by the statement of the Greek philosopher Aristotle that "there [should] be a law that no deformed child live" (cited in Scheerenberger, 1983 p. 12), and of cultures segregating individuals with mental illness or retardation in horrid institutions where they lived among excrement and rats, such as those exposed by Dorthea Dix in the mid-1800s. On balance, however, poor treatment has far outweighed the humane treatment of individuals with disabilities, both nationally and internationally.

In this country, the balance began to equalize slowly in the 1970s as a result of hard-fought court decisions and legislative lobbying. Prior to this, students with disabilities had limited educational opportunities. Students with mild disabilities could enter public schools until such time as the academic work became too demanding. Students with more severe disabilities could attend state-funded schools or charitable institutions. Students whose families had adequate resources could receive an education in private schools or through tutors. Children with disabilities could also simply not attend school, being cared for at home or in institutions, or contributing to the family through labor at home or in the workplace. These options, of course, depended a great deal on the education laws of the states in which the student resided, the economic status of the parents, and the attitude of the family and immediate community.

Litigative Actions

The struggle for public education for students with disabilities has a long history in the court system (see Baca & Cervantes, 1989; Rothstein, 1990; Turnbull, 1986; Weber, 1992). In *Beattie v. Board of Education* (1919), the Wisconsin public schools were allowed to refuse entrance to a student of normal intelligence who had cerebral palsy on the basis that the physical appearance of the student, described by the school board as producing a depressing and nauseating effect on the class, would be detrimental to the education of other students. This unfavorable decision mirrored the public attitudes of shame and fear about individuals with disabilities at that time. By the 1970s, however, public opinion had slowly evolved to the point that most states were providing education to at least some students with disabilities. Taking momentum from the civil rights movement of the 1960s, parents and advocates pushed the courts to determine the specific parameters of the rights of individuals with disabilities to public education and to other typical liberties.

In two cases reminiscent of the *Beattie* case some fifty years earlier, the issues of educability and the value of providing instruction to children with certain types of disabilities were addressed. In *Pennsylvania Association of Retarded Citizens v. Commonwealth of Pennsylvania* (1971) and in *Mills v. Board of Education of the District of Columbia* (1972), school districts were sued for refusing to include students with severe disabilities in public school programs. The outcome in both cases set precedent for the free appropriate public education for all students regardless of the severity of their disabilities. The *Mills* case also set the precedent that the exclusion of students with disabilities from public education was a direct violation of the due process and equal protection clauses of the Fourteenth Amendment.

Other important cases of that period involved the discriminatory treatment of CLD students, especially in relation to the diagnosis of mental retardation. In *Diana v. California State Board of Education* (1970), for example, the court established that students tested for potential placement in special education must be assessed in their native or primary language. In *Arreola v. Santa Ana Board of Education* (1968), the court set precedent for due process prior to placement in special education programs. In *Larry P. v. Wilson Riles* (1972), the court ruled that African American students could not be placed in special education on the basis of IQ tests that result in racial imbalance in regular and special education classrooms.

Legislative Actions

In concert with positive developments in the courts, legislative actions have made significant improvements in the delivery of services to students with disabilities (see Baca & Cervantes, 1989; Ballard, Ramirez, & Weintraub, 1982; National Information Center for Children and Youth with Disabilities, 1991; Winzer, 1993). Prior to the 1950s, federal legislation related to disability issues was scarce and tended to address specific disability categories such as deafness or blindness. By the 1960s, however, legislation had been passed to authorize training programs for personnel in areas including mental retardation and serious emotional disturbance and for research and demonstration projects for the education for students with disabilities. In 1965, Congress passed the Elementary and Secondary Education Act (ESEA), the most comprehensive education package to be undertaken at the federal level that also included funding to students with disabilities. Five years later, the ESEA was amended to consolidate increasing legislation dealing with students with disabilities under the Education of the Handicapped Act. These actions, along with a favorable litigative climate and interest in expanding vocational rehabilitation opportunities, helped to set the stage for two landmark pieces of legislation for individuals with disabilities: the Rehabilitation

Act of 1973 and the Education of All Handicapped Children Act of 1975, now known as the Individuals with Disabilities Education Act (IDEA).

The Rehabilitation Act

The Rehabilitation Act of 1973 deals with issues of vocational rehabilitation, employment, and discrimination against individuals with disabilities. The original act established: (1) priority for rehabilitation services to those with the most severe disabilities; (2) initiation and expansion of programs for underserved populations; (3) expansion of employment opportunities; (4) elimination of architectural barriers; (5) development of written rehabilitation plans; (6) research and demonstration projects; and (7) protection of discrimination in any program receiving federal assistance. The act was amended in 1983 to include demonstration projects related to the transition of youth with disabilities to the workplace and in 1986 to provide for programs of supported employment.

Section 504

The most famous part of the 1973 Rehabilitation Act is Section 504, often referred to as "the civil rights act for individuals with disabilities." Section 504 states that "no otherwise qualified individual with handicaps in the United States...shall, solely by reason of her or his handicap, be excluded from participation in, be denied benefits of, or be subjected to discrimination under any program or activity receiving federal assistance." According to Section 504, an individual with handicaps is "any person who (i) has a physical or mental impairment which substantially limits one or more major life activities, (ii) has a record of such an impairment, or (iii) is regarded as having such an impairment." Major life activities include caring for one's self, performing manual labor, walking, seeing, hearing, speaking, breathing, learning, and working.

Under Section 504, any public elementary or secondary school program must provide students with disabilities with many of the same benefits mandated by the IDEA, which is described in the following section. These benefits include an annual search for all unserved students with disabilities; a free appropriate public education, including regular or special education and related services; an education, to the maximum extent possible, among peers who are not disabled; nondiscriminatory evaluation and placement; procedural safeguards; and an equal opportunity to participate in nonacademic and extracurricular services. In the case of a student found to have a disability under Section 504 but not under IDEA, the public school is still obligated to meet the requirements stated in the 504 regulations. For example, a student with an inherited genetic disorder such as Fragile X Syndrome must be protected from discriminatory actions and provided with an education to meet her individual needs, even though special education services may not be required.

The Individuals with Disabilities Education Act

In 1975, the most comprehensive of all previous federal enactments related to the education of students with disabilities was signed into law by President Gerald Ford. This legislation, known as the Education of All Handicapped Children Act (EHA), went into effect in October 1977 following the establishment of final regulations. The EHA guaranteed a free, appropriate public education for students with disabilities, ages five to twenty-one, and provided states with financial assistance for meeting specific legislative requirements. Since 1975, the EHA has been amended on three occasions. In 1983, it was amended to expand incentives for the establishment of early intervention, preschool special education, and transition programs. In 1986, the EHA was amended to lower the age of eligibility for services to age three by the 1991–92 school year and to assist states in providing programs for students with disabilities, ages zero to two, inclusive, and their families. The latest amendments to the EHA were signed into law by President George Bush in 1990. This legislation changed the name of the EHA to the Individuals with Disabilities Education Act (IDEA) to emphasize nondiscriminatory "person-first" nomenclature. Other changes included the addition of autism and traumatic brain injury as categories of disability, an emphasis on service to students from minority populations in discretionary programs, and the inclusion of transition services on the individualized education program (IEP) no later than age sixteen.

The IDEA assists states in providing a free, appropriate public education to students with disabilities, ages three to twenty-one. Under the IDEA, SEAs must meet minimum requirements in order to be eligible for federal financial assistance. These requirements include a state policy that ensures all students with disabilities a free, appropriate public education and a corresponding detailed plan that must be approved every three years at the federal level. Similarly, at the state level, LEAs must submit an application and be approved in order to receive their share of the federal financial assistance. One critical aspect of the IDEA is that students with disabilities or their families may sue SEAs or LEAs for failing to provide appropriate services. The 1986 amendments to the IDEA actually encourage such suits to be filed by requiring that the losing education agency pay attorneys' fees and/or money damages to the students involved. To advocate successfully for students and their families under the IDEA, educators should have knowledge of the disability categories included in the act and of the requirements for procedural safeguards, evaluation procedures, development of individual programs, and placement in least restrictive settings. (Descriptions of the disability categories appear in Chapter 1. Each of the other areas is described in the following sections.)

Procedural Safeguards and Parent Involvement

The IDEA was constructed to include a system of checks and balances to decrease errors in the diagnosis and treatment of students and to increase the input of parents in the special education process. These checks and balances include requirements for: (1) parental consent and notification; (2) the composition of the group that will make decisions about a student's educational future; and (3) parental and student rights, especially in cases where parents are not satisfied with decisions made by the agency.

Parental Consent and Notification.   Parents must be informed and give their consent at every step in the special education process. Parental consent means that the parent has been fully informed, in his or her native language or other form of communication, of all information related to the activity for which consent is desired. Agencies carry the responsibility for assuring that efforts to involve parents in this way have been taken. In the case of parents who do not speak English, this responsibility means that efforts to reach parental consent include the use of translation services in oral, manual, or written communication.

The IDEA stipulates that written or other notice should:

• Be available in the native language of the parents, unless clearly not feasible
• Explain the procedural safeguards related to the special education process
• Be given prior to meetings or other actions related to evaluation or placement issues

The Multidisciplinary Team Approach.   The IDEA requires that a multidisciplinary team or group approach be used in the evaluation of students for special education services and in any subsequent decision-making about the content of the student's educational program. The team considering placement decisions is to be knowledgeable about the student, the meaning of the evaluation data, and placement options.

Meetings to initiate, develop, revise, or review special education services must include the following team members:

• A representative of the public agency
• The student's teacher
• One or both of the student's parents
• The student, if appropriate
• Other personnel invited at the discretion of the agency or parent

- A member of the evaluation team or a professional knowledgeable about evaluation procedures and the results of the evaluation, if the meeting is to discuss an initial evaluation
- A specialist in the area of learning disabilities, if such a disability is suspected

Parental and Child Rights. To protect the interests of students who are being evaluated for or who are receiving special education services, the IDEA requires that agencies provide for due process. Parents and students who disagree with an agency's actions or lack of action may challenge the decision through a structured procedure called a due process hearing. Students who do not have parents have the right to representation in all special education matters by an appointed surrogate parent.

The IDEA gives parents the right to:

- Inspect all relevant records
- Request an independent evaluation
- Request an impartial due process hearing
- Appeal in the courts if necessary

Evaluation Procedures

The IDEA addresses the process of evaluating students for special education services in several ways. First, agencies are required to engage in "child-find" activities that include efforts to identify and locate students suspected of needing special education services. Second, agencies are to conduct child-find activities and all subsequent evaluations in a nondiscriminatory manner. Third, once a student has been identified as needing special education services, a comprehensive reevaluation must take place every three years.

The IDEA requires for all students that:

- Evaluations must be provided and administered in the student's native language or other mode of communication, unless clearly not feasible.
- Tests and other evaluation materials must be validated for the purpose for which they will be used and must be administered by trained personnel in accordance with test administration procedures.
- Evaluations must include assessment in all areas related to the suspected disability and in specific areas of educational need.
- Tests for students with impaired sensory, manual, or speaking ability must accurately represent the child's ability.
- No single procedure may be used as a sole criterion in the evaluation process.
- Evaluations must be conducted by a multidisciplinary team including at least one specialist with knowledge of the suspected disability area.

In the case of suspected learning disabilities, the IDEA also requires:

- An observation of the student by a professional other than the child's regular teacher
- A written report of the evaluation results, including discussions on
  1. Relevant behavioral and medical findings
  2. Whether a severe discrepancy exists between achievement and ability that cannot be corrected without special education services
  3. The effects of environmental, cultural, and economic factors

- Certification in writing by all team members as to whether the evaluation report reflects their views and the written conclusions of team members who do not agree with the report

The Development of the Individualized Education Program

If the members of the multidisciplinary team, including parents, agree that a student is eligible for special education services, the IDEA requires that an individualized education program (IEP) describing those services be developed within thirty days of such a determination. Thereafter, meetings to revise or review the IEP must occur at least once annually and prior to the beginning of the school year.

The IEP must include:

- A description of the student's present level of functioning
- Annual goals, including short-term instructional objectives
- Specific educational services to be provided, including related services such as transportation, counseling, and parent training
- The extent to which the student will be able to participate in regular education
- A description of necessary transition services for students at least sixteen years of age
- Projected dates for the initiation and duration of services
- Criteria for evaluating annual progress of objectives

Placement in the Least Restrictive Environment

The IDEA stipulates that all placement decisions consider that students with disabilities are to be educated, to the maximum extent possible, with students who do not have disabilities.

The IDEA requires agencies to:

- Provide for a continuum of service options from the regular classroom to institutional or other settings based on the individual needs of the student

- Consider segregated placement, whether in a separate school or classroom, only when the nature or severity of the condition is such that education in regular classes cannot be satisfactorily achieved even with the use of supplementary aids or services
- Ensure that students with disabilities have access to the same variety of educational programs and services available to students without disabilities
- Ensure placement as close as possible to the student's home
- Ensure placement in a school that the student would attend if no disability existed, unless the IEP stipulates otherwise

Other Features of the IDEA

As part of each SEA's plan to provide an education for students with disabilities, the IDEA requires a comprehensive system of personnel development. The SEA must ensure an adequate supply of qualified personnel in its region, describe how these personnel will be prepared for their responsibilities, and maintain a data system on the current status of and projected need for qualified personnel and on the development of personnel in institutions of higher education. The IDEA also provides for a number of discretionary programs in which SEAs and other appropriate agencies compete for funding. These discretionary programs are important not only because of their financial benefit but also because they help to establish priorities for the field of special education. This funding includes opportunities to establish centers and services that meet unique needs, such as providing for students in rural areas; programs for personnel training, research, and model demonstration projects in areas including collaboration and inclusion; programs for the development of technology and instructional media; and programs for infants and toddlers. The most recent reauthorization of the IDEA specifically addressed the need for projects focused on CLD students, particularly in the area of personnel preparation.

The IDEA and CLD Students

While the IDEA contains a number of strong mandates concerning CLD students suspected of or identified as having disabilities, several serious omissions compromise the effectiveness of the act. One omission relates to data collection: SEAs are not required to provide specific information on the number of students with LEP and disabilities who receive special education services or who are eligible to receive such services. Relatedly, SEAs do not have to address the issue of personnel preparation for these students in their state plans. Obviously, if SEAs are not required to identify the population they are to serve, they cannot easily be held accountable for not serving that population. A second omission relates to the development of goals and objectives for the IEP. While the IDEA makes provisions for culturally and linguistically appropriate assessment, it makes no comparable provisions for culturally and linguistically appropriate instruction. A result is that students with LEP who are accurately diagnosed with a disability may be served under IEPs that do not address proficiency in the native language and/or in English. This is especially true if members of the multidisciplinary team have little knowledge of the language and cultural issues involved. A third, related omission involves placement in the least restrictive environment. According to the IDEA, students with disabilities should be educated along with their peers to the maximum extent possible. In the case of students with LEP, however, the guidelines do not specify whether the peer group should include, when possible, members of the student's own language and cultural group. Hypothetically, students with LEP could be included exclusively in settings where their peers do not share their language. This would be especially true for students who do not have culturally and linguistically appropriate IEPs. These omissions should be addressed in future reauthorizations of the IDEA, giving SEAs and LEAs more specific rules of operation and strengthening the relationship between disability and diversity concerns.

PROTECTING THE RIGHTS OF CLD STUDENTS WITH DISABILITIES

Despite the legal strides toward educational equity for CLD students and students with disabilities, the rights of students with dual needs often continue to be ignored by school districts. One difficulty is that educators may not be fully aware of the legal aspects involved in serving these students, especially if they work in states with weak policies governing bilingual or ESL education. A second difficulty is that educators may not realize or wish to acknowledge that legal references to students with LEP include students who also have disabilities and that legal references to students with disabilities include students who also have LEP. Comments such as, "We don't need to provide proficiency testing or bilingual services for this student; he's special ed," or "Don't refer her; she's in the ESL class—she can't get both ESL and special ed," illustrate common misperceptions. Often, legislation and court decisions involving bilingual/ESL or special education do not specifically mention students with both diversity and disability characteristics; however, this does not mean that membership in one group excludes membership in the other. In Section 504 of the Rehabilitation Act, for example, public schools are prohibited from discriminating against students on the basis of disability. We understand this to be true regardless of students' racial/ethnic origin. Similarly in cases such as *Castañeda v. Pickard* (1981), special education issues may not be specifically mentioned, yet the rulings obviously apply to students with LEP who also have disabilities. A third difficulty is that educators may not take the time or effort to integrate state and federal legislative actions and case law surrounding the needs of these students and develop comprehensive school policies. A large part of our role as advocates is to clarify misperceptions and point out the sources of legal support for our arguments.

One source for this legal support is the courts. As described, a number of decisions highly favorable to the specialized instruction of students with LEP and to students with disabilities have been made since the early 1970s. In the small number of cases argued specifically on behalf of CLD students with disabilities since the passage of the IDEA, court opinions have strongly reflected and integrated the intent of federal legislation and legal decisions on bilingual and special education issues (see Baca & Cervantes, 1989; Fernandez, 1992; Fernandez & Pell, 1989; Weber, 1992). Three cases in New York City—*Jose P. v. Ambach* (1979), *United Cerebral Palsy v. Board of Education of the City of New York* (1979), and *Dyrcia S. v. Board of Education of the City of New York* (1979)—resulted in a combined judgment that specifically affirmed the right to bilingual special education services and required the district to take actions including collecting census data by language group, hiring additional bilingual staff, and filing with the court a description of bilingual programming for students with LEP and disabilities. In *Y. S. v. School District of Philadelphia* (1986), which included a Cambodian refugee who, plaintiffs argued, was misclassified as cognitively disabled after failing to benefit from a program that offered ESL instruction without a native language component, a settlement resulted in the district revising the ESL curriculum and developing appropriate remedial plans for Asian students with LEP, including students with disabilities. In *League of Latin American Citizens et al. v. Florida Board of Education* (1990), the plaintiffs contended that the state had failed to monitor the adequacy of services to students with LEP, including those with disabilities. A consent agreement included provisions that districts provide equal access to appropriate services for all students with LEP and that IEPs reflect appropriate language programming.

Another source of legal support comes from the federal legislation described earlier in the chapter, including the Civil Rights Act of 1964, Section 504 of the Rehabilitation Act, and the BEA. One of the most powerful pieces in this body of legislation is the IDEA, which contains a number of mandates that strongly protect the rights of CLD students suspected of or identified as having disabilities. These mandates include the use of nonbiased assessment measures and strategies, assessment in the native language, communication with parents in the native language, the consideration of cultural and environmental factors prior to making a diagnosis of learning disabilities, and an extensive due process procedure. Another component of the IDEA that benefits CLD students with or at-risk of disabilities is child-find activities, which are helpful in identifying children from underserved populations and in providing early intervention services. In addition, the

IDEA requires an IEP based on the unique needs of the student. Although language and cultural needs are not specifically mentioned in the development of the IEP, educators can refer to the BEA and to civil rights legislation on race and national origin as the basis for including culturally and linguistically appropriate instruction.

Future Legal Actions

Public discussion and litigation concerning the educational rights of CLD students with disabilities are likely to continue as increasing numbers of U.S. citizens from CLD backgrounds as well as immigrants and refugees enter public schools largely unprepared to meet their needs. As this occurs, the insertion of regulations specific to CLD students with disabilities and their families appears inevitable in future reauthorizations of legislation such as the IDEA and the BEA, and in state laws and school codes. This has already happened in Illinois, where in 1992 legislation was enacted that specifically addressed the rights of students with LEP and disabilities, the only legislation of its kind in the nation (see Box 2.1). This legislation is likely to serve as a model for legislation in other states, as it addresses the major concerns of the field of bilingual special education. The act includes many of the components noted in favorable court rulings related to bilingual education, including the training of personnel, use of appropriate curriculum, and development of state standards, with attention to federal special education mandates.

Several components of the act have considerable importance in terms of their potential to influence state delivery systems over the long term. One of its powerful components is the mandate for a detailed annual census of students who come from homes in which a language other than English is spoken and who receive special education services. Without this information, which is not specifically required at the federal level nor well documented at the state level, we cannot estimate whether we are underidentifying, overidentifying, or serving appropriate numbers of CLD students. We also cannot plan for future program needs. Another powerful component of the act is the mandate establishing credentials for bilingual special educators. Having state requirements encourages colleges and universities to provide course work they might not ordinarily offer, especially in times when institutions of higher education are streamlining programs. Having state requirements also assures that educators have the appropriate training and language background to serve students adequately. Finally, a third component of the act that has the potential for broad influence across the state system is the mandate that subcommittees on bilingual special education issues be established on state advisory councils. If advocates are able to work effectively on these committees, then the needs of CLD students with disabilities will not be ignored as new issues arise.

**BOX 2.1   Education for CLD Students with Disabilities:
Illinois Public Act 87-0995**

Illinois Public Act 87-0995, signed into law in September 1992, is a unique, comprehensive piece of legislation that addresses bilingual special education issues at the state level. A model of grass-roots efforts, this legislation resulted largely through the experiences of Mrs. Juana Ramos, a parent of a Spanish-speaking child with Down's syndrome who was enrolled in a special education program in the Chicago public schools but who was not receiving bilingual services. After numerous meetings with school officials, Mrs. Ramos was successful in obtaining a bilingual special education teacher for her son's classroom. This teacher was eventually removed, however, because she did not meet all of the requirements for permanent credentials. When she was replaced by yet another monolingual teacher, Mrs. Ramos sought help from Dr. Miryam Assaf-Keller, a special education university professor. The women approached State Senator Miguel del Valle, of the 2nd legislative district of Illinois, who had been listening to an increasing number of complaints from the Latino community about the lack of bilingual services for students with disabilities. Senator del Valle formed a group of parents, community representatives, and professionals to suggest changes to the Illinois School Code and was successful in passing the resulting legislation. The act is viewed by Illinois educators as the beginning of a national trend to deal with persistent problems in providing adequate service delivery to CLD students by legislative means. The act amended the Illinois School Code to include:

Student and Program Issues

- A detailed annual census of children of non-English backgrounds, birth through 21 years, who receive special education services
- Assessment and placement of students with LEP that reflect linguistic, cultural, and special education needs
- Eligibility for special education only with the recommendation of a state-approved bilingual special educator (if one is available)
- Development of the definition of "culturally and linguistically appropriate IEPs"
- IEPs that reflect cultural, linguistic, and special education needs
- Integration of students with disabilities and LEP with bilingual peers

Personnel Issues

- Creation of credentials for bilingual special educators
- Data collection on shortage of bilingual special educators
- Scholarships to obtain bilingual special education credentials
- Identification of "qualified" colleges and universities to provide course work

Standards and Monitoring Issues

- Establishment of subcommittees on bilingual special education issues on state advisory councils
- Establishment of standards for development, implementation, and monitoring of bilingual special education programs
- Incorporation of monitoring procedures to verify implementation of the standards

Recommendations

When federal legislation and case law are considered, schools are more likely to meet their legal obligations to CLD students with potential or identified disabilities if students are perceived and treated first as learners who have a right to instruction that meets their language and cultural needs and second as learners who may also require special education services as a result of a disability. School district policies for the assessment and instruction of CLD students with disabilities should be approached with this rule in mind.

Assessment Procedures
From a bilingual/ESL perspective, schools have an obligation to identify students with LEP and to monitor their progress once placed in appropriate programs. This obligation extends to CLD students with disabilities, regardless of the severity of the condition. While some schools may be sensitive to assessing the language proficiency of students with mild disabilities, the proficiency of students with more significant disabilities (e.g., moderate and severe mental retardation, autism, or multiple impairments) may be overlooked as educators deal with what they perceive as more pressing concerns. From a special education perspective, schools have an obligation to identify CLD students with potential disabilities and, if they are found to have a disability, to monitor their progress on the annual IEP and in the three-year reevaluation process. School policy should make it clear that all CLD students are to be screened for language proficiency and disabilities and that students with LEP and disabilities are to be monitored for progress in the language acquisition process as part of the typical special education evaluation procedures.

Instructional Programs
From a bilingual/ESL perspective, schools have an obligation to provide appropriate instruction to students with LEP and to ensure that such instruction is based on sound theory and has been adequately implemented and evaluated. This obligation extends to students with LEP in special education programs and, as such, influences the development of the IEP and decisions about placement in least restrictive settings. From a special education perspective, schools have an obligation to make program decisions that consider the individual needs of students, provide access to the same services available to students without disabilities, and allow for maximum integration in general education. The merging of these two perspectives dictates that the IEPs of students with LEP should address issues of language and culture in a manner similar to how such issues are or should be addressed in the instruction of students in general education bilingual programs, provided of course that the individual needs of students are met. For example, students with disabilities should have goals and objectives on their IEPs that address native language and ESL instruction. Taking this example a step fur-

ther, IEPs should indicate, when appropriate and to the maximum extent possible, that such instruction be carried out in the context of the general education bilingual classroom. The merging of these two perspectives also dictates that special education programs for students with LEP and disabilities meet the same criteria as programs for students without disabilities, that is, adequately implemented and evaluated instruction based on sound theory.

In summary, we have attempted to synthesize legal developments in the education of students with LEP, students with disabilities, and students with dual needs and to assist educators in making informed decisions about policies for assessment and instruction. In essence, the struggle for appropriate education for CLD students and students with disabilities has been one of changing longstanding social attitudes. If we wish to reach the goal of educational equity for all students, we must consider the role of language, culture, and disability on teaching and learning as well as our own role in promoting or obstructing the legal strides that have been made.

REFERENCES

Ambert, A. N., & Melendez, S. E. (1985). *Bilingual education.* New York: Garland.

Andersson, T., & Boyer, M. (1978). *Bilingual schooling in the United States* (2nd ed.). Austin, TX: National Educational Laboratory.

Arreola v. Santa Ana Board of Education, No. 160–577 (Orange County, Cal., 1968).

Aspira of New York v. Board of Education of the City of New York, 394 F. Supp. 1161 (S.D.N.Y. 1975).

August, D., & Garcia, E. E. (1988). *Language minority education in the United States: Research, policy, and practice.* Springfield, IL: Charles C. Thomas.

Baca, L. M., & Cervantes, H. T. (1989). *The bilingual special education interface* (2nd ed.). Columbus, OH: Merrill.

Ballard, J., Ramirez, B., & Weintraub, F. (1982). *Special education in America: Its legal and governmental foundations.* Reston, VA: Council for Exceptional Children.

Bilingual Education Act of 1968 (In Elementary and Secondary Education Act Amendments, P.L. 90–247) 81 Stat. 816.

Bilingual Education Act of 1978 (In Elementary and Secondary Education Act Amendments, P.L. 95-561) 92 Stat. 2268.

Brown v. Board of Education of Topeka, 347 U.S. 483, 74 S.Ct. 686, 91 L.Ed. 873 (1954).

Castañeda v. Pickard, 648 F.2nd 989 (5th Cir. 1981).

Civil Rights Act of 1964, P.L. 88-352, 78 Stat. 241.

Coleman, J. S., Campbell, E. Q., Hobson, C. J., McPartland, J., Mood, A. M., Weinfield, F. D., & York, R. L. (1966). *Equality of educational opportunity.* Washington, DC: U.S. Government Printing Office.

Crawford, J. (1991). *Bilingual education: History, politics, theory, and practice* (2nd ed.). Trenton, NJ: Crane.

Department of Health, Education, and Welfare Guideline, 33 Fed. Reg. 4956 (1968).

Department of Health, Education, and Welfare Memorandum, Identification of Discrimination and Denial of Services on the Basis of National Origin, 35 Fed. Reg. 11, 595 (1970).

Diana v. California State Board of Education, No. C-70, RFT (Dist. Ct., N. Cal., 1970).
Dyrcia S. v. Board of Education of the City of New York, 79 C. 2562 (E.D.N.Y. 1979).
Education for All Handicapped Children Act of 1975, P.L. 94-142, 89 Stat. 773.
Education of the Handicapped Act Amendments of 1983, P.L. 98-199, 97 Stat. 1357.
Education of the Handicapped Act Amendments of 1986, P.L. 99-457, 100 Stat. 1145.
Elementary and Secondary Education Act of 1965, P.L. 89-10, 79 Stat. 27.
Equal Educational Opportunities and Transportation of Students Act of 1974 (In Elementary and Secondary Education Act Amendments, P.L. 93-380) 88 Stat. 484.
Fernandez, A. T. (1992). Legal support for bilingual education and language-appropriate related services for limited English proficient students with disabilities. *Bilingual Research Journal, 16,* 117–140.
Fernandez, A. T., & Pell, S. W. J. (1989). The right to receive bilingual special education. *West's Education Law Reporter, 53,* 1067–1081.
Fitzgerald, J. (1993). Views on bilingualism in the United States: A selective historical review. *Bilingual Research Journal, 17,* 35–56.
Fleischman, H. L. & Hopstock, P. J. (1993). *Descriptive study of services to limited English proficient students.* Arlington, VA: Development Associates.
Improving America's Schools Act of 1994, P.L. 103-382, 108 Stat. 3518.
Individuals with Disabilities Education Act of 1990, P.L. 104-476, 104 Stat. 1103.
Jose P. v. Ambach, 3 EHLR 551:245 (E.D.N.Y. 1979).
Keyes v. Denver School District No. 1, 576 F. Supp. 673 (Colo., 1983).
Larry P. v. Wilson Riles, C-71-2270 US. C, 343 F. Supp. 1306 (N.D. Cal. 1972).
Lau v. Nichols, 414 U.S. 563 (1974).
League of Latin American Citizens et al. v. Florida Board of Education, No. 90–1913 Civ. Scott (S.D. Fla., 1990).
Lyons, J. J. (1994). The view from Washington: A cause for celebration. *NABE News, 18,* 1, 22–24.
Mills v. Board of Education of the District of Columbia, 348 F. Supp. 866 (D.D.C. 1972).
National Information Center for Children and Youth with Disabilities (NICHCY) (1991). The education of children and youth with special needs: What do the laws say? [Special Issue] *NICHCY News Digest, 1.*
Pennsylvania Association of Retarded Citizens v. Commonwealth of Pennsylvania. 334 F. Supp. 1257 (E.D. Pa., 1971).
Rehabilitation Act of 1973, P.L. 93–112, 87 Stat. 355.
Rehabilitation Act Amendments of 1983, P.L. 98-221, 98 Stat. 17.
Rehabilitation Act Amendments of 1986, P.L. 99-506, 100 Stat. 1807.
Rothstein, L. F. (1990). *Special edition law.* White Plains, NY: Love Pub.
Scheerenberger, R. C. (1983). *A history of mental retardation.* Baltimore: Paul H. Brookes.
State *ex rel.* Beattie v. Board of Education, 169 Wis. 231, 172, N.W. 153, 154 (1919).
Turnbull, H. R. (1986). *Free appropriate public education: The law and children with disabilities.* Denver: Love Pub.
United Cerebral Palsy of New York v. Board of Education of the City of New York, 79 C. 560 (E.D.N.Y., 1979).
Weber, M. C. (1992). *Special education law and litigation treatise.* Horsham, PA: LRP.
Winzer, M. A. (1993). *The history of special education.* Washington, DC: Gallaudet University Press.
Y. S. v. School District of Philadelphia, CA. 85–6924 (E.D. Pa., 1986).

3

SEPARATING MILD DISABILITIES FROM CULTURAL AND LINGUISTIC DIFFERENCES: ASSESSMENT PROBLEMS AND APPROACHES

In this chapter we discuss current methodological, educational, and theoretical problems affecting the differential diagnosis of normal second-language learning from mild disabilities and from giftedness in culturally and linguistically diverse (CLD) students. Four current problems in the differential diagnosis of CLD students will be identified and discussed, and their interrelations will be pointed out. The first two problems are methodological, and refer to the difficulty of differentially diagnosing CLD students and to the correlation between cognitive and language development in CLD students. The third problem is educational, and refers to the need to change educators' attitudes in order to reach accurate diagnostic decisions for CLD students. The fourth problem is theoretical, and refers to the lack of robust psycholinguistic models that can be used for understanding how CLD students develop and for constructing accurate assessment and instructional methods. In addition, four traditional and contemporary assessment approaches (psychometric, "missionary," behavioral, and "ethnic researcher") will be reviewed in light of seven aspects: assessment and diagnostic principles, objectives, assessment and evaluation procedures, diagnostic categories and placement decisions, missions and goals of the educational program, intervention strategies, and educational program evaluation. In this chapter the term "ethnic researcher" will be used, instead of "ethnic educator," to refer to research conducted by scholars who depart from the mainstream perspective. Thus, this chapter gives an overview of major problems encountered by educators when trying to conduct a differential diagnosis of CLD students using current assessment practices and approaches.

Moreover, this chapter is related to the vision statement of this book in that it discusses traditional and contemporary assessment models as well as theoretical, educational, and methodological problems that educators face. This discussion of assessment models and problems is done from an "ethnic educator" perspective in order to present a new paradigm that can enlighten practitioners when facing the most challenging laws and regulations. In relation to the vision statement of this book, the most important thesis presented in this chapter is that educators can critically evaluate their attitudes by becoming aware of the powerful effect of their personalities and cultural and linguistic identities on the assessment and instruction of CLD students.

METHODOLOGICAL, EDUCATIONAL, AND THEORETICAL PROBLEMS AFFECTING THE ACCURATE ASSESSMENT OF CLD STUDENTS

Presently, educators face a complex decision when they assess, diagnose, and place CLD students due to the presence of methodological, educational, and theoretical problems. The first two problems that we will discuss are methodological: (1) the difficulty of differentially diagnosing normal second-language learning from genuine disabilities in CLD students; and (2) the psychometric properties of standardized tests that result in the correlation of cognitive and linguistic development reflected on common processes measured by artificially independent discrete point tests of language proficiency, intelligence, and achievement. The third problem is educational, and refers to the preparation of personnel who can appropriately serve CLD students, especially in relation to the attitudinal change needed to gain awareness and sensitivity of how educators' knowledge affects their educational and diagnostic decisions. Finally, the fourth problem is theoretical, and refers to the lack of developmental theories for CLD students that support assessment, diagnosis, and placement decisions. The first three problems are intimately related, because if we educators are going to succeed at differentially diagnosing mild disabilities from cultural and linguistic idiosyncrasies, given the psychometric problems of currently used standardized tests, then we need to become aware of our attitudes toward CLD students. Thus, it is our main argument in this chapter that there is need to raise educators' awareness and responsibility levels as they become advocates and mentors of CLD students, and to develop robust psycholinguistic theories that explain how CLD students develop.

The Difficulty of Conducting a Differential Diagnosis in CLD Students

The difficulty of differentiating disabilities from normal second-language learning in CLD students is considered a methodological problem of assessment. A well-known major assessment principle states that diagnoses, placements, and instructional decisions have to be based on a battery of measures that comes from multiple sources and areas of information (i.e., medical history, parents' interviews, teachers' ratings, class observations, use of the language by the student in different social and academic contexts, representative products of school performance, etc.). That is, evaluators need to use a multidimensional battery of standardized tests and other qualitative measures for assuring an accurate assessment of CLD students. As discussed in Chapter 2, the Individuals with Disabilities Education Act of 1990 (IDEA), formerly known as the Education for All Handicapped Children Act, also requires that no single procedure should be used as a sole criterion in the evaluation process for identifying children in need of special education services. Moreover, in order to accomplish a multidimensional assessment process, multiple informants need to participate in the assessment of CLD students. In addition, the IDEA requires that a multidisciplinary team participates in the assessment and diagnostic process, in the development of an individualized educational program (IEP), and in the placement of CLD students. Furthermore, in order to conduct a differential diagnosis between normal second-language learning and genuine disabilities, as supported by the IDEA requirements, evaluations should:

1. Be administered in the child's native language
2. Be validated for the purposes for which they will be used (screening, diagnosis, placement, development of an IEP)
3. Be administered by trained personnel in accordance with administration procedures
4. Include assessment in all areas related to the suspected disability and in specific areas of educational need

For the specific case of differentially diagnosing normal second-language learning from genuine learning disabilities, and in light of the IDEA requirements, assessment procedures should:

1. Involve other professionals, besides the classroom teacher, in observations of the child's behavior
2. Discuss in a written report relevant behavioral and medical findings, and whether discrepancies exist between achievement and ability that need special education services

3. In a written report, discuss the effect of environmental, cultural, and economic factors

This last requirement of the IDEA is particularly relevant for CLD students,
who may be influenced by external factors that hinder their development. In
addition, the presence or absence of discrepancy of diagnostic decisions in
the multidisciplinary assessment team should be documented in the report.
This latter requirement of the IDEA is important, given the current assessment procedures for CLD students that lack validity and reliability. Then,
because of these methodological problems in assessment instruments, contradictory results will be found when using multiple assessment procedures.
As a result, different assessment team members can use these contradictory
results of assessment procedures as evidence for defending multiple diagnostic decisions.

The assessment principles discussed above, which are related to the
presence of a multidisciplinary assessment team and multiple assessment
procedures, reveal a major point: the conceptual difference between assessment and diagnosis. Assessment refers to test taking and test scoring by an
evaluator. Diagnosis refers to the decision of whether CLD students present
intrinsic and/or extrinsic problems based on a battery of measures. Reaching
a differential diagnosis is a complex process that demands that the evaluator
understand the constructs being measured and the internal and external
assessment principles being applied. Moreover, evaluators need to have a
sensitivity toward and an awareness of minority and majority students'
developmental characteristics, and a willingness to assume an advocacy role
for CLD students.

Diagnosis is also a very powerful classification process, as it labels CLD
students as having internal and thus genetic conditions, and/or external and
thus environmental conditions as the sources of handicaps and disabilities.
Labeling forms part of our current educational system, for it is the means
through which we can secure additional educational and psychological services for CLD students. For instance, as discussed in Chapter 2, the IDEA
addresses the identification of children in need of special education services
by using a nondiscriminatory evaluation process. According to the IDEA,
once a child is identified as needing special education services, a reevaluation is required every three years. However, identification involves labeling,
and the labeling process can also have major negative consequences, such as
alienation and stigmatization, and can be the source of emotional and learning problems in CLD students. In addition, due to the state of assessment
procedures for CLD students, there is a high risk of mislabeling, with very
harmful social, ethical, and educational consequences. Labeling also serves
as the basis for making predictions about the educational successes and
needs of CLD students, which also causes positive or negative expectations

in educators as they attribute the educational performance of CLD students to internal and/or external causes.

Furthermore, due to the present lack of robust theories underlying assessment instruments, we need to be very cautious about diagnosing and labeling CLD students. Ethical, social, and educational implications of false positive and false negative misclassifications are very powerful. A false positive misclassification refers to the misdiagnosis of a CLD student as being in need of special services who in fact has no genuine handicaps or disabilities. A false negative misclassification refers to the misdiagnosis of a CLD student as normal who in fact has genuine handicaps or disabilities. False positive misclassifications are more common, especially among CLD students, due to the presence of two languages and two cultures. As discussed in Chapter 2, during the late 1960s and early 1970s court cases were milestones in the struggle to avoid discriminatory treatment when diagnosing intelligence abilities in CLD students. Moreover, court cases have raised important assessment issues for CLD students, such as avoiding the misdiagnosis of mental retardation by using the children's first language for tests (i.e., Diana v. California State Board of Education, 1970) and by using multiple measures of performance instead of a single IQ test (i.e., Larry P. v. Wilson Riles, 1972). These provisions were incorporated into the IDEA largely to address the overrepresentation of CLD populations, such as Hispanic and African-American students, in special education programs.

In addition as we discussed in Chapter 2, the IDEA includes as major components the identification of children who may be suspected of having disabilities using nondiscriminatory assessment procedures. Moreover, if disabilities are found when using accurate assessment procedures, an IEP should be developed. Then the child should be placed, to the extent possible, in a regular education classroom. However, we are still dealing with major methodological flaws in our assessment and diagnostic process used with CLD students that result in unvalid and unreliable assessment instruments, misdiagnoses, and misplacements. Thus, even though there are federal laws designed to prevent the misdiagnosis and misplacement of CLD students, we are still facing problems when trying to diagnose normal second-language learning from genuine disabilities differentially.

Thus, we propose that due to the present state of assessment instruments, the diagnostic process is an "art" rather than a technique, because evaluators need to piece together information coming from different assessment approaches that have contradictory principles and assessment objectives. Therefore, evaluators face a decision-making process when they conduct an assessment and diagnostic procedure with CLD students. Furthermore, as mentioned in Chapter 2, no single piece of federal legislation secures appropriate assessment and instructional services for children who are both CLD and have genuine disabilities. However, both federal laws for limited English proficient (LEP) children and for children with disabilities make reference to both groups. According to federal legislation, children with disabilities also have the right to culturally and linguistically appropriate education. When using federal legislation such as the Bilingual Education Act of 1978, students are categorized as LEP. However, in this book, we consider that the term "LEP" has negative connotations, and thus we prefer to use the more positive term "culturally and linguistically diverse" (CLD).

In the sections that follow we elaborate on the issues discussed above, including the influence of educators' attitudes on assessment and diagnostic decisions for CLD students, and traditional and contemporary assessment approaches.

Psychometric Properties of Standardized Tests

A second major methodological problem is the psychometric properties of standardized tests that result in the correlation between cognitive and linguistic processes in measures of language proficiency, academic achievement, and verbal and nonverbal intelligence. Most tasks included in assessment instruments of first- and second-language proficiency and academic achievement do not only measure linguistic skills per se but cognitive processes included in intelligence measures (see, e.g., Alexander, Schallert, & Hare, 1991; Anderson & Pearson, 1984). For instance, measures of pronunciation included in language proficiency assessment instruments may in fact assess a cognitive process—auditory discrimination. In addition, reading comprehension is considered a linguistic skill in language proficiency and achievement assessment instruments, while current theory (e.g., Anderson & Pearson, 1984) suggests that it is a cognitive process. Finally, vocabulary, often considered a linguistic ability, is based on the cognitive process of verbal conceptual development.

Most assessment instruments present language proficiency and achievement as independent dimensions from intelligence, and assume that differing patterns of performances on the three dimensions will differentially diagnose between genuine disabilities and normal second-language learning. Unfortunately, language proficiency measures cannot be statistically or conceptually distinguished from either achievement or intelligence measures. Indeed, intelligence is measured tangentially by subtests of traits labeled language proficiency, reading ability, or writing ability, but none of them assesses the interface between cognitive and language development.

As a result, most intelligence and achievement measures underestimate the actual potential of CLD students, especially when according, to the Bilingual Education Act, they have limited English proficiency (see Chapter 2). The lack of valid and reliable assessment procedures for evaluating intelligence, achievement, and language proficiency in CLD students has resulted in the disproportionate representation in special education of students in the process of learning English as a second language. Moreover, several authors have pointed out that intelligence and achievement assessment instruments are confounding the normal process of learning English as a second language with disabilities. For instance, Oller (1991) pointed out that intelligence and achievement measures have as an implicit goal to assess language skills and verbal intelligence. According to Oller, these measures assess first-language skills and have many deficit-oriented categories (e.g., language disorders, learning disabilities, and mental retardation). As a result, as Oller stated, American educators are misinterpreting the lack of proficiency in English as a second language as a widespread intelligence deficit among CLD students. Pointing to the same problem, De George (1988) suggested that tests in English confound content knowledge with language proficiency, and that oral English-language proficiency tests do not measure academic language.

A resulting methodological problem of the correlation between cognitive and linguistic processes in CLD students is to identify causes and effects. Gonzalez (in press) conducted a research study designed to explore the association between language proficiency in Spanish and English, phonological strategies, and reading readiness as measured by standardized tests and qualitative assessment methods in CLD students. The general conclusion was that first- and second-language proficiency and reading readiness were causal factors for the specific phonological strategy used by CLD students. CLD students may thus show different patterns of phonological development in comparison to mainstream students that can be misinterpreted as disorders. This study can be interpreted as identifying the presence of idiosyncratic patterns of learning and development in CLD students due to the fact that they are bilingual and bicultural.

It can be concluded that presently it is very difficult to differentiate first- and second-language proficiency from cognitive development because of the methodological problems of assessment instruments used with CLD students.

The Influence of Educators' Attitudes on Understanding the Needs of CLD Students

The first two methodological problems discussed above are intimately related to the problem of how our attitudes as educators influence our understanding of the needs of CLD students. That is, if we are going to succeed at differentially diagnosing mild disabilities from cultural and linguistic idiosyncrasies, given the psychometric problems of currently used standardized tests, we need to become aware of our attitudes toward CLD students. We need to raise educators' awareness of and responsibility levels for becoming advocates and mentors of CLD students. One way of raising awareness is to include in teacher education programs a historical account of the struggle in this nation for equal access to educational opportunity and equitable outcomes, as mentioned in Chapter 2. In this way educators can learn how the American educational system has changed in the last forty years in response to social and professional movements. There has been a movement for adapting assessment and instructional methods to help individuals achieve to the best of their potential. Moreover, educators must realize that educational equity does not mean that they should treat every child in the same way, but that there is the need to meet the unique needs of CLD students to avoid discrimination in the educational system. In addition, another major current problem in the assessment of CLD students who may be suspected of needing special education services, as mentioned by the IDEA (see Chapter 2), is the need for a comprehensive system of personnel development that can ensure an adequate supply of qualified professionals across the United States.

That is, the assessment of CLD students necessarily involves an *awakening experience* in educators, as we are currently living through a transitional period of change for the better (see Gonzalez, 1993a, 1993b). Some of these improvements are:

1. A restructuring period in American schools, as reflected in new assessment models
2. Changes in the theories and philosophies underlying the instruments
3. Diagnostic and placement decisions based on interdisciplinary committees, which link assessment and instruction

Furthermore, a real change will only happen if all educators realize that the most important tool for assessment is their own personality. To come to this realization many of us need to undergo an *awakening experience* through which we can open our minds and reflect on our own attitudes, philosophies, and beliefs underlying our diagnostic decisions. Much has been written and said about biases in standardized assessment instruments that lack validity and reliability. However, we are just beginning to realize the enormously pernicious power of biases in educators' attitudes, beliefs, and lack of conceptual understanding of how CLD students learn and develop at normal or above-normal levels when they are surrounded by a different sociocultural and linguistic environment. Educators, scholars, and practitioners who are determined to make a difference and to model a change let us know that when there is a will and a positive attitude, and when we accept the challenging responsibility of assessing and diagnosing CLD students accurately, an *awakening experience* starts in which we realize, "¡Si, se puede!!" ("Yes, we can make it!!").

Presently, there is a major need for new assessment models, instruments, theories, and philosophies that will lead us to restructure how we educate teachers and evaluators of students. Educators in academia and research and professional educators in the "trenches," who make diagnostic decisions every day for a diverse group of CLD students, need to share a common philosophical understanding of how these students develop and learn. It has been our experience that wearing three different hats has enhanced our vision by bringing together the interface of three related dimensions of the problem of the assessment of CLD students:

1. Doing heuristic research for generating new models and procedures for assessment
2. Teaching courses on the assessment of CLD students or relating general courses for pre- and in-service educators to important assessment issues
3. Participating as evaluators and consultants in efforts to improve assessment procedures and as members of assessment teams in school districts

Presently, we are facing a paradigmatic shift between standardized instruments derived from the psychometric approach and qualitative assessment methods derived from the ethnic researcher approach (both are discussed below). It is important to nurture educators involved in the evaluation of CLD students, because they are facing two opposite perspectives that produce contradictory diagnoses. That is, given the state of the assessment models and instruments that are being used for assessing CLD students, evaluators can come to opposite conclusions depending on the philosophies, attitudes, beliefs, and theories they adopt. As a result, we can no longer claim that the complex decision-making process of reaching a differential diagnosis between genuine disabilities (e.g., learning disabilities, language disorders, and mental retardation) and the normal process of learning English as second language is objective. At present educators still hold this misconception, as they tend to believe that standardized tests can be used for reaching "objective" diagnostic decisions. However, *this belief is a fallacy*, because instrument development involves the selection of theories underlying the operational definitions of the constructs to be measured "objectively." In fact, instrument development may show the subjective agreement of the individuals who developed and operationally defined the constructs. Our best claim thus can probably be that instrument development involves a collection of objective intersubjectivities, but not a purely objective process per se.

Moreover, presently educators hold not only misconceptions but also many myths that result from the methodological problems of standardized tests that lack validity and reliability for CLD students. One of these myths is the belief that language proficiency is the only sign of intelligence, which means that CLD students in the process of learning English are viewed as less intelligent than monolingual students who are native and fluent English speakers. However, this popular belief is far from the truth about the genuine potential of CLD students. For instance, Gonzalez (1991, 1994, 1995) found that the nonverbal cognitive development of kindergarten and first-grade bilingual Spanish/English children was above normal levels when assessed with qualitative methods. In contrast, standardized language and intelligence tests, even nonverbal intelligence tests, underestimated the genuine verbal and nonverbal potential of these CLD students (see Gonzalez, 1991, 1994, 1995).

Another popular myth among educators is the assumption that if CLD students show a high performance on standardized tests of English-language proficiency, then their scores in other intelligence and achievement standardized tests should be valid and reliable. This assumption is inaccurate, because CLD students have different cultural and linguistic backgrounds that most of the time are not reflected in the content and norms of standardized tests. Therefore, their genuine potential for intelligence development and achievement levels is not reflected in their performance in these standardized tests. Moreover, there is a difference between the functional oral language proficiency measured by standardized tests and the academic language proficiency needed for attaining high achievement levels.

The attitudinal change needed for breaking these myths is difficult to achieve because of the internal barriers that prevent educators from being aware of their personal responsibility. When we have taught academic courses for graduate-level in-service teachers and undergraduate-level preservice teachers, we have felt that a "shield," in the form of their attitudes, prior knowledge, and cultural and linguistic backgrounds, prevented the teachers from openly considering, reviewing, and discussing concepts portraying a different view of how to educate CLD students. The attitudinal change that educators need to undergo in order to become advocates for CLD students will only happen with the proper peer support. It is our own responsibility as educators to be the leaders in this movement to assume advocacy roles and to dispel the professional myths of helplessness. An attitudinal change is required because educators must remember that their personality is the major tool for assessment and includes their own:

1. Ethnic-cultural-linguistic identity
2. Personal and professional commitments to specific schools of thought that defend different assessment models and instruments
3. Beliefs and theories about how CLD students learn and develop
4. Personal backgrounds and experiences with CLD students

Indeed, the differential diagnosis between genuine disabilities (e.g., learning disabilities, language disorders, and mental retardation) and the normal developmental process in CLD students is a very complex problem that, given our current theories and assessment instruments, is far from being an objective process. We need to become aware of the subjectivity involved in diagnostic decisions and the placement of CLD students in a regular, special education, bilingual, or bilingual special education classrooms. The current problem of the overrepresentation of CLD students in special education classes and their underrepresentation in gifted classes is just one reflection of the subjectivity involved in the diagnostic process. Our voices are yelling for increased professional awareness of the importance of exploring our own attitudes and levels of commitment for becoming advocates of our CLD students. We educators need to remember that our voices come from our hearts and brains and cultural and linguistic identities, that is, from our own subjectivity. Each educator has a unique personality, the result of the interface between personal and professional identities, which is the most important instrument for evaluating CLD students. For more detailed studies and findings see Gonzalez, Bauerle, Block, and Felix-Holt (in press), and Gonzalez and Felix-Holt (1995).

In summary, to restructure the current assessment procedures used in the school system with CLD students, school personnel need to be educated differently. We need to provide educators with an awakening experience that will help them to overcome their shields that protect their old attitudes. This awakening experience will open a whole new world of fresh conceptual, cultural, and individually based understandings and philosophies on the assessment of CLD students.

The Lack of Theories for Explaining Development in CLD Students

Finally, if we educators are going to succeed in differentially diagnosing genuine disabilities from normal second-language learning given the state of current standardized tests, then we need to change our attitudes and also to develop robust psycholinguistic theories that explain how CLD students develop. We must generate theories that can explain the cognitive, linguistic, emotional, and social development of CLD students, who are different from mainstream students because they are exposed to bilingual and bicultural environments. The critical area in which there is a lack of robust theoretical models is in the explanation of the process of first- and second-language acquisition and cognitive development in bilingual students. It is important to recognize that bilingual students have different rates of development compared to monolingual students and that the bilingual process is an idiosyncratic one. For instance, Swain (1981) pointed out that bilingual language development is four to five months behind monolingual language development, because the bilingual student has more vocabulary and linguistic rules to acquire and differentiate. Moreover, bilingualism enhances cognitive development in the areas of creativity, flexibility, concept formation, and metalinguistic awareness (i.e., the ability to think about linguistic conventions, to separate referents from labels, to use language creatively and humorously, and in general to reflect critically about language use).

Currently, we are still looking for the "panacea," the valid and reliable instrument that can accurately assess and diagnose CLD students. However, this quest for the panacea, which corresponds to an educationally applied interest, cannot be successful without the construction of theories for explaining how CLD students learn and develop across cognitive, linguistic, social, and emotional areas. Thus, we are calling for the development of multidimensional theories that can explain how CLD students learn and develop and that will serve as a basis for constructing valid and reliable assessment instruments. Due to this need for an underlying multidimensional theory, methodological, educational, ethical, and social problems arise when current assessment instruments are used for diagnostic and placement decisions (see, e.g., American Educational Research Association, American Psychological Association, & National Council on Measurement in Education, 1985; Messick, 1989). Indeed, multiple methodological problems affecting the accurate assessment of CLD students have been pointed out by a number of researchers (e.g., Cummins, 1981; De Avila & Havassy, 1974; Mercer, 1979; Oller, 1979). Some of these methodological problems are:

1. Lack of appropriate norms for CLD students
2. Use of unnatural and ambiguous stimuli, such as literal translations of standardized tests in English
3. Dialectal variations in the non-English language
4. Assessment of language skills only in English and not in the student's first language
5. Use of verbal standardized tests that are not valid and reliable for CLD students and lack of use of nonverbal qualitative assessment methods
6. Tests that do not measure only linguistic skills per se but also cognitive processes commonly measured by intelligence tests

In addition, theories specifically developed for CLD students can help to solve the educationally applied need for alternative assessment procedures that can assist in making accurate diagnostic decisions. When CLD students have been assessed and diagnosed accurately, then appropriate placement decisions can be reached for meeting their individual needs. Different placement possibilities exist for CLD students, including bilingual education, English as a second language, special education, bilingual special education, and mainstream classrooms. For instance, when appropriate theories are used for developing assessment instruments for young CLD students, emphasis is placed on nonverbal behaviors, such as the model and qualitative assessment method QUEST, constructed by Gonzalez (1991, 1994, 1995 for the model; see also Gonzalez, Bauerle, & Félix-Holt, 1994a, 1994b, for case studies), which will be explained and illustrated through a case study in Chapter 5. In addition, it is critical to assess young CLD students using qualitative nonverbal assessment methods because they are still in the process of acquiring both their first and second languages. Moreover, these qualitative assessment methods should include culturally appropriate materials and tasks, and should be administered in the first and second languages by a bilingual and bicultural examiner. Furthermore, information gathered when using qualitative assessment methods can be directly applied by educators in developing educational programs that meet the unique needs of CLD students.

In conclusion, solving the theoretical and methodological problems will help to shed light on educational and applied problems, including:

1. How to diagnose first- and second-language proficiency, intelligence, and achievement levels accurately in CLD students
2. How to develop educational programs that optimize cognitive, linguistic, emotional, and social development of CLD students

ASSESSMENT APPROACHES: EDUCATIONAL IMPLICATIONS FOR CLD STUDENTS

In this section we will discuss four assessment approaches, with an emphasis on their educational implications for CLD students: the traditional psychometric, missionary, and behavioral approaches, and the contemporary ethnic researcher approach (for a summary of this discussion, see Gonzalez & Yawkey, 1993). Even though these are not the only assessment approaches available, the traditional and contemporary models discussed are the most important ones in reference to CLD students. Seven aspects of these four approaches will be analyzed: (1) assessment and diagnostic principles; (2) objectives; (3) assessment and evaluation procedures; (4) diagnostic categories and placement decisions; (5) missions and goals of the educational program; (6) intervention strategies; and (7) educational program evaluation.

In general, there are a number of similarities across the underlying principles of assessment approaches, such as the inclusion of internal and/or external factors as possible explanations for the causes of "learning problems." However, there are also a number of differences across the underlying principles, such as the objectives for using assessment instruments. Indeed, the assessment of complex constructs, such as intelligence, may be better accomplished by using several assessment approaches that can be merged in a multidimensional or holistic approach. Indeed, a multidimensional view of assessment may be especially useful for measuring complex constructs in diverse populations. That is, when we are assessing CLD students, we may find multiple sources of differences coming from individual, cultural, ethnic, and linguistic domains. For instance, the construct of intelligence may open up in multiple kinds of intelligences that are culturally and linguistically bound, and that at the same time share a universal trend. As a result, an evaluator may decide to integrate more than one approach for conducting an assessment process, resulting in a holistic assessment approach for CLD students. However, special consideration needs to be given to the compatibility or opposition of underlying principles and objectives across assessment approaches.

The Psychometric Approach

This traditional approach has many assessment and diagnostic principles. The first one is the identification of internal causes for "learning problems" that are related to genetic, neurological, and maturational factors. That is, this approach follows the medical model in which the symptoms of the "patient" are seen as the expression of "internal diseases" that can be either "cured" by offering some treatment, if available, or considered "terminal," if no cure is known. However, within the medical model, a foolproof "cure" has not been found yet for "internal learning problems" such as learning disabilities or language disorders in CLD students.

A second related principle is that solutions for internal learning problems cannot be found in external factors (e.g., a mismatch between the student's potential and the educational materials and methods, or educators' linguistic and cultural knowledge and belief systems and attitudes). Therefore, it is very easy for educators who apply the medical model endorsed by the psychometric approach to avoid professional responsibility and not to develop empathy, commitment, and an advocacy role for CLD students who are diagnosed as having learning problems.

A third related principle of this approach is that the psychological constructs that we assess and diagnose, such as intelligence or language development, can be quantitatively measured in an exact manner. That is, skills and abilities can be measured validly and reliably by standardized tests. This principle is related to the assumption that abilities or skills are inherited in specific limited values. Individual differences are thus seen as being caused by these internal genetic factors that are fixed and determined in the prenatal stage. However, an important point in the psychometric characteristics of standardized tests is that any given instrument is normed only for the particular sample that participated in the norming process. In another linguistic and cultural context, this standardization process is meaningless, and therefore any interpretations and information derived from these standardized tests for diagnostic decisions are biased due to the lack of validity and reliability. Another major point is that these standardized instruments lack construct validity; in other words, the theories about how children develop have major differences when monolinguals are compared with bilinguals (e.g., in intelligence and language development). We cannot assume that standardized instruments developed for monolingual mainstream students are meaningful and harmless when translated for CLD students. We need to reconstruct the standardized instrument from the beginning by first redefining what we think about the cognitive and language development of CLD students. That is, this reconstruction should follow the philosophy of the "ethnic researcher" approach to be discussed later in this chapter.

A fourth principle of the psychometric approach is that skills and abilities measured through valid and reliable standardized tests can be compared across students in order to identify individual differences. This principle is also related to the three principles discussed above, because individual differences are expected as skills and abilities are believed to be inherited. Then, emphasis is placed on performance as a product, because scores reflect the number of correct or incorrect responses that the student produced. In addition, for the purpose of diagnosis, standardized instruments compare the performance of a student to a standard based on chronological age and level of skill achieved with a norm (norm-referenced tests) or a criterion (criterion-referenced tests). The emphasis is on following specific administration procedures in most norm-referenced and some criterion-referenced tests in order for results to be comparable to established norms and scores. When using standardized scoring procedures, age scores, developmental quotients, grade equivalents, standard scores, or percentiles are computed for the purpose of comparing performance between students. The use of standards as criteria for reaching diagnostic decisions place CLD students in at-risk situations due to the presence of multiple languages and ethnicities, even within a specific cultural group. For example, Hispanic children can come from different ethnic groups (e.g., Puerto Rico, the Andes region in South America, or metropolitan centers such as Mexico City) that form a cultural and a language group (i.e., they may speak different varieties of the Spanish language, although the language system is the same). Presently, American schools have children representing more than 150 different languages, making the availability of standards for every linguistic group almost an impossible task.

Thus, a number of factors must be considered when evaluators are matching test norms to the performance of CLD students, such as:

1. The correspondence of the student's characteristics with those of the norm group
2. The number of cases in the group, which influences the stability and accuracy of the test scores

3. The relevance of the group, in order to avoid inappropriate racial, ethnic, cultural, and linguistic biases when testing CLD students

A fifth related principle in the psychometric assessment approach states that performance and competence can be predicted by standardized tests, as skills and abilities are considered to be stable since they are determined by innate and inherited factors that are supposed to be continuous across development. A sixth related principle of this approach is that skills and abilities can be subdivided in a number of discrete competences and perfor-mances that can be measured independently by standardized tests. For instance, the measurement of the degree of bilingual proficiency has been a special problem, because language proficiency is a holistic process that stan-dardized tests subdivide unnaturally into many areas, such as phonology, lexicon, morphology, syntax, semantics, and pragmatics at the receptive and expressive levels (Damico, 1991). Other standardized tests subdivide lan-guage proficiency in terms of modalities of processing, such as listening, speaking, signing, interpreting, reading, writing, and thinking (Oller & Damico, 1991).

Measuring first- and second-language proficiency is critical, because the dominant language of CLD students needs to be determined in order to decide whether dual-language assessment is needed. Different authors have proposed an integrative and holistic approach for simultaneously assessing the different and complex skills embedded in the construct of language pro-ficiency (for a historical summary of the origins of the holistic approach, see Damico, 1991; Oller & Damico, 1991). Thus, standardized tests measuring first- and second-language proficiency follow the discrete point approach that artificially divides the intimate interrelationships between cognitive-lin-guistic processes into unnatural areas. For instance, interacting cognitive and linguistic processes are measured by using separate standardized tests of language proficiency, intelligence, and achievement. This subdivision of skills and abilities is unnatural and results in the misconception that in the real world students can use their skills and abilities separately. In fact, we can only express our skills and abilities through holistic performances that reflect interactions across areas.

In sum, four objectives are derived from the assessment and diagnostic principles of the psychometric approach:

1. To identify internal causes of learning problems
2. To measure skills and abilities using standardized tests
3. To compare performance across individuals using norms
4. To predict performance, as skills and abilities measured are considered to be stable

Diagnostic categories and assessment procedures of the psychometric approach are deficit-oriented, since internal factors are identified as the causes of learning problems categorized as disabilities. When deficit-oriented diagnostic categories are used with CLD students, any deviations from the norms are considered to be the result of neurological dysfunctions, developmental delays, or "sleeper effects" that have been inherited. Because no external factors are considered within this diagnostic approach, the medical view of learning problems may generate testing for its own sake, mislabeling, and misdiagnosing CLD students. As explained, the differential diagnosis of CLD students is a more complex "art" in which a knowledgeable educator carefully selects assessment models and instruments that match the students' cultural and linguistic idiosyncrasies, and that are administered with flexibility to follow their unique ideas and developmental levels.

The ultimate objective of labeling CLD students when using standardized tests and following psychometric assessment objectives thus is to demonstrate that they obtained lower scores compared to majority children due to internal factors, such as race. Defenders of this approach want to demonstrate a racial and therefore an innate inferiority of CLD students that prevents high performance levels and causes learning problems. The negative social and ethical implications of mislabeling and misdiagnosing arise from misunderstanding how CLD students develop, and from misusing standardized instruments that were created based on philosophies and theories developed for mainstream students. Mislabeling and misdiagnosis then become powerful tools that negatively affect teachers' and parents' expectations and attitudes.

Placement decisions that are based on the psychometric approach, which endorses mainstreaming CLD students, results in acculturation and the maintenance of the status quo. The assumption is that very little can be done for improving learning by changing educational external factors, since the causes of learning problems are believed to be internal. This approach therefore opposes offering enriched multicultural or bilingual classes for meeting the idiosyncratic needs of CLD students. The educational program based on this approach has the goal of measuring and comparing learning across students as a "product." That is, students' competence and performance in standardized tests are translated into quantitative measures of learning as reflected in scores that become powerful tools for securing funds and services within the current school administrative system. In practice, what we have generated with this emphasis in quantitative approaches for measuring learning is an emphasis in "teaching-to-the-test" across the nation. As a result, content is not learned conceptually but memorized temporarily for performing at high levels in standardized tests. However, this major misconception of the learning process does not take into consideration individual differences of CLD students, their idiosyncratic interests, and the central role of their intrinsic motivation for being successful. Thus, the mission of the educational program derived from the psychometric approach is to maintain the status quo of the American society, that is, to acculturate and mainstream CLD students.

Intervention strategies derived from this approach are based on the philosophy of inclusion for CLD students. For instance, transitional bilingual education programs will be offered to transfer students to an English-only educational environment as early as possible, or remedial educational programs that "water down" the curriculum will be provided for matching the students' "internal learning problems." Educational program evaluation within this approach also emphasizes the measurement of learning as a "product" that can be compared across students by using standardized tests and norms.

Educational Implications of the Psychometric Approach
Translating the first principle of the psychometric approach to the educational setting, we can see that it is very easy to assess CLD students and come to the diagnostic conclusion that innate factors are the causes of learning problems. As a result, students are labeled and educators blame the "victims," since internal factors are believed to cause learning problems. Thus, CLD students are at-risk of being misdiagnosed as having internal learning problems, such as disabilities, when they are assessed following the medical model. Moreover, the assumption that the learning problems of CLD students are internal is associated with the misconception that the causes are racial and genetic. Different "treatments," or "prescriptions," for these "internal diseases" expressed as "symptoms" labeled "learning problems" can be then developed, such as medication, therapy, individualized educational programs, and special education.

In relation to the second principle of the psychometric approach, within the medical model a definite "cure" for internal learning problems has not yet been found. Thus CLD students who are mislabeled and misdiagnosed most commonly as "learning disabled" or "mentally retarded" (Ortiz & Yates, 1983) are placed in special education classrooms in which mainly rote memorization and automatic drills are emphasized (Commins & Miramontes, 1989). As a result, an ideal environment for a self-fulfilling prophecy has been created, because students act based on learned helplessness, and because teachers' attitudes and behaviors are based on low expectations. Teachers are trained to attribute the lack of success in these understimulating classrooms as the expression of the lack of potential and internal abilities in students. That is, teachers are trained to avoid assuming responsibility for CLD students' lack of learning in the unsuccessful educational settings that have been created by them.

The basis for this misconception is transmitted by teachers trained according to psychometric principles regarding the existence of "neurological dysfunctions" that are caused by irreversible internal, genetic, and innate factors. Given these "innate restrictions," educators can only "remediate" this structural problem by providing a matching low-level environment. As Gonzalez and Yawkey (1993) pointed out, "Students who graduate from institutions of higher education become thoroughly indoctrinated in this approach . . . [and it] continues to nurture the status quo in teacher training and student development" (p. 47).

A major flaw in the third principle of the psychometric approach, which states that psychological constructs may be quantitatively measured in an exact manner, is revealed by the overrepresentation of CLD students in special education programs. If diagnoses of psychological constructs, such as intelligence and language development, based on standardized tests were accurate, every cultural group would be equally represented in every category along the continuum of giftedness-abnormalities. That is, the assumption that standardized test measure internal causes of learning problems is a major flaw, given that no one instrument can claim to differentiate between learned information and innate potential, skills, or abilities. Defenders of the psychometric approach blame CLD students for not having had the opportunity to learn the mainstream cultural information that they are being tested for in intelligence standardized tests. Oller (1994) referred to this nonsense as the "monoglottosis" or "terminal monolingualism" that afflicts some educators, psychologists, administrators, and legislators who defend the psychometric approach. Oller (1994) advocated that educators refrain from making bilingual children accountable for their school failure. He recommended that educators use dual-language and culturally appropriate assessment procedures to do justice to the superior potential of challenged bilingual children that numerous research studies have demonstrated.

In relation to the fourth, fifth, and sixth principles of the psychometric approach (referring to the comparison and prediction of skills and abilities across students to identify individual differences using discrete point standardized tests), educators assume that development emerges in sequential phases and that specific inherited genetic traits are nonadditive (Gonzalez & Yawkey, 1993). That is, educators do not stimulate the whole child, but reinforce and test only discrete concepts. When comparing students across these discrete genetic traits, "students not demonstrating high discrete point totals become the *failure* of society" (Gonzalez & Yawkey, 1993, p. 46). Thus, emphasis is placed only on the products, and teachers are only counting the number of successes or correct responses in standardized tests. As Gonzalez and Yawkey (1993) pointed out, "These 'failures' and 'successes' become another stage in the ongoing movement in the survival of the species" (p. 46). Thus, specific idyosincracies are disregarded when comparing students to group norms, because the influence of cultural and linguistic factors on students' cognitive processes and learning strategies are not taken into account.

The "Missionary" Approach

This traditional assessment approach is adopted without sensitivity to minority cultures and languages by researchers who use mainstream theoretical and assessment models to try to understand how CLD students develop. In an earlier paper (Gonzalez & Yawkey, 1993), we called this the "missionary" approach, as it uses "experts" from the mainstream community who act as ambassadors to minorities. It follows the participant observer approach of early anthropological studies, because researchers act as translators or mediators who maintain the status quo of the acculturation model. This approach has some similarities with the psychometric approach in terms of assessment and diagnostic principles. For instance, the "missionary" approach also attributes learning problems to internal causes. Therefore, external factors cannot solve these internal "learning problems," resulting also in blaming the victim. The principle that skills and abilities can be validly and reliably measured and predicted in a quantitative form, can be subdivided into discrete competences and performances, and can be compared across individuals is also present in the "missionary" approach.

In addition, the "missionary" approach has both overt differences and underlying similarities with the psychometric approach in relation to assessment objectives. A major overt difference is that the "missionary" approach is interested in adapting and translating standardized tests to reflect the cultural and linguistic context of different minority groups. Even though translations and adaptations of a number of standardized tests exist presently, they lack validity and reliability, as their underlying theories and philosophies have been developed for mainstream groups. The adaptation of assessment methods and techniques can have harmful negative consequences for CLD students, resulting in misclassifications and mislabeling. An inappropriate placement (e.g., special education classroom) may produce the misdiagnosed condition (e.g., mental retardation) as a result of a self-fulfilling prophecy or of the effect of external educational conditions in development, such as the lack of opportunities to develop internal potentials. However, misdiagnosed deficit-oriented conditions are believed to be the result of internal learning problems by both the psychometric and "missionary" assessment approaches.

A major underlying similarity of the two approaches is related to their objectives when using standardized tests: to demonstrate internal or racial causes for the presence of low scores and learning problems among CLD students compared with mainstream students. In addition, the objective for assessment, as reflected in the principles of both approaches, relates to a mainstream perspective that defends the acculturation model. That is, they are interested in studying the differences of CLD students from a cross-cultural perspective, within which being different means being an "exotic alien" who needs to be acculturated. In fact, the word "alien" has two connotations in English: a "foreigner" and an "extraterrestrial."

In terms of assessment and evaluation procedures, there are also major similarities across both approaches, because they use standardized tests as major tools for assessment. As mentioned, the "missionary" approach's interest in the adaptation and translation of standardized tests for different minority groups is a major overt difference related to the assessment objectives between these two approaches. However, their underlying principles for assessment and the use of the tests serve the same purposes.

Diagnostic categories used in the "missionary" approach are also very similar to the ones supported by the psychometric approach. Both approaches have deficit-oriented diagnostic categories that identify the internal causes of learning problems. For CLD students, these internal causes are racially and genetically related. Therefore, placement decisions are remedial and compensatory, which is reflected in the overrepresentation of CLD students in special education programs (Ortiz & Maldonado-Colon, 1986; Ortiz & Yates, 1983) and their underrepresentation in gifted education programs (Frasier, 1991; Renzulli, 1991). The objective of an educational program that follows a "missionary" approach is to acculturate CLD students in order to maintain the status quo in society. This acculturation model opposes multi-cultural and developmental bilingual education programs that maintain both first and second languages and the minority culture of students. Intervention strategies of the "missionary" and psychometric approaches are also similar, as both include remedial and compensatory strategies that reflect the assumption that external factors cannot change the presence of internal learning problems in CLD students.

When conducting educational program evaluations, the "missionary" approach uses the same tools as the psychometric approach—standardized tests that are believed to measure accurately the performance and competence of CLD students. Any lack of improvement reflected in test and retest procedures is believed to be the result of the lack of innate skills and abilities, and not of inappropriate and low quality educational programs. The corollary of the "missionary" approach is that CLD students are failing and dropping out of the present educational system not because they lack the opportunity to succeed, but because they lack the internal abilities and skills and cultural educational values needed to take advantage of their opportunities in the mainstream school culture. However, this reasoning cannot explain the current massive dropout rates and the obvious failure of the American educational system. Presently, we need to accept that the educational system is in crisis and that external educational factors are causing learning problems in CLD students, before it is too late for the future social and economic well-being of the United States.

Educational Implications of the "Missionary" Approach

From educational programs and teacher-training perspectives, there are many implications of the "missionary" approach. As we focus on school practices in classroom programs, this approach in many ways reflects the societal attitude toward immigrants after World War I. Educational and recreational programs focused on "saving" children from their primitive, "un-American" pasts. For example, seesaws and monkey bars were put in playgrounds to train children to use proper behavior and to extinguish "tribal" behavior. In large cities, for example, afterschool programs in team sports were initiated to train adolescents in "societal fair play" so they would not resort to "savage" activity.

Against this attitude, which still exists (albeit more subtly) in today's schools, the teacher using the "missionary" approach views development and learning as fixed rather than fluid. The CLD students thus progress through developmental stages fixed by time and dictated by their genes. As in Macbeth's caldron, developmental traits bubble forth at certain times. For example, young CLD children might be environmentally immersed in a sea of easels, crayons, paper, watercolors, and so forth to nurture aesthetic traits that are thought to bubble forth, between the ages of three to five. Similar to the seesaws and monkey bars, the easel and watercolors become markers that set nurturing limits on traits, with development determined by genes. The lack of progress made by students using this approach is explained by heredity—"Her pretend play is not well developed—she only speaks Spanish!" The "missionary" teacher, as a "social crusader," might use other internal causes to explain away learning differences between CLD students and majority students, such as, "Well, she was adopted by a family friend!" and "The child is biracial; his father is white!" Since the facts that these CLD students speak Spanish, are adopted, are biracial, and so forth cannot be helped, no solution sets are possible, because external factors are controlled by internal ones.

In addition, educational programs and school practices in this approach are viewed as "ambassadors," or one-way bridges to the dominant culture. From this perspective, non-CLD students would be asked to model understandings, skills, and positive attitudes to CLD students to "help them become more like us!" As noted by Gonzalez and Yawkey (1993), the practice of school programs of reporting test achievement by native-language groups is also an example of the "missionary" (as well as the psychometric) model: "For example, the mean scores for Anglos, Hispanic Americans and Khmer-speaking children are 67, 51, and 59, respectively. The implication is that this division of scores by culture (each with its own arithmetic means) solves problems of individual and group representation" (p. 47).

In this example of the use of arithmetic mean test scores, the test instruments themselves may be translated into native languages. School practices and programs serving as "ambassadors" to cultural and linguistic groups might in turn separately document and publish the Spanish, Khmer, and Anglo group means of tests given in native languages. This program practice is an example of a "missionary" educational endeavor because it represents "pacification," since group means are compared and testing instruments of this type stress discrete point evaluation. Relatedly, in educational practice the "missionary" approach would view the tests translated into native language to be second-best compared to the English-language version. This "armchair missionary" approach becomes a self-fulfilling prophecy—with the "natives" coming out second-best when compared cross-culturally.

Teachers following the "missionary" approach view themselves at early and middle childhood levels as guiders, modelers, and as arrangers of the learning environment! Students "get-what-they-get" based on what they have: good genetic input equals good genetic output! Secondary teachers in this model view themselves as dispensers of content, based on logic similar to that used by the early childhood and elementary teachers. Tendencies toward looking for and finding weaknesses in CLD students would also be characteristic of this approach. Similar to the psychometric model, the "missionary" approach, with its emphasis on finding pathologies based on reductionism from native to Anglo (standard) cultures, is clinically oriented.

From a teacher-training program perspective, there are several implications of the "missionary" approach. The intent of these preservice and inservice programs would be to sensitize the teachers to various cultures. Here, cross-cultural comparisons would be specific. From a "missionary" perspective, we see one potential outcome of cross-cultural comparisons as mental "file cards," all categorized neatly by cultures and attributes. For example, the language groups might have headings such as Russian, Spanish, Chinese and so forth. Next, attributes found in the culture might be identified, such as the types of housing, transportation, educational schooling, and so forth. This type of learner education programs would ultimately appear to be extremely biased, with rather stereotypic outcomes. Conversely, these cross-cultural comparisons might also appear in a "stripped-down" version in a "missionary" approach. In this teacher education program, there might be one major course in education departments or colleges called "diversities," which would emphasize core similarities cross-culturally (Gonzalez & Yawkey, 1993). Here, the search is for cultural imperatives and common cultural core elements that ultimately support and subtly stress enculturation. Relatedly, there might be required diversity-identified courses outside education departments for students. As college students take one three-credit required diversity course among the twelve credits required for English, one three-credit diversity course among the twelve credits required for history, and so forth, such courses become "add-ons" to the core thrust of similarities and enculturation.

Another implication of the "missionary" approach for teacher training focuses on developmental views. Since this approach has a heredity-orientation toward human behavior, it becomes extremely important to understand growth and development. Courses developed around evolving motor, personality, and language traits and so forth would emphasize specific traits at work from birth onward in students. Ways to prepare classrooms to nurture these traits become pedagogical practices in this approach. Further, the traditional view on assessment is critical to the "missionary" approach. As such, these teacher education programs emphasize the usual "straight-line," clinical model of diagnosis and remediation in courses on testing, or simply have the students model the ways they were evaluated in college classrooms.

In sum, maintaining the status quo is a key long-range goal of the "missionary" approach in classroom practices and teacher education programs. "More-of-the-same" practices, policies, and procedures in working with culturally and linguistically diverse students are the long-range outcome and prognosis of the "missionary" approach.

The Behavioral Approach

The major assessment and diagnostic principle of this traditional approach is that external factors cause learning behaviors and development. That is, learning problems are the result of external factors that can be changed, such as negative behaviors that have been reinforced by the environment or desirable behaviors that can be learned by imitation given the presence of models or rewards. As a result, a learning problem can be solved by modifying and shaping the student's behaviors in the classroom and at home, by changing the way the teacher and parents respond to the student's behaviors, by providing appropriate role models to imitate, or by any other change in the surrounding environment. A second principle for assessment and diagnosis of this approach is that the particular ages at which behaviors take place are not important. Therefore, comparisons across individuals are not important either, as behaviors are not supposed to be the result of internal maturational factors, as the psychometric approach argues. A third principle is that concrete behaviors are the only trait that can be measured objectively by quantitative dimensions, such as structured observations or task analysis. The behavioral approach is not interested in measuring abstract constructs that are expressed through psychological traits, such as intelligence or personality. A fourth principle states that complex behaviors can be subdivided in simple and discrete behaviors in order to facilitate their objective measurement and treatment. In fact, because the behavioral approach has a major interest in concrete and observable behaviors, complex behaviors are reduced to multiple simple behaviors. As a result, this approach cannot measure and explain complex behaviors.

Because of the assessment objectives of this approach is to identify the environmental causes of someone's learning problems, the comparison of students to norms or criterions is avoided. A second assessment objective is to collect information on external causes of behaviors observed in a particular individual given specific external conditions. This information is assumed to be most useful for educational program planning. A third assessment objective is to collect information that emphasizes which skills the student has acquired and which skills remain to be learned. This approach uses different assessment instruments, such as task analysis, applied behavioral analysis, criterion-referenced tests, and curriculum-based tests. Mostly, task analysis is used for dividing a skill into smaller subskills for skill sequencing and response chaining. This assessment approach does not emphasize the use of diagnostic categories related to identifying the learning problems as internal, such as mental retardation or learning disabilities. The emphasis on diagnosis is on identifying the external factors that are affecting the students' behaviors and on developing a plan for changing the external conditions or situations associated with an undesirable behavior. Placement decisions are related to how the external conditions can be improved through means such as providing an environment that stimulates students to respond positively or that responds adequately to students' socially desirable behaviors.

The mission of the educational program is to provide an environment that can control and positively influence the students' social behaviors and learning, that is, to control the external factors in order to change the students' behaviors to meet socially acceptable standards. Intervention strategies are based on the use of behavior modification techniques (e.g., operant conditioning, shaping, behavior generalizing, discriminating, etc.), the provision of role models to imitate, and the application of social learning principles. The educational program is evaluated according to observable behavioral changes that have occurred in students due to the modification of the external environment.

Educational Implications of the Behavioral Approach
The implications of the behavioral approach for educational school-based programs and teacher training are markedly and vastly different from the "universal" idealisms of the "missionary" approach. From an educational schooling perspective, the behavioral approach is commonly viewed as the one most often used in classrooms, especially among elementary, secondary,

and special teachers. Whether implicitly or explicitly, teachers, parents, and students are increasing pushing for the "correct" or the "right" answers, the "correct" way. School programs that stress dichotomous correct-and-incorrect responses, discreteness and exactness in learning, and rote memorization represent the behavioral application to classroom settings. Here, in order to apply behavioral principles to the classroom, teachers view the student's brain as a rather passive receptacle into which learning comes.

However, within this approach students must also be active, since they must physically and mentally respond (i.e., emit behaviors) to "catch" the skills being "thrown" out by the teacher. In this sense, the students are seen as miniature adults or as processing computers. With the continuing explosions of knowledge, college content is pushed to twelfth grade, twelfth-grade content is moved to eleventh and tenth grades, and so forth. At the end of the continuum, preschool becomes an academic primary-grade program model— all thought to "give the student a better mind!" With the constant press for better minds, higher SAT scores, and improved vocabularies, behavioral classrooms stress convergent outcomes, not divergent discoveries. This classroom pressure is one of a number of pressures which are thought to cause students to lose their creative and pretend-play processes by the end of first grade (e.g., see Trostle & Yawkey, 1990). Under behavioral approaches, these teacher attitudinal frames include "push-down" subject matter and "add-on" curricula. In addition, they represent opinions, such as "they haven't met criterion" (Steffens, 1992, p. 395), if students miss the standard on-target behavior.

The classroom teacher is interested in training specific skills and subskills that are identified through task analysis, in which the teacher asks the following four questions (Peters, Neisworth & Yawkey, 1985, p. 146):*

1. What concepts must children know in order to complete the task?
2. What kinds of attentional skills must they have?
3. What kinds of physical movements are necessary?
4. What behavior sequences must children perform?

These four guiding questions not only define task analysis but also provide excellent insight into the focus, intent, and delivery of behavioral classroom practices and programs. Relatedly, learning criteria are demonstrated through observing physical responses and verbal labels as they occur *in situ*. Since motivation for learning lies outside students, the behavioral approach relies heavily on using reinforcement contingencies to shape students'

*All Peters, Neisworth and Yawkey quotes on pages 80, 81, 86, and 87 are from *Early childhood education: From theory to practice* by D. L. Peters, J. T. Neisworth and T. D. Yawkey. Copyright © 1985 by Brooks/Cole Publishing Company, Pacific Grove, CA 93950, a division of International Thomson Publishing Inc. By permission of the publisher.

behaviors (see Peters, Neisworth, & Yawkey, 1985, pp. 156–161, for detailed explanations of the types of reinforcers and their uses).

The behavioral approach in the classroom is educational engineering. The structure is provided by the teacher, and teaching technology and mechanics "shape" the teacher's and the students' responses. The classroom philosophy is that all students can learn. Here students do not fail as learners. It is rather the teachers who fail if the task analysis and the reinforcement contingencies they employ do not increase the students' learning (Peters, Neisworth, & Yawkey, 1985).

From a teacher-training perspective, preservice and in-service education is aimed at becoming proficient in using behavioral techniques and practices. Various courses are offered to develop proficiencies in behavioristic psychology, reinforcement contingencies, task analysis, and so forth. Other course work focuses on selecting and/or designing classroom materials characterized by self-correction and automatic feedback in learning, such as "talking" typewriters and language machines, with which students model oral language statements to criterion immediately after hearing them, and computer games. Classroom scheduling by subject blocks stresses the significance of content mastery. Teacher training in separate skill-oriented subjects is primary, and the conceptual relations among subjects are secondary (Gonzalez & Yawkey, 1993; Yawkey & Juan, 1994). Recess and other breaks from course work become times for students to release energy after studying and learning. Within higher education, behaviorally oriented teacher training offers courses in data collection, analysis, and interpretations relative to engineering the student's learning. Techniques for pinpointing base-line behaviors show operants existing prior to treatment (i.e., the initiation of appropriate reinforcement contingencies). Reinstituting base-line contingencies (i.e., removing of reinforcement contingencies) might be emphasized with certain behaviors (e.g., learning skills) versus other (e.g., emotive behaviors such as crying) to determine the reliability and validity of treatment conditions.

Within the behavioral teacher training program, differences among and between cultures are minimized. Given that all individuals, regardless of cultural and linguistic group, emit physical and verbal responses, diversities are not as critical to learning and development as with other approaches. In teacher-training programs built from this approach, the recognition of cultural and linguistic differences would fall to reinforcement contingencies. Here, the key that unlocks the school door for CLD students is finding relevant reinforcement contingencies that motivate them to learn. For CLD students, this key is emphasized. Finally, classroom learning and teacher training under the behavioral approach are quite different in conceptualization and role. Training for culture acquisition is primary; cultural and linguistic diversity is secondary.

The "Ethnic Researcher" Approach

This contemporary approach is based on developmental principles that assume the interaction between internal and external factors that combine differently across individuals. Ethnic researchers depart from mainstream theories to develop studies and generate explanations, taking into account the cultural and linguistic diversity of students. In this chapter we apply the term to assessment models. The first assessment and diagnostic principle assumes that individuals have potentials that can be actualized or expressed differently in various sociocultural environments. Then, in the "ethnic researcher" approach the assessment of external factors is considered to be central for an accurate diagnosis of CLD students. The assessment of external factors across settings and informants includes the collection of information by a multidisciplinary team of evaluators. By examining the student's performance across settings, erroneous interpretations of that performance (e.g., the six-hour mentally retarded child) can be reduced.

A second principle assumes that these potentials by definition are unlimited and therefore that fixed quantitative values cannot be assigned to potentials. These unique potentials of each student can thus only be appreciated through qualitative descriptors. Unlike the psychometric and "missionary" approaches, this approach does not compare these potentials across individuals. Instead, the "ethnic researcher" approach considers that potentials can be assessed and diagnosed using qualitative ranges or possible values of the potentials expressed at a particular point by specific, idiosyncratic interactions between internal and external factors. A third principle is that assessment is focused on the process, as the students' strategies for learning, their developmental stage, and their potential for learning are described within a range of possible expressions of this potential given an adequate educational environment. Therefore, information derived from qualitative assessment methods can be directly used for instruction without the need for translating technical concepts, such as information obtained from standardized instruments. A fourth principle states that these potentials can be further developed, a concept that is acknowledged by the continuity of development from lower to higher levels throughout life. As a result, this approach is constructivistic in nature, as it assumes that development, whether continuous or stagelike, occurs due to the interaction of internal and external factors.

Some developmental approaches may be based on a cognitive-stage perspective, others on the idea that development is continuous (i.e., that progress through life occurs in a smooth and stable fashion). Stagelike approaches consider that students go through qualitative changes, or milestones, in their thinking and other developmental areas that enable them to achieve at higher levels as they mature. Stagelike theories have a structuralistic or hierarchical position, as they consider that students mature from lower to higher development. The stages perspective assumes as the criterion for assessment the identification of the hierarchical stages of development associated with approximate maturational-developmental age levels, where chronological age is not important. The emphasis is on the sequence of stages a student goes through and the abilities associated with each stage (a process-based approach). Students are given problem-solving tasks, and examiners observe and probe how students interact with the environment in play situations. There is evidence that cognitive-based scales are useful in the assessment of CLD students, as discussed in Chapter 5 in relation to Gonzalez's (1991, 1994, 1995) qualitative assessment model.

The objective for assessment in the "ethnic researcher" approach is to value the unique characteristics of each individual and to respect individuals' cultural and linguistic differences. The major goal is to demonstrate that CLD students develop at normal or above-normal levels but express their potential differently due to the presence of two cultures and two languages. In addition, the potential for learning must be differentiated from the knowledge acquired.

The "ethnic researcher" approach uses mostly qualitative assessment methods, such as developmental problem-solving tasks, unstructured observations of students in different environments, surveys and interviews with parents and teachers, teacher-made criterion-referenced measures, and portfolio assessment. These alternative assessment approaches are discussed in Chapters 4 and 5. All of these qualitative methods are useful for developing and planning educational programs, as they measure skills mastered by an individual student. This approach assumes the presence of potentials in the sociocultural and linguistic environment that can be nurtured, and the interaction of internal and external causes of learning problems in CLD students. These assumptions are reflected in qualitative assessment methods as well as in diagnostic categories and placement decisions.

According to the "ethnic researcher" approach, the diagnostic process demands deep knowledge of the constructs being evaluated as well as awareness of the influence of cultural and linguistic factors on the development of CLD students. Thus, with this approach evaluators need to put together multidisciplinary pieces of information in order to reach accurate differential diagnoses and placement decisions. Then, considering the lack of valid and reliable assessment instruments and theories explaining development in CLD students, it is better to conceptualize the diagnostic process as an "art" rather than as a technique. As explained in the first section of this chapter, it is important to make an accurate differential diagnosis between the normal process of second-language learning and genuine disabilities in CLD students. For instance, Duran (1989) reported that Hispanic bilinguals were diagnosed as mentally retarded when cutoff scores on IQ tests were used with no additional data to support this diagnosis. Gonzalez (1991, 1994, 1995) found that standardized tests of nonverbal intelligence (see Brown, Sherbenou, & Dollard, 1982) underestimated kindergarten and first-grade bilingual Hispanic children's cognitive nonverbal abilities, which resulted in mislabeling them as mentally retarded. In fact, Gonzalez (1991, 1994, 1995) reported that these same bilingual children showed normal to superior cognitive developmental levels when assessed by a qualitative assessment method that took linguistic and cultural factors into consideration. Thus, misdiagnosis results from biased standardized tests, and leads to an over-representation of CLD students in special education (see, e.g., Ortiz & Maldonado-Colon, 1986; Ortiz & Yates, 1983) and an underrepresentation in gifted education programs (see, e.g., Frasier, 1991; Renzulli, 1991).

Assessment procedures used by the "ethnic researcher" approach include primarily qualitative assessment methods, sometimes with the addition of standardized tests that are used to fulfill legal demands. However, we need to keep in mind the need to protect CLD students from misdiagnosis and mislabeling. Thus, evaluators and educators must act as advocates for CLD students. Standardized tests may be used within an "ethnic researcher" approach, but for different reasons than within the psychometric and the "missionary" approaches. The "ethnic researcher" approach strives to prove that CLD students are different from majority children, and that being different does not mean being abnormal due to internal or racial causes. In fact, the cultural diversity of CLD students is valued and celebrated as an enrichment for their development. Moreover, when using standardized tests within an "ethnic researcher" approach, the emphasis is not on comparing students but on understanding individual strengths and weaknesses for developing individual educational plans. It is important to highlight that the same instruments may be used differently depending on the philosophical principles of the assessment approach. This same idea was also highlighted when the influence of evaluators' attitudes and beliefs on the diagnosis of CLD students was discussed above.

The mission of the "ethnic researcher" approach is to depart from mainstream theories as new models for explaining the uniqueness of CLD students are developed. Our current belief that the diagnosis of CLD students can be an "objective" process is a fallacy, as the evaluator can select subjectively different instruments coming from various assessment models in order to defend their own beliefs, values, and theoretical philosophies. That is, the identification of internal or external causes of possible at-risk conditions in CLD students expresses the evaluator's biases and subjectivities. Ethnic researchers have as a mission and goal to introduce and model change in the educational and social system by generating change in the mainstream attitudinal system. They have an insightful understanding of symbolic and linguistic expressions of the culture and their influence on how CLD students think and develop, which results in an insider's perspective.

Ethnic researchers may come from minority or majority backgrounds, and they share a social and ethical responsibility for acting as committed advocates of CLD students. They have an empathic view of current social, ethical, and educational problems resulting from mislabeling and misdiagnosing. They do not view the CLD students as an "interesting case for solving traditional cross-cultural problems," as researchers following the psychometric and "missionary" approaches do. Instead, ethnic researchers accept the challenge of understanding CLD students, as they are genuinely interested in validating the experience of growing up in culturally diverse environments.

Educational strategies are based on developmental principles that emphasize nurturing internal potentials by offering a positive educational environment that values cultural and linguistic diversity as an enrichment. Educational strategies include stimulating students to be an active learner by respecting their individual interests and stimulating their strengths. Students are also encouraged to learn by discovery while developing intrinsic motivation for learning. Stimulation of the "whole" student is emphasized by nurturing all aspects of students' personality development, including cognitive, linguistic, emotional, and social areas.

Educational program development is based on qualitative assessment methods that give information that can be directly applied for planning instruction. Students' strengths and weaknesses are identified in order to nurture potentials and to stimulate the development of skills and abilities at higher levels. Instruction is individualized as unique characteristics and needs as well as idiosyncratic interests and motivations for learning are respected and acknowledged. Within a developmental curriculum, individual differences of CLD students are expected, valued, and celebrated. Educational program evaluation is based on understanding growth in students' unique processes for learning. For example, developmental qualitative assessment methods or portfolio assessment may be used for understanding progress in students' learning processes and potential for learning.

In sum, major methodological, educational, and theoretical problems encountered in current assessment practices when conducting a differential diagnosis with CLD students are related to assumptions held by traditional and contemporary assessment approaches. These assumptions carry with them some misconceptions and myths that are transmitted to educators during the training process. It has been proposed in this chapter that educators need to participate in an awakening experience in order to gain awareness and sensitivity for realizing the influence of their own attitudes and beliefs on their assessment practices with CLD students.

Educational Implications of the Ethnic Researcher Approach

Moving from the behavioral approach to the "ethnic researcher" approach, we make the transition from "schooling for the masses" (Popkewitz, 1992) to "schooling for the individual." School practices and program views provide students with an opportunity to become active individuals who continually develop their thinking and linguistic processes. "Ethnic researcher" programs in schools stress developing and nurturing concepts (e.g., objects that float and sink) rather than training skills (e.g., the weight and lack of porousness that explain why objects sink). Within this approach, school programs offer sense experiences through real objects, field trips, experimentation, demonstration, and so forth. There is great regard for the malleability of thinking and "languaging" due to the effects of external situations and internal factors. Here, maturational biological processes can be altered based on external experiences as the student and environment interact.

Another critical implication of the "ethnic researcher" approach is the lack of emphasis on products or discrete points or terminal standards of excellence. Schooling practices here stress process—the various markers, modes, and ways that individuals use to analyze and problem-solve critically to arrive at products. Getting to point A is more important developmentally than point A itself. Gonzalez and Yawkey (1993) note that "emphasizing more process '*outcomes*' in the classroom also permits educators to focus on following student's lines of thinking along points in time" (p. 48). Processes might involve observing how students interact or what a child does in mixing paints or conducting a chemical experiment in the laboratory. Processes also mean collecting samples of students' work in portfolios and using other performance assessment techniques (e.g., interviews and demonstrations). Both observational and performance assessment techniques provide ample evidence for reliably assessing students' work while checking on their progress across time. Assessing work and checking progress along developmental continua are twin components of teacher and classroom operations. Development occurs in uneven spurts as children move toward adult thinking. Attempting to increase development and learning deliberately and significantly by manipulating environmental contingencies external to students is meaningless in the "ethnic researcher" approach. Students' rate of learning is an individual process and relates to the quality of their social and physical experiences, the extent of their thinking, and their biological maturation (Peters, Neisworth, & Yawkey, 1985).

Since cultural transmission is one of several nurturing factors in the student's development, the "ethnic researcher" approach values cultural and linguistic differences. Social experiences include the influence of family, peer group, and schooling as well as social language and social culture. Differences of languages, customs, ideas, cultures, and religions are all significant because they assist in nurturing and facilitating the individual's thinking and "languaging." The impacts of these social and cultural encounters help provide students with opportunities to imitate, model, and create. Having "Taco Day," "Vietnamese New Year," and other targeted, glossy, one-shot approaches to diversity are not examples of the "ethnic researcher" approach (Gonzalez & Yawkey, 1993). Instead, cultural and linguistic experiences are celebrated as diversity through subject, actual experiences and activities, and learning about self (specifically cultural identity). As noted, these diversities are extenders for development and provide massed experiences for enrichment. "Here, the classrooms become mosaics of students' personalities as well as social, emotional and cultural overlays" (Gonzalez & Yawkey, 1993, p. 48). Within the "ethnic researcher" classrooms, teachers come to realize that the contributions and potential of each CLD student can be expressed within and across cultures.

As a related part of social experiences, the "ethnic researcher" classroom reaches out to and uses the family to strengthen its school program. As cited in Yawkey and Juan (1993, p. 18), Garcia (1992a), stresses that "the family unit creates opportunities for the child to learn values" (p. 79). Values in both the family and the classroom stress cooperation, group attachment, status (Yawkey & Juan, 1993), and so forth. Here, classroom and family potentials are harnessed because they both have similar value systems and both target, nurture, and care about the same developing student.

A final classroom implication noted by Gonzalez and Yawkey (1993) is the integration of curricular areas. Peters, Neisworth, and Yawkey (1985) see this as a twofold thrust in this type of classroom. Meeting the individual developmental needs of all students through classroom experiences is one goal. Another goal is to work with the whole student—the motive self, intellectual self, cultural self, and so forth (Peters, Neisworth, & Yawkey, 1985). Integration in this context means understanding and using varied experiences and activities at the classroom that respect individual developmental growth and the whole-child concept. It means applying multiple experiences and encounters that emerge and are delivered in large, small, and individual groups (Yawkey, 1992). This use and variety of group modes are ideal in the "ethnic researcher" classroom because of their suitability to demonstration, exhibition, library research, and so forth.

From another perspective, integration means taking a broad-fields approach to subject matter at early and middle childhood. At the preschool, kindergarten, and primary grades, the "ethnic researcher" classroom most likely uses themes and thematic units. In P.I.A.G.E.T. Programs, for instance, thematic units include self, family, living things, and transportation (Yawkey, 1992). Whole subject matter concepts are spun around and focus on these broad themes. This thematic orientation provides meaningful experiences from multiple perspectives focused on a unitary set of common learnings (e.g., transportation). At the upper elementary level, examples of this broad-fields integration of subject matter are language and literacy, which unite subjects such as reading, language arts, and social studies. Similar integrating thrusts can be used with learning science and mathematics. In secondary education, this integration can be coupled with teaming and collaborative endeavors.

From classroom to teacher training, the implications of the "ethnic researcher" approach support and nurture reformist practices in pedagogy. One critical implication is that teacher programs must train preservice and in-service teachers to develop and implement alternative methods of teaching and learning. For example, alternative assessment methods within an "ethnic researcher" approach suggest multiple evaluations of the student's current rather than past learning. A corollary in student learning is the use of multiple methods of process discovery and product conceptualization; for example, interviews, demonstrations, exhibitions, and other innovative, individualized techniques. Negroni (1992) stated that "different people learn in different ways and it is the role of the teacher to adapt teaching techniques to learning styles" (p. 379). From an "ethnic researcher" approach, multiple teaching modes cue into individualized instruction as well as large, small, and individual groups, while still focusing on whole-student development.

A related implication is that teacher-training programs provide practice in using experiential and active learning modes to develop and enhance learning (Garcia, 1992b). The "ethnic researcher" approach regards the experiential and active modes as critical elements of the interactive processes occurring between students and their environments. Didactic and related lecture and recitation methods rely almost exclusively on the auditory sense, whereas experiential and active modes use all the senses, thereby increasing the probabilities of meaningful learning. Garcia (1992b) feels that the didactic approach also relies heavily on the traditional skills approach, in which students remained largely in their seats for instruction. Experiential and active learning modes require practice to be used properly in small and individual groups. Relatedly, teachers need to identify with the students and guide them to understanding the group tasks and what they need to complete.

Another implication of the "ethnic researcher" approach is the active use of the native language. Garcia (1992b) sees effective teachers as using mediated teaching and instruction through the utilization of both English and native languages. To prepare to teach CLD students, trainees will need to know or learn native languages. The need for more foreign-language learning and teaching has been debated for decades. However, with the adoption of the "ethnic researcher" approach in teacher-training programs, another language in addition to English is critical.

In both classroom and teacher-training practices and programs, the adoption of the "ethnic researcher" approach with CLD students will demand many changes in the basic structure of what to teach and how to teach as well as in the college curricula required to match these much needed classroom changes that are occurring rapidly.

In summary, in this chapter we have discussed educational, methodological, and theoretical problems and major assessment models as well as their practical implications for the assessment, diagnosis, placement, and instruction of CLD students. Particularly, the philosophies and assumptions held by different contemporary and traditional assessment models have been discussed in reference to teachers' expectations, attitudes, and belief systems.

REFERENCES

Alexander, P. A., Schallert, D. L., & Hare, V. C. (1991). Coming to terms with the terminology of knowledge. *Review of Educational Psychology 61* 315–343.

American Educational Research Association, American Psychological Association, & National Council on Measurement in Education. (1985). *Standards for educational and psychological testing.* Washington, DC: American Psychological Association.

Anderson, R. C., & Pearson, P. D. (1984). A schema-theoretic view of basic processes in reading comprehension. In P. D. Pearson (Ed.), *Handbook of reading research* (pp. 255–293). New York: Longman.

Bilingual Education Act of 1978. (In Elementary and Secondary Education Act Amendments, P.L. 95-561) 92 Stat. 2268.

Brown, L., Sherbenou, R. J., & Dollard, S. J. (1982). *Test of Nonverbal Intelligence (TONI).* Austin, TX: Pro-Ed.

Commins, N. L., & Miramontes, O. B. (1989). Perceived and actual linguistic competence: A descriptive study of four low-achieving Hispanic bilingual students. *American Educational Research Journal 26*(4), 443–472.

Cummins, J. (1981). The role of primary language development in promoting educational success for language minority students. In California State Department of Education, Office of Bilingual Education, *Schooling and language: Minority children* (pp. 3–49). Los Angeles: California State University, Evaluation, Dissemination, and Assessment Center.

Damico, J. S. (1991). Descriptive assessment of communicative ability in limited English proficient students. In E. V. Hamayan & J. S. Damico (Eds.), *Limiting bias in the assessment of bilingual students* (pp. 157–217). Austin, TX: Pro-Ed.

De Avila, E., & Havassy, B. (1974, November–December). The testing of minority children: A neopiagetian approach. *Today's Education,* 60–74.

De George, G. P. (1988). Assessment and placement of language minority students: Procedures for mainstreaming. *NEW Focus 3 (Winter).*

Diana vs. California State Board of Education, No. C-70, RFT (Dist. Ct. N. Cal., 1970).

Duran, R. P. (1989). Assessment and instruction of at-risk Hispanic students. *Exceptional Children 56*(2), 154–158.

Education for All Handicapped Children Act of 1975. PL No. 94–142, 84 Stat. 773.

Frasier, M. M. (1991). Disadvantaged and culturally diverse gifted students. *Journal for the Education of the Gifted 14*(3), 234–245.

Garcia, E. E. (1992a). Hispanic children: Theoretical, empirical, and related issues. *Educational Psychology Review 4*(1), 69–93.

Garcia, E. E. (1992b). Teachers for language minority students: Evaluating professional standards. In *Proceedings of the Second National Research Symposium on Limited English Proficient Student Issues: Focus on Evaluation and Measurement:* Vol. 1 (pp. 383–414). Washington, DC: U.S. Department of Education, Office of Bilingual Education and Minority Languages Affairs.

Gonzalez, V. (1991). *A model of cognitive, cultural, and linguistic variables affecting bilingual Spanish/English children's development of concepts and language.* Doctoral dissertation, The University of Texas at Austin. (ERIC Document Reproduction Service No. ED 345 562)

Gonzalez, V. (1993a). Assessment of language minority students: An awakening experience. *NABE News* 17(2), 2, 9–10, 26.

Gonzalez, V. (1993b). Special voices. *NABE News* 16(6), 23, 26.

Gonzalez, V. (1994). A model of cognitive, cultural, and linguistic variables affecting bilingual Spanish/English children's development of concepts and language. *Hispanic Journal of Behavioral Sciences* 16(4), 396–421.

Gonzalez, V. (1995). *Cognition, culture, and language in bilingual children: Conceptual and semantic development.* Bethesda, MD: Austin/Winfield.

Gonzalez, V. (in press). Models for the relationship among language, language proficiency, phonological strategies, and levels of reading readiness in bilingual Spanish/English children. In V. Gonzales (Ed.), *Language and cognitive development in second language learning: Educational implications for children and adults.* Needham Heights, MA: Allyn & Bacon.

Gonzalez, V., Bauerle, P., Black, W., & Felix-Holt, M. (in press). Influence of evaluator's beliefs and cultural–linguistic backgrounds on their diagnostic and placement decisions for language-minority children. In V. Gonzalez (Ed.), *Language and cognitive development in second language learning: Educational implications for children and adults.* Needham Heights, MA: Allyn & Bacon.

Gonzalez, V., Bauerle, P., & Felix-Holt, M. (1994a). A qualitative assessment method for accurately diagnosing bilingual gifted children. *NABE '92–'93 Annual Conference Journal,* 37–52. Washington, DC: National Association for Bilingual Education.

Gonzalez, V., Bauerle, P., & Felix-Holt, M. (1994b). Theoretical and practical implications of assessing cognitive language development in bilingual children with qualitative methods. In V. Gonzalez (Chair), *Alternative qualitative approaches for assessing, identifying, and instructing Hispanic bilingual students in gifted and talented educational programs.* Symposium conducted at the 23rd annual international conference of the National Association for Bilingual Education, February, Los Angeles.

Gonzalez, V. & Felix-Holt, M. (1995). Influence of evaluators' prior academic knowledge on the diagnosis of cognitive and language development in bilingual Hispanic kindergarteners. *New York State Association for Bilingual Education (NYSABE) Journal* 10(1), 34–45.

Gonzalez, V., & Yawkey, T. D. (1993). The assessment of culturally and linguistically different students: Celebrating change. *Educational Horizons* 72(1), 41–49.

Individuals with Disabilities Education Act of 1990 P.L. 101-476, 104 Stat. 1103.

Larry P. v. Wilson Riles, (C-71-2270). US. C., 343 F. Supp. 1306 (N. D. Cal. 1972).

Mercer, J. R. (1979). A policy statement on assessment procedures of the rights of children. *Harvard Educational Review 44,* 125–141.

Messick, S. (1989). Meaning and values in test validation: The science and ethics of assessment. *Educational Researcher 18*(2), 2–11.

Negroni, P. J. (1992). Transforming American education: Making it work. In *Proceedings of the Second National Research Symposium on Limited English Proficient Students' Issues: Focus on Evaluation and Measurement:* Vol. 2, (pp. 371–391). Washington, DC: U.S. Department of Education, Office of Bilingual Education and Minority Languages Affairs.

Oller, J. W., Jr. (1979). *Teaching the language-different child to read.* Columbus: Merrill.

Oller, J. W., Jr. (1991). Language testing research: Lessons applied to LEP students and programs. In *Proceedings of the First Research Symposium on Limited English Proficient Students' Issues: Focus on Evaluation and Measurement:* Vol. 2 (pp. 42–123). Washington DC: U.S. Department of Education, Office of Bilingual Education and Minority Languages Affairs.

Oller, J. W., Jr. (1994). Challenged bilinguals. *NABE News 17*(4), 15–16 & 18.

Oller, J. W., Jr., & Damico, J. S. (1991). Theoretical considerations in the assessment of LEP students. In E. V. Hamayan & J. S. Damico (Eds.), *Limiting bias in the assessment of bilingual students* (pp. 77–110). Austin, TX: Pro-Ed.

Ortiz, A. A., & Maldonado-Colon, E. (1986). Recognizing learning disabilities in bilingual children: How to lessen inappropriate referrals of language minority students to special education. *Journal of Reading, Writing, and Learning Disabilities International 2*(2), 43–56.

Ortiz, A. A., & Yates, J. R. (1983). Incidence of exceptionality among Hispanics: Implications for manpower planning. *Journal of the National Association for Bilingual Education 7*, 41–53.

Peters, D. L., Neisworth, J. T., & Yawkey, T. D. (1985). *Early childhood education: From theory to practice.* Monterey, CA: Brooks/Cole.

Popkewitz, T. S. (1992). A political/sociological critique of teacher education reforms: Evaluation of the relation of power and knowledge. In *Proceedings of the Second National Research Symposium on Limited English Proficient Students' Issues: Focus on Evaluation and Measurement:* Vol. 1 (pp. 287–314). Washington, DC: U.S. Department of Education, Office of Bilingual Education and Minority Languages Affairs.

Renzulli, J. S. (1991). The national research center on the gifted and talented: The dream, the design, and the destination. *Gifted Child Quarterly 35*(2), 73–80.

Steffens, J. E. (1992). Teacher training program for specific LEP students instructional needs. In *Proceedings of the Second National Research Symposium on Limited English Proficient Student Issues: Focus on Evaluation and Measurement:* Vol. 2 (pp. 393–416). Washington, DC: U.S. Department of Education, Office of Bilingual Education and Minority Languages Affairs.

Swain, M. (1981). Time and timing in bilingual education. *Language and Learning 31*, 1–15.

Trostle, S. R., & Yawkey, T. D. (1990). *Integrated learning activities for young children.* New York: Allyn and Bacon.

Yawkey, T. D. (1992). *1987–1990 Three-Year Report of Title VII Academic Excellence Project P.I.A.G.E.T. Cycle I* (Technical Report 295). University Park: The Pennsylvania State University.

Yawkey, T. D., & Juan, Y. (1994). Linking assessment and instruction with language-minority students: Extending the match. *NABE News 17*(3), 9, 18, 34.

4

SEPARATING MILD DISABILITIES FROM CULTURAL AND LINGUISTIC DIFFERENCES: RECOMMENDED ALTERNATIVE ASSESSMENT PRACTICES

In Chapter 3, we looked at various assessment models and their implications for teaching: the psychometric, "missionary," behavioral, and "ethnic researcher" approaches. The term, "ethnic researcher" is used consistently throughout this chapter because it implies that scholars have developed this current research approach. Any assessment methodology rests on the philosophy and psychology of learning, and on whether educational professionals essentially believe in and use that methodology in making decisions relative to children's problems in school performance (Cummins, 1984; Gonzalez & Yawkey, 1993). This fourth chapter is related to the vision statement of this book, because it discusses recommended alternative assessment models from an "ethnic researcher" perspective. We recommend that educators endorse new methodologies coming from a developmental and constructivistic philosophies for improving current assessment practices used with CLD students across the United States.

A major need at present is the development of alternative assessment methods reflecting assessment principles and objectives of the "ethnic researcher" approach (see Chapter 3) that take into consideration the student's first language (L1), second language (L2), and minority culture. This major contemporary need derives from sociohistorical assessment practices that go back to the beginnings of the establishment of the American public schools. Since that time the most commonly used assessment model is the psychometric approach. Accordingly, and given its past and present widespread usage, school personnel are well versed in its assessment methods, which include both intelligence and achievement tests. Based upon a deficit- and disorder-oriented psychoeducational philosophy, intelligence tests are believed to assess the quantity of intellectual abilities possessed by students based on and derived from normed populations. The Stanford-Binet test is a very common example of the psychometric assessment method. An achievement test is another form of psychometric assessment. With this method, achievement instruments assess the extent to which CLD students have acquired academic matter content. Some well known examples of achievement tests include the Metropolitan Achievement Test, the California Achievement Test, and the Iowa Test of Basic Skills.

Given that the psychometric model prevails in assessment practices conducted in American schools, and that this model may be least appropriately used with CLD students, the intent of this chapter is to present alternative assessment methods. We will discuss prereferral intervention strategies and models, assessment objectives, and alternative assessment procedures for accurately assessing CLD students, including portfolio, observation, and performance assessments.

PREREFERRAL INTERVENTION STRATEGIES AND MODELS

Prereferral intervention strategies are the "gatekeepers" for avoiding biases and inequalities when assessing CLD students. Even though we may be using valid and reliable assessment instruments, such as alternative assessment methods, we need to avoid "testing for its own sake." We need to refer appropriately CLD students who are in genuine need of testing due to real at-risk characteristics. Testing when there is no genuine need can also lead to biases and inequalities, especially when assessment objectives are not clear. Ball and Harry (1993) pointed out the powerful role of teacher referral in maintaining the inequalities of the educational system. Once CLD students are referred by teachers, it is very difficult to stop the inequalities of the labeling and placement process given the state of currently used standardized procedures. Then, as Ball and Harry (1993) noted, it is from this teacher-selected pool that CLD students continue to be overrepresented in special education categories. The problem is that these CLD students are misdiagnosed and misplaced, and, as explained in Chapter 3, disabilities are created by external factors. Therefore, currently special education services create rather than solve problems that result from normal CLD students.

As also mentioned in Chapter 3, and as highlighted by Ball and Harry (1993), separate fields, with their corresponding federal laws, create our present problems of assessing and educating CLD students. Misdiagnosis results when biased assessment procedures derived from the medical model underlying the field of special education are used when assessing CLD students. Moreover, most federal laws and commonly used assessment procedures within special education still conform to the traditional psychometric and "missionary" approaches that rely on the medical model. As explained in Chapter 3, this model assumes the presence of internal factors that cause learning problems, which in CLD students become racial and ethnic biological causes. Thus under the medical model, CLD students are treated unequally due to the use of discriminatory assessment procedures. Furthermore, when CLD students are referred for evaluation, they are at-risk of being misidentified as being in need of special education services. The result is a waste of not only economic and educational resources but most importantly of our most precious treasure, our young multicultural and multilingual children, the richness human resource of our nation.

Thus, the problem is that these CLD students who are at-risk of being misidentified as being in need of special education services come from different cultures and may also be bilingual. A bridge therefore needs to be created between special education, multicultural education, and bilingual education to serve appropriately CLD students in the American educational system. The interface between these three fields needs to include the integration, adaptation, and modification of the federal laws and assessment procedures currently used within each area. Numerous practical recommendations have been given by different authors for adapting and modifying assessment procedures when trying to integrate the fields of special education and bilingual education when assessing CLD students. For instance, Holtzman and Wilkinson (1991) proposed that assessment personnel need to avoid potential biases when they are faced with the double task of fulfilling legal requirements and providing adequate data for decision-making. They offered as guidelines for the fair assessment of CLD students: prereferral intervention, situational analysis, direct observation, establishment of the dominant language, dual-language testing, informed selection of a test battery, and careful data interpretation. The model and qualitative assessment method developed by Gonzalez (1991, 1994a) follows the assessment principles and objectives of the "ethnic researcher" approach (see Chapter 3), which coincide with current recommendations for improving our assessment practices with CLD students. Within an "ethnic-researcher" perspective, the major assessment objective is to prove the existence of culturally and linguistically bound potentials, abilities, and skills.

From the multiple strategies that have been suggested by Holtzman and Wilkinson (1991), we are going to expand on the prereferral intervention in this section. The idea of a prereferral intervention incorporates the classroom teacher as an important agent in the assessment process. The classroom teacher becomes a gatekeeper who can prevent the derivation of CLD students to evaluation processes that automatically place them in an at-risk situation given current assessment procedures. Moreover, the idea of a prereferral intervention links assessment with instruction, as learning taking place in the classroom needs to be evaluated primarily by the teacher before any referral is even initiated. The classroom teacher must assume the responsibility of creating learning situations that match the individual needs of CLD students. Therefore, the success or failure of the learning situation is directly related to the external factors that are created by classroom teachers such as methodologies and materials, expectations, familiarity with and sensitivity to the students' culture and language, respect and value for the uniqueness of each student's characteristics, commitment to understanding the students' backgrounds and needs, and mostly teachers' attitudes about their role in the academic and social development of their CLD students.

Teachers' attitudes can be changed from perceiving internal causes for learning problems to viewing their own teaching as an important external factor that can create learning problems. Gonzalez (1994b) demonstrated that an attitudinal change in preservice and in-service teachers can occur if higher education courses in multicultural teaching provide them with an opportunity to: (1) examine how their own cultural and linguistic backgrounds influence their own educational process; and (2) discuss the presence or absence of their prior knowledge for understanding how CLD students develop. It has been our experience as instructors of preservice and in-service teachers that in order to acquire new and much needed knowledge about how CLD students develop, they need to effect an attitudinal change. Teachers tend to develop negative attitudes toward much needed multicultural education courses that build strong "shields" preventing the acquisition of new knowledge. Several authors (e.g., Cummins, 1984; Ortiz, García, Wheeler, & Maldonado-Colón, 1986) have reported that referral, evaluation, and diagnostic procedures reveal the absence of adequate understanding among teachers of the impact of bilingualism, cultural, and other differences on learning processes. Thus, lack of knowledge is a major problem in educators that can only be overcome if educators change their attitudes about how CLD students develop.

In addition, several studies have been conducted (see, e.g., Lloyd, Kauffman, Landrum, & Roe, 1991) to identify the major reasons that teachers cite for referring students for evaluation and possible placement in special education. Lloyd et al. (1991) found that in schools with a high enrollment of minority students (36–41% of the school population), regular classroom teachers were the primary source of referral, and they tended to refer most often male students of seven years of age. The most common reasons for referrals were reading and written language problems, followed by behavior problems. Teachers tended to refer students who were performing below expectations in academic areas and who also showed behaviors that threatened the teacher's control of the classroom. That is, teachers were referring students based on the assumption of the presence of internal learning problems within the student and thus were implicitly denying any responsibility for the presence of teaching problems within the regular classroom. The reasons for referral never even questioned the teachers' perceived competence, showing that teachers were educated within the medical model. As a result, regular classroom teachers tend to assume the presence of internal factors when assessment, diagnosis, placement, and instructional processes are implemented.

Then, part of the attitudinal change and the acquisition of new knowledge needed in teacher education models is the infusing of the idea of linking assessment with instruction, which underlies prereferral intervention models. Giving teachers the opportunity to participate in the prereferral intervention process empowers them as central agents in the task of preventing the misdiagnosis and misplacement of CLD students. By being included in the prereferral process, teachers gain awareness that it is their responsibility to become advocates for CLD students. Teachers can begin to assume responsibility in the educational process when they realize how much a difference their decision of referring or not referring a student can make for the future social and educational well-being of that individual. It is by gaining awareness of their responsibility in this process that teachers begin to own the educational process. Other members of the multidisciplinary assessment team, such as educational diagnosticians and school psychologists, need to support teachers' efforts for trying out different instructional methods and materials in the first and second language of CLD students over a long period. CLD students need to be given enough developmental time to nurture their potentials for learning and avoiding premature referrals for evaluation. This need coincides with the assessment principles and objectives of the "ethnic researcher" approach when making diagnostic and placement decisions (see Chapter 3), specifically when potentials are differentiated from acquired learning when assessing CLD students.

Wilkinson and Ortiz (1986) found that Hispanic students who had been diagnosed as learning disabled were performing at lower levels on verbal and performance scales of IQ tests and at the same level on achievement scales after three years in special education. In the case of CLD students, developmental delays or normal English-as-a-second-language-learning cases can be confounded very easily with learning disabilities. Developmental delays are related to maturational factors that are influenced by nutrition, health care, and educational opportunities. That is, those delays that may be present in CLD students can be related to external economic and social factors. Normal English-as-a-second-language-learning cases are related to normal developmental times of young bilinguals acquiring two languages simultaneously. Some young bilingual children may show developmental levels in both languages that are at times even six months below "normal" monolingual developmental levels. However, this need for a longer developmental time for learning two languages simultaneously will be outgrown naturally and quickly after the first milestones in oral language development are reached at seven or eight years of age. Thus, both developmental delays and normal English-as-a-second-language-learning cases in CLD students are related to external conditions and not to internal neurological dysfunctions for language processing, as assumed by the medical model definition of learning disabilities. As Wilkinson and Ortiz (1986) reported, special education placements are not appropriate for CLD students who do not have any internal problems but who instead are in need of developmental time in a rich educational environment. However, these CLD students are often misplaced in special education environments that create for them external educational problems and inappropriate conditions that hinder their otherwise normal cognitive and linguistic development.

According to Ortiz (1992), these externally caused learning problems in CLD students that are misdiagnosed most commonly as learning disabilities, language disorders, and mental retardation can be prevented by implementing effective prereferral strategies. Inappropriate referrals made primarily by teachers can be prevented, as Ortiz suggested, by modifying instruction and classroom management in the regular classroom, and by supporting the teachers' efforts to intervene as *teaching* problems (and not *learning* problems) arise when serving CLD students. Ideally, according to Ortiz, we could prevent not only inappropriate referrals but also these teaching problems by changing the role of the teacher within the regular classroom, community, and society at large. This change of roles will only happen by promoting a change in educators' attitudes regarding the conceptualization of how to educate CLD students appropriately. Educators need to assume responsibility for the teaching problem and stop identifying learning problems as internal to CLD students. One way of modifying instructional methods would be for the teacher to implement a bilingual developmental program that uses both the first and second languages of students, and that also stimulates their holistic development. That is, not only do cognitive and academic areas need to be stimulated, but emotional developmental areas, such as self-esteem; cultural, ethnic, and linguistic identity; and social values of the minority culture also need to be respected and nurtured. In addition, teachers need to promote the students' active participation in learning by using cooperative learning strategies, meaningful learning content, and the stimulation of higher-level critical thinking skills. Moreover, teachers need to be assertive about their abilities for implementing these instructional strategies. This assertiveness can be achieved by teachers who believe in the underlying multicultural education philosophy of these methods generated by a change of their attitudes toward learning problems in CLD students.

In relation to specific prereferral intervention practices with CLD students, Ortiz (1992) recommends clinical teaching as a problem-solving process that implements several alternatives for improving academic and behavior problems in the classroom. These alternative clinical teaching processes include the documentation of adaptations of instructional programs within the regular classroom, including teaching basic skills, reteaching skills using significantly different strategies, and refocusing instruction when problems continue. Ortiz also recommends consultation models, especially collegial rather than expert models, as teachers need to own the process of improving their teaching skills and methodologies in order to assume responsibility for appropriately educating CLD students. When experts act as consultants for generating solutions, learning problems of CLD students are conceptualized as existing within the students. In fact, solutions can be generated and implemented only if teachers accept the responsibility for teaching problems within their own classrooms.

According to Ortiz (1992), problem-solving teams (Chalfant & Van Dusen Pysch, 1981) can also be effective prereferral models for preventing the misdiagnosis of CLD students, if teachers are knowledgeable about appropriate placements options, such as special education, Title I programs, migrant education, bilingual education, and English-as-a-Second-Language programs. Advantages of problem-solving teams relate to the establishment of a collaborative learning community within schools by providing continuous training for improving educators' skills for solving teaching problems when educating CLD students. However, as Ortiz (1992) pointed out, prereferral strategies and models need to be adapted to the idiosyncratic needs of CLD students, which differ across schools and communities.

In sum, as pointed out in Chapter 3, a "magic" instrument, a panacea for validly and reliably assessing and diagnosing CLD students, does not and cannot exist. Similarly, the "magic" prereferral model cannot be applied for solving teaching and learning problems that may arise when serving CLD students. However, several state-of-the-art prereferral intervention strategies and models for appropriately serving CLD students were discussed in this section.

ASSESSMENT OBJECTIVES

After prereferral intervention strategies and models have been adapted and implemented in schools with specific needs, appropriate referrals of CLD students who are in genuine need of special education services can be made. However, even though referrals may be appropriate, it is still important to review assessment objectives in order to assess CLD students validly and reliably. The first major objective of assessment—screening—assures the presence of a gatekeeping process for a successful diagnostic process. Screening is a way to differentiate students who do not need follow-up from those who need further assessment and diagnosis. There are several kinds of screening measurements, such as standardized tests, developmental problem-solving tasks, interviews, and home language surveys, which are derived from different assessment approaches (i.e., psychometric, "missionary," behavioral, and "ethnic researcher") that have different underlying assessment principles and objectives. For instance, an objective of standardized tests, used in a traditional psychometric assessment approach, is to compare students' performance with norms. But standardized tests need to be used with caution with CLD students, as norms do not represent all the linguistic and cultural groups. Moreover, CLD students can be at-risk for being misidentified as being in need of further assessment just because they are in the process of learning English as a second language or because they have been socialized in a bicultural environment.

Once screening has been accomplished, the other three major assessment objectives—the identification and diagnosis of at-risk students, program development, and program evaluation—need to be implemented. However, due to the state of assessment practices used in the American school system, CLD students are at-risk for being misdiagnosed as having disabilities. Three categories of at-risk factors can be identified when diagnosing students:

1. Internal conditions present at birth due to genetic disorders that can be medically diagnosed at the neurological level, causing developmental disabilities
2. Internal conditions present at birth, called "sleeper effects" (e.g., premature birth or susceptibility for environmental agents), that put students at high risk for developing handicaps or disabilities
3. Extreme conditions present in the physical and sociocultural environment (e.g., lack of proper nutrition during a sensitive developmental period or a dysfunctional family) that can prevent internal potentials from developing fully due to a lack of opportunity

The third objective of assessment, program development, has the purpose of placing students and generating an individualized educational program (IEP). Information gathered in the assessment and diagnosis process is used in developing an IEP. This information is collected using a battery of assessment instruments in the areas of competence, performance, motivation and attitudes, the sociocultural environment, and family strengths and needs. Primarily qualitative assessment methods can be used, as they provide information that can be directly applied to the development of educational programs by classroom teachers without much further training.

In developing educational programs, both internal and external factors need to be assessed. Internal factors may include competence and potentials. Competence assessment refers to skills that the student has mastered as measured by traditional assessment approaches, including the psychometric, "missionary," and behavioral approaches. The measurement of potentials for learning is emphasized by the "ethnic researcher" approach, which includes qualitative assessment methods. As external factors are also important from the "ethnic researcher" and behavioral approaches, the description of the characteristics of the sociocultural environments in which the student is immersed (e.g., school, home, community, and neighborhood) is also included. Some of the instruments that can be used are naturalistic and structured observations, task analysis, environmental rating scales, and teachers and parents rating scales. Family strengths and needs have also a central part of external factors that include an awareness of current family functioning and the identification of linguistic and cultural differences with the mainstream school culture. Some of the instruments that can be used for this purpose are home visits, home language and cultural surveys, observations of students' behaviors at home, and interviews with parents and students.

The fourth objective of assessment, program evaluation, serves the purpose of reconsidering placement decisions and the impact of educational programs on student progress. Instruments that can be used for program evaluation are students' accomplishment of stated educational goals and product evaluations such as portfolio assessments. Usually standardized tests are used for program evaluation because they are norm referenced and can be used for comparing individual students to their peers.

In the following section, we will review three categories of alternative assessment procedures—portfolios, observations, and performance assessments—which can be used for different assessment objectives, as discussed above.

ALTERNATIVE ASSESSMENT METHODS

Portfolio Assessment

Portfolio assessment processes (Yawkey & Juan, 1993) are described by Jasmine (1992) as "a method of evaluating . . . a student based on a collection of the student's work" (p. 6).* Gonzalez and Yawkey (1994), Hakuta (1992), and Jasmine (1992) note that these processes show credibility in the assessment

---

*All Jasmine (1992) references taken with permission from TCM 145-*Portfolio assessment for your whole language classroom*, pp. 6, 9, 11, 16, and 47. Published by Teacher Created Materials, Inc.

of students. Yawkey, Gonzalez, and Juan (1994) assert that portfolio processes, when used appropriately by professionals, are more reliable than psychometric assessment, especially with CLD students. Portfolio assessment (especially with appropriate use) is described as credible and reliable because this process is both based in part on observation and rests ownership with students and teachers. Portfolio is part of authentic education and constructivist philosophy because it provides adaptive, two-way feedback between learner and environment (Yawkey, Gonzalez, & Juan, 1994), which Jasmine (1992) calls "real" learning. Relatedly, portfolio assessment processes may provide greater transfer of literacy and biliteracy understandings at microtransfer and macrotransfer levels (see a detailed description in Gonzalez & Yawkey, 1994; and Hakuta, 1992). In addition, portfolio assessment processes anchor classroom performance within contextual settings of the classroom using present and real groups of students rather than artificial, removed, and normed groups. Jasmine (1992) notes that the "portfolio approach has helped to give us what amounts to a whole new philosophy of evaluation and assessment" (p. 6).

Relatedly, according to a document entitled *Reading Framework for the 1992 National Assessment of Educational Progress* (1992, p. 24), portfolio assessment processes also:

1. Provide information on students' self-selected reading outside of school
2. Offer information about what is actually happening in classrooms during reading instruction
3. Permit an examination of students' daily reading responses
4. Begin to involve teachers directly in the assessment

In developing and using portfolio assessment, thought must be given to its constituent processes, including which assessment samples to collect, when to collect them, and how to evaluate them. The examples of these processes are taken from Title VII P.I.A.G.E.T. (Promoting Intellectual Adaptation Given Experiential Transforming) Programs, a national model for early childhood and family education.

In P.I.A.G.E.T. Programs, the collection process in portfolio assessment is done by listing. Staff is encouraged to list of all items that they wish to be included in each student's portfolio. The collectables are representative of the student's work and targeted for collection on a systematic basis. In addition, some P.I.A.G.E.T. Programs have the students make decisions about what they want in their portfolios. In other instances, Jasmine (1992, p. 11) recommends that the "teacher can also add ... to the portfolio ... papers [or products] that the student did not choose but that you feel are meaningful" (p. 11). Also, Jasmine (1992, p. 47) says that student papers should be included, such as writing samples, journal entries, reading responses and checklists, and problems and solutions in math, social studies, science, and so forth. Other collectable items are "anecdotal records, conference records, interest inventories, teacher-made tests (e.g., unit tests, open-ended tests), student evaluations of teacher, district test scores, standardized test scores" (Jasmine, 1992, p. 16). At the end of each marking period (or whatever time period is used), the students can decide which items to take home to share with their family.

The decision as to when to collect assessment samples varies across P.I.A.G.E.T. Programs, according to classroom cites. The important idea here, however, is to collect on a *systematic* basis. In some P.I.A.G.E.T. Programs, this means every marking period throughout the school year. Other workable time periods include four times per month across three months, for our migrant site programs, or other workable, manageable periods, depending on the classroom. Relatedly, Jasmine (1992) asks that each item in the collection be dated, to "make the eventual selection process easier and much more meaningful for evaluation purposes" (p. 9). Jasmine (1992) also suggests that each classroom have a "Portfolio Monitor"—"someone who takes on the responsibility of keeping the files in order" (p. 9). Here, organizing items within each portfolio by day or time period (or perhaps alphabetically) and taking turns as "Portfolio Monitor" are critical responsibilities. Moreover, in order to show validity, reliability, and credibility, portfolio assessment must decide how to evaluate with clarity and precision. Evaluation criteria can be identified and explained for each of the portfolio items (Yawkey, 1994).

Based on *Reading Framework* (1992) and Yawkey (1994), Yawkey, Gonzalez, and Juan (1994, p. 139) offer the following examples of evaluation criteria:*

1. Thoroughness of children's work samples.
2. Variety and type of products shown in the portfolio.
3. Children's generations of ideas and interpretations required by various . . . examples.
4. Types of understandings, skills, and attitudes . . . exemplified in the work samples.
5. Examples of . . . transfer between native and English language . . . levels.
6. Reliability of assessment of portfolio items with other related work samples not included in the portfolio.

As an alternative method of evaluation, portfolio assessment has great promise. In addition, as professionals realize its importance, coupled with continuing increases in the number of language minority students, this assessment method will become more significant in schooling processes.

*Provided by permission of Dr. Phillip Feldman, editor, *Reading Improvement.*

Observation

Observation assessment methods are as old as the field of American psychology and its application to human behavior. Here, observation refers to watching what students say and do and then writing down what had happened. The difference between usual, everyday observation and this form of observation is the way in which this observation is done. Observation as an assessment method is conducted systematically with written notes in some form. "Systematic" may mean observing the same actions or statements across different settings, such as inside the classroom and on the playground, or observing these actions or statements every other day for four times a month. The systematic procedures used are selected to fit the purposes and goals of the observer.

Observation can be made of student's behaviors. An example of an observed behavior is, "Samuel completed reading the chapter in his literature book!" Observation can be targeted for products completed such as "building castles from sand" or "mixing four substances to get the chemical compound." Observation assessment can be made of processes used in arriving at solutions to problems. Here, processes observed might be generalization, problem-solving, and analysis of the situation. Finally, observational assessment can also be made of the environment. For example, a description of the environment can be portrayed by the types of materials included within, their placement, and the functions they serve.

Data collection based on these types of observation can then be summarized in a number of ways. There can be a descriptive summary of the observation, where the exact set of events are written narratively:

1. Juan read five chapters in the history book and took a 100-item true-false test on the content of these chapters.
2. Zoraida tied her shoes today for the first time.

In addition, frequency measures can be used to summarize these observations:

1. Eight out of ten times Brian handed in his homework in mathematics across a three-week period.
2. Brian received a score of 80 percent for turning in eight of his mathematics homework papers during the three-week grading period.

Finally, duration, the length of time in which particular actions or events occurred, can also be used to summarize observations: "Maria played with her doll for thirty seconds across five consecutive time blocks!"

As teachers begin to use observation assessment methods seriously for CLD students in some systematic fashion, relevant criticisms of these methods must be addressed. For observation assessment methods to have credibility and reliability, teachers must guard against these criticisms and make every effort to account for them as part of their data collection. For example, one of the greatest criticisms of observation assessment methods is their subjectivity (Cohen & Spenciner, 1994; Gallagher & Kirk, 1989). A second major criticism is the potential of confounding influences during the observations (Cohen & Spenciner, 1994; Salkind & Ambron, 1987).

Relative to the criticism of subjectivity, critics point out that the use of observation assessment methods becomes "beauty in the eyes of the beholder." That is, the results of the assessment vary between teachers, even when they are evaluating the same children displaying the same behavior from one setting to another (Gallagher & Kirk, 1989). To minimize this variability of results between evaluations of teachers watching the same children and the same behaviors, several steps can be taken. First, the behaviors, products, processes, or environment to be observed must be definable and hence more objective. (Examples of defining behaviors, products, processes, and environmental aspects to be observed were provided in the above paragraphs.)

After defining the behaviors specifically, the next step is training. For example, within the minority-language P.I.A.G.E.T. Programs, teachers and paraprofessionals are trained in using observation assessment methods (Yawkey, 1993). Training consists of instruction, role-playing, and practice in actually observing, scoring, and rating the process or behavior, and then discussing the results of these procedures (Yawkey, 1993). The training procedure of observing, scoring, or rating and then discussing minimizes problems in qualitative assessment and produces the excellent credibility and high coefficients of reliability of observation assessment methodology.

A second procedure for minimizing the variability of results between raters in observation assessment methods is to understand the influence or impact of the observer on students. The teachers here understand that their presence in the classroom changes the behavior of the children they are observing. For example, the teacher may be new to the classroom setting. This newness has the potential of changing students behavior simply because of the novelty of the observer. Being unobtrusive in the classroom to minimize adult novelty is difficult. One suggested method used in P.I.A.G.E.T. Programs is qualitative assessment, which is conducted in a part of the room that is away from direct, mainline activity. Within preschool/ kindergarten classrooms, this would mean setting up an operational base away from large motor activities, such as children's pounding or cycling. Perhaps a quiet area in the classroom, where children are working at literacy or cultural centers, is more unobtrusive and thus more conducive to assessment. An additional suggestion for becoming more unobtrusive is using one-way mirrors in gallery-type or laboratory classrooms. Teachers have also used videotaping to be more unobtrusive.

Related to the attempt to become more unobtrusive in observation assessment methods is the teacher's attempt to reduce distractions. Events happen in classrooms as observations are being conducted that can distract from their accuracy. Simply following the guidelines of not attending to potential distractions and of not interacting with students as observation assessment is in progress can be used with success. In addition, as children see adults writing and taking notes, they often ask, "What are you doing?" In P.I.A.G.E.T. Programs training sessions, it is suggested that the observer simply tell the students what they are doing in an honest, straightforward manner. In the majority of situations, this answer is enough for the students, who return to their former activity. Taking into consideration the need for definitions and unobtrusiveness will definitely reduce major criticisms of biases perceived to be characteristic of observation assessment methods.

In summary, there are several common guidelines for observation as assessment methodology (for details, see Cohen & Spenciner, 1994; Salkind & Ambron, 1987).

1. Identify exactly what is to be observed. Be specific and know what you are watching as a part of the ongoing behavior stream in classroom settings.
2. Record the time, date, and duration of your observation.
3. Number your observations of the same children across days. Important here is a systematic context and an easy, readily available reminder that this is, for example, the third observation of Juan, Tom, Hector, and Zoraida.
4. Make notes of what you are observing in a descriptive, specific form that tells exactly what occurred. Also, jot down any unexpected events that happened during your observation. However, when taking notes of these occurrences, it is helpful to note that they were "unexpected."
5. Keep notes of your interpretations of what happened.

Within observation assessment methods, there are several forms of evaluation, as described in the following paragraphs: anecdotal records, rating scales, and checklists.

Anecdotal Records

Anecdotal records are a major type of an observation assessment method. As an observation measure, anecdotal records are defined as records of observed behaviors taken systematically of student's ongoing development and achievement. Like all observation measures, anecdotal records are ways of obtaining and documenting information about what students do and say.

Anecdotal records in the form of either mental or written notes are used heavily in teaching. In turn, these notes become: (1) part of permanent record files; (2) a basis for student or parent-teacher conferences; (3) a method for assigning grades to student performances; and (4) an ongoing record of growth and achievement. When used as an alternative method of assessment, anecdotal records must be written down on a systematic and ongoing basis to target student behaviors. Based on anecdotal records, teachers can observe easily by comparing student behaviors across time; teachers can also document any increases, decreases, or continuation of these behaviors.

In writing anecdotal records, a setting is identified by specifying the observation date, location (e.g., English language arts, social studies), grade of or age level of the child, and time and duration of the observation. This explanation of the situation provides a contextual social base line that helps the recorder to write better and more accurate anecdotes. In addition, situational contexts provide the reader (e.g., another teacher, parent, administrator, or social worker) and the target student with a more meaningful understanding of the behavior or behaviors that were recorded. Examples of contextual or situational identifiers include

1. Completing a homework assignment to write a descriptive summary of a Spanish novel.
2. Drawing the major parts of the human body in health and physical education class.

In writing anecdotal records, there are several considerations. First, we recommend that you identify a location or behavioral setting for your record. Generally speaking, the location should also include items such as the observation date, the student's grade or age, the total observation time, your name, and the child's name. Second, straightforward descriptions of the child's behavior are best to reduce subjectivity. Here, we recommend checking your written description for nonsubjective writing. Third, we recommend that you consider jotting down other students' reactions to the target child's behavior. Here, these responses include inappropriate and appropriate behaviors. The critical point is to include a *balance* of appropriate and inappropriate actions. Fourth, we recommend that all words and terms critical to the behaviors be defined in context of the narrative. For this reason, there are words that are misleading and should be avoided. Common examples include words such as happy and sad. Fifth, several observations of the same behaviors at different times, locations, and on different days should be made. After these five ideas are used to construct your anecdotal records, writing of the behaviors can begin. These ideas will insure greater reliability, authenticity, and use of anecdotal records for alternative evaluations.

Anecdotal records contribute much information for assessment. They, like other alternative assessment methods, can be used together to paint accurate evaluative episodes of ongoing student performances.

Rating Scales

Rating scales are a most interesting form of observation assessment because they are easy to develop, quick to use, and ideally suited to observational methodologies. Rating scales are measures of observed performance that typically show degrees of change, with each degree designated by a numeral. Cohen and Spenciner (1994) call this common type of rating scale the Likert, or numerical, scale, which is detailed in the following paragraphs. For excellent detailed descriptions of other types of rating scales (e.g., semantic differential, graphic and visual analog scale, descriptive inventory, and problem-solving rating scales, see Cohen & Spenciner, 1994, and Puckett & Black, 1994).

There are several easy guidelines to follow in constructing a Likert rating scale. First, identify a series of specific student performances that you feel are goals, objectives, or outcomes of other learning (Yawkey, 1992b). Like other types of observation assessment methods, these goals or outcomes that you generate can be focused on behaviors, products, and processes or a combination of these three descriptors.

In mathematics, examples of behavioral descriptors for CLD preschool children are:

1. Using ordinal location of objects from first to eighth in the native language
2. Recognizing squares and circles
3. Counting items from one to ten in English

In science, examples of process descriptors for culturally and linguistically diverse children in fifth grade include:

1. Identifying the phases of weather changes from sunny to rainy conditions
2. Experimenting with various objects and determining why some are and some are not attracted by magnets
3. Solving by trial and error crossword puzzles about dairy products

These goals or outcomes generated as behaviors, products, and processes can be made for language arts, music, social studies, art, chemistry, physics, and all other content subjects and areas of growth and development such as physical, socioemotional, and language.

After identifying these goals or outcomes, a second guideline in developing a Likert rating scale is listing the goals or outcomes from top to bottom along the left-hand side of a piece of paper. You may cluster these goals or outcomes by any category, such as science, Spanish language, and child's play world. Third, across the top of the paper, degrees of performance are identified in columns.

There are many examples of these Likert degrees of performance. Yawkey (1992a, 1992b) uses always, regularly, sometimes, and never; and master, mastered with assistance, and did not master. Other examples are never, often, and always; and never, sometimes, frequently. Other degrees of performance can also be used (e.g., for self–esteem, happy, neutral-no feeling, and sad).

Finally, each degree of performance can be quantified by assigning it a high to low numerical equivalency. For example, from Yawkey (1992c), numerical equivalences of four points are assigned to "regularly," three points to "often," two points to "sometimes," and one point to "never." Two examples follow of Likert rating scales from P.I.A.G.E.T. Programs (Yawkey, 1992b, 1992c). Figure 4.1 shows the Likert rating scale and part of the items to illustrate easily and simply how the items and scale are scored.

This rating scale can be used as a summative measure in language minority programs. Depending on the type of agency serving CLD students, the school districts, for example, could administer these rating scales as pretests in September and as posttests in June, with ten months between administrations. Because of the needs of their populations, migrant programs typically run on cycles that match the planting and harvesting season for crops. Migrant programs targeting fruit crops such as apples and peaches in

FIGURE 4.1   Likert Rating Scale for Young Children's Behaviors

	Regularly	Often	Sometimes	Never
1. The child runs				
2. The child jumps				
3. The child climbs				
4. The child plays with others				
5. The child hops				
6. The child uses blocks				
7. The child draws				
8. The child strings beads				
9. The child rides tricycles				
10. The child cuts paper				

From Yawkey, T. D. (1992b). *1987–1990 Three-year report of Title VII Academic Excellence Project P.I.A.G.E.T. Cycle I (Technical Report 295)*. University Park, The Pennsylvania State University, modified with permission.

the northeastern United States have a pretest to posttest cycle of twelve to fourteen weeks. Accordingly, Likert rating scales may be preadministered in mid-June and postadministered in the beginning of October. An essential point is that Likert rating scales are so versatile that their administration ranges from ten months to twelve weeks, pre- and postusage. That is why they can serve real authentic assessment needs. Relatedly, the reliability coefficients on rating scales are not necessarily low and unreliable because they use observation as a basis. For example, in an outside evaluation of P.I.A.G.E.T. Programs, Herbert (1994, p. 11) found that the rating scale yielded a very high pretest *alpha* coefficient of .96 and a posttest *alpha* of .95.

Figure 4.2 shows another Likert rating scale as used in developmental bilingual programs for young children. This instrument is the Daily Observation Card (Peters, Neisworth, & Yawkey, 1985), modified here to show utility as a rating scale used as a formative measure in developmental bilingual programs such as P.I.A.G.E.T. This rating scale is used primarily in activity or learning centers in which teachers observe children in small groups work-

FIGURE 4.2　Likert Rating Scale: Daily Observation Card

1. _____ Subject Content 2. _____ Observation Date 3. Uses: a. English (Check) b. Native Languages 　　　 c. Both	Process Descriptors				
	Exploring Characteristics of Items	Showing Make-Believe Play	Following through with Decisions	Working in Groups	
Student's Name	Observation Ratings				Interpretation
1.					
2.					
3.					
4.					
5.					
6.					
Process Observation Mastery Scale:	4. Mastery of Process Descriptors 3. Partial Mastery of Process Descriptors 2. Mastered with Teacher/Peer Assistance 1. Did Not Master				

ing to master behaviors, products, or processes. As teachers observe the children, they rate the degrees of performance for each descriptor. They also rate the children on their level of understandings. The numerals used range from four (showing mastery) to one (demonstrating no mastery). This formative measure is used regularly with the children. For example, in developmental bilingual programs, children can be observed monthly or every two weeks. The descriptors may or may not change given the results of the observations. This type of formative Likert rating scale is a very practical and useful tool for evaluating culturally and linguistically diverse children at work in various learning centers throughout the day.

Thus, the formative Likert rating scale can be used by the teacher for ongoing diagnosis, such as for grouping children:

1. By learning *strength* for more advanced work
2. By learning *need* toward observed mastery
3. For *practice* and *reinforcement*
4. For *exploring* materials and objects prior to their use in formal lessons

The same problems and criticisms of biased information, subjective observations, and so forth that are leveled at developing and using all observation measures are also leveled at Likert and other forms of rating scales (see Puckett & Black, 1994). You can use the following list to check the quality, credibility, and utility of the rating scales that you develop for observational assessment:

1. Did I define the terms I use specifically so they are not open to broad interpretations by others?
2. Did I use the rating scale in systematic fashion with the same students over several time periods?
3. Did I use observed facts in an unbiased manner in writing interpretations of students' learning and development?
4. Did I rate the same students in a number of subject and/or growth areas to get a better mosaic of the learning and development of the whole student?

Checklists

Checklists, another form of observation assessment, are excellent instruments to use with other alternative evaluations. This type of assessment, in various forms, was used in the very beginning of the American public school system. The major problem with these types of checklists defined by age is that not all children show same concepts at the same age. Age-based or for that matter norm-based checklists do great disservice to students—especially

CLD students and others who do not fit age and/or norm criteria (e.g., handicapped). A more developmentally appropriate definition of a checklist is an observation measure of the presence or absence of particular performance items. In the context of this definition, the use of the checklist based on developmental perspectives is enormous. Examples of particular performance items used to develop checklists include observed likes and dislikes, choices, products, processes, characteristics of objects (e.g., toys) in the environment, observed feelings, curricular concepts, and traits. With the wide range of possibilities for developing checklists, these forms of observation assessment tend to be current and change from year to year depending on the students and program (Puckett & Black, 1994).

In preparing a checklist, the performance items are identified and listed along the left-hand side of the paper. The procedures of identifying and listing performance items are exactly the same as those used for Likert rating scales. They can also be clustered or grouped in any way depending on the teacher's, student's, and/or program's need. Checklists also can be developed for all subject areas and developmental growth domains such as perceptual-motor, language, and intellect (thinking). Since checklists focus on the observed absence and presence of performance, just two columns are used in the checklist, unlike the Likert rating scale.

Accordingly, the teacher simply watches carefully and determines whether the performance is observed or not observed. If the performance is observed, the teacher marks a check (✓) in the appropriate column. No check is made if the performance is not observed. High to low numerical equivalents may be assigned, such as two points for an observed performance and one point for an unobserved performance.

Figure 4.3 (on p. 112) illustrates an observation checklist with observed performance items checked. Figure 4.4 (on p. 113), a subject concept checklist, shows where the children's names are to be written. Yet even though children's names will appear, comparing children on performance acquisition must be avoided when using this or other alternative assessment measures. Instead, use these instruments to document entering and exiting performances, such as prereferral performances in conjunction with other alternative assessments (Puckett & Black, 1994).

There are several common limitations in using the checklist as an observation measure. In addition to the usual criticism about the subjectivity of all qualitative instruments, a checklist shows only the presence or absence and not degrees of performance items. Its yes-or-no quality and the fact that it represents current performance (which changes readily) should be kept in mind as this assessment tool is used. When the student's performance is specifically defined, checklists have the greatest utility. Otherwise, performance items lack context if they are too broad.

FIGURE 4.3   Observation Checklist

Daily Observation

Directions: Use this checklist as children first arrive in the morning.
Check all that apply.

	Child 1	Child 2	Child 3
1. Name and age	*Y.G.* 3	*M.G.* 4	*G.B.* 3
2. Child's entrance into room			
a. Entered room willingly	✓		✓
b. Clung to parent		✓	
c. Entered room reluctantly			
d. Other (specify)			
3. Reaction to the environment			
a. Freely explored	✓		✓
b. Curious but hesitant to move out		✓	
c. Reluctant to explore			
4. Relationship to others			
a. Sought contact with other children	✓		✓
b. Sought contact with teacher			
c. Remained apart from the group		✓	
d. Rejected advances made by others			
e. Aggressive toward others			
5. Response to materials			
a. Chose materials freely (specify)	blocks		blocks
b. Needed help in selecting materials		✓	
c. Behaviors seemed to lack direction			

From *Asssessment of Young Children* by Libby G. Cohen and Loraine J. Spenciner. Copyright ©
by Longman Publishers. Reprinted with permission.

Performance Assessment

Observation and performance are both large categories used for grouping
individual alternative instruments. Both address current problems of student evaluation, such as how to meet standards of school reform, and both
have the potential to address the six national goals of America 2000 (Baker,
1992). Portfolio instrumentation was presented as an example of performance assessment separately, apart from its performance category, because
it is well known and very widely used (French, 1992). Moreover, performance assessments (like portfolios) show particular actions and behaviors in
completing products or processes for which there are established criteria or
standards of appropriateness (Cohen & Spenciner, 1994).

FIGURE 4.4 Checklist: Subject Area Observed Concepts Listing

	Time Periods											
	1st Four Weeks— Student's Name						2nd Four Weeks— Student's Name					
Subject Areas and Concepts 1. Check (√) if observed 2. Circle: English; native language 3. Date: _____	1.	2.	3.	4.	5.	6.	1.	2.	3.	4.	5.	6.
A. Language Arts 1. Identifying body parts 2. Showing emotions through puppets 3. Composing oral stories 4. Writing child's name in capital letters												
B. Mathematics 1. Seriating varying numbers 2. Sorting objects by number and color 3. Showing sets of objects (3, 8, 9) 4. Measuring tables and desks with a 12″ ruler												
C. Music 1. Making common rhythm instruments 2. Playing home-made rhythm instruments 3. Recognizing and naming brass instruments 4. Tapping out fast and slow beats												
D. Reading 1. Using visual recall and memory of words 2. Alphabetizing words 3. Role-playing and acting out action words 4. Completing a computer word game												
E. Science 1. Experimenting with oxygen 2. Examining rock particles under a microscope 3. Growing plants from seeds 4. Exploring properties of floating and sinking												
F. Social Studies 1. Identifying holidays in native and American cultures 2. Making maps of the school and family neighborhoods 3. Role-playing community helpers 4. Reading stories about different countries												

In addition to portfolios, other performance assessment instruments include:

1. Long- and short-range student projects (Yawkey, 1992a)
2. Stories, essays, and other narratives
3. Interviews
4. Students demonstrations of a particular item or aspect
5. Community, religious, and social actions that help solve associated issues (e.g., food for the homeless, abuser help-lines)
6. Student group examinations in which students assist in setting up and carrying out the project
7. Exhibitions (French, 1992)
8. All other means by which students create and share their work done in naturalistic environments and for real situations

For example, a sixth-grade class focuses on a historical and cultural event for a four- to six-week period. In this project, they gather idea from books, classroom resource people, encyclopedias, and so forth, and identify special interests and aspects that are part of the event. The students, working individually or in small groups of no more than three, develop an "A-B-C" event book. In a book on the U.S. Civil War, for example, they match the letter "A" with "Appomattox," "B" with the "Battle of Gettysburg," and so forth, writing an essay and sketching a picture about each event. They repeat the same process until all twenty-six letters are used.

In this example, the "A-B-C" event book, as a performance assessment product, showed several attributes of performance assessments. As a performance assessment task, this project had to be done over several weeks rather than, for example, in one hour of one day (Baker, 1992). In addition, the students individually or collectively helped to build part of the assessment criteria (e.g., neatness) for its evaluation. Further, the students needed to show high levels of developmental thought in doing and completing the performance assessment task. Logical, abstract thought and many intelligences (e.g., linguistic, mathematical) can be demonstrated through performance assessment (Gardner, 1991). Also, many curricular areas need to be used in doing and completing the performance assessment task (Baker, 1992). In the "A-B-C" event book, history, language arts, cultural studies, art, and reading were just a few of the areas used to solve the real problems arising from doing the book.

On a more global level, Baron (1992) sees the same ingredients of performance assessment at work in this "A-B-C" event book:

1. The first [principle shaping assessment work] is that we view our assessment tasks as "bits of curriculum"... to "put their [the students] learning together"—to integrate and synthesize separate bits of knowledge...!

2. The second is that we are designing our tasks to represent what our students should know rather than what they may currently be learning in their classes.
3. The third principle is that we view ourselves and our teachers as learners in the development processes. (p. 209)

Performance assessment in application thus becomes "bits of curriculum" (Burstall, 1990; cf. Baron, 1992), representations of what students should (rather than currently) know, and teachers and students together are viewed as developmental and lifelong learners. As student-sized curriculum bits, performance assessment actually becomes a return in public education to learning-by-doing rather than learning-by-pencil. This learning-by-doing historically has been characteristic of cultural arts, music, art, and crafts, while learning-by-pencil was characteristic of pedagogy and related social sciences (Walters, 1992). Here, performance assessment tasks are personally and individually rewarding because they intrinsically motivate the students. They are drawn to doing a performance assessment task individually or in groups because they have a stake in initiating, developing, implementing, and collaboratively evaluating it. Viewed from Gardner's (1991) perspective, performance assessment and developmental tasks go hand in hand, because the students' performances rise, individually and/or as a group, to their levels of developmental thinking. Similarly, performance assessment and its respective product-oriented tasks from Piagetian constructivist perspectives show creative and constructive thinking—that is, adaptive intelligences (Piaget, 1962, 1965, 1967). For instance, Piaget gives the following example of creative and constructive thinking showing adaptive intelligence. A child begins to make a sailboat and chooses soft pine wood as the medium. With a knife, the child whittles and whittles, becoming self-motivated and focused on this task.

Becoming self-absorbed with the goal, the child's criteria of academic excellence are:

1. Completing the sailboat
2. Fastening the sail
3. Seeing if it floats—just like a real sailboat!

This developmental movement in thought toward creative and constructional performance is adaptive intelligence, which is intermediary between work and play performance (Piaget, 1962, 1965, 1967).

Relatedly, the ideas of Cohen and Spenciner (1994) focus on several strategies or guidelines for functional, useful performance measures. First, students need to use their current knowledge not to find *one* solution set to the task but *sets* of solutions. When we take nonperformance assessment instruments such as multiple-choice or true-false tests, we answer the questions based on what we have learned after study.

By contrast, performance assessment tasks evaluate:

1. What we know now
2. What we can do now

Second, Cohen and Spenciner's guidelines imply prior discussion and common understandings about broad base lines as to what performance may or may not be acceptable. These common understandings must be broad yet understandable enough for students to attempt to identify sets of solutions and give them ample time to focus and test several of them. This suggests a repertoire of broad understandings yet specific behaviors that could be used as standards to assess the completed task. Some of these behaviors could be identified by the students. The previously mentioned A-B-C event book was, in part, assessed using a "neatness" criterion suggested by the students. The students understood this criterion, and in their predraft "dummy" copies of the book made every effort to use erasers and legible penmanship and to proof their narrative.

Third, the feedback loop shows how well the performance task meets the standards of excellence. Cohen and Spenciner's fourth guideline suggests demonstrating learning in multiple ways, for example, with different objects in different settings. Within P.I.A.G.E.T. Programs (Yawkey, 1992b), real experiences help students use numbers, language, and so forth with various objects (e.g., blocks, books, and puppets) and in various settings (e.g., classroom and home). Additionally, and in the P.I.A.G.E.T. Home Programs, culturally and linguistically diverse parents are shown through extensions how to work with the same concepts (i.e., primary colors) at home, in the mall, and at their relatives' homes (Yawkey, 1992b). These real, developmental encounters in using these sets of solutions in many ways give the added edge to meaningfulness and relevancy.

Baron (1992) identifies several extremely useful prerequisites to using performance assessment tasks effectively:

1. Significant and sustained professional development opportunities to provide time for teachers to: identify the "big ideas" in their discipline; understand and develop a new vision of learning and teaching; develop a repertoire of new instructional strategies, and develop a sense of efficacy.
2. Permissions from state and school administrators that "less is more" and that the job of teachers, in David Hawkins' words, is not "to cover the curriculum but to uncover the curriculum" (Duckworth, 1987).
3. New curriculum materials that support depth over breadth.
4. Appropriate stakes and incentives so that administrators, teachers, and students will be willing to take risks and try new approaches.

5. Time for teachers to develop new assessment tasks and refine them through the many iterations required.
6. Time for teachers to develop shared understandings of quality and to have conversations about how to provide their students with rich opportunities to foster it.
7. Time for teachers to score students' work and develop common standards.
8. Other high stakes tests may also need to change. We frequently hear from teachers: "We think this is the right way to teach and assess but we are too busy preparing our students to take the College Board Achievement Tests."
9. Some restructuring may be required to provide opportunities for students and teachers to achieve the higher standards we value: e.g., different configurations of class time will be required for more sustained student projects and conversations. Finally, common planning time will be necessary for teachers to work with other teachers and/or other content experts to understand what quality is and how to best achieve it. (p. 228)

In the beginning of this section on performance assessment, we listed examples of performance assessment tasks, such as projects, written narratives, and action groups to solve meaningful problems. Inherent in using performance assessment tasks are several criticisms. The main criticism is the large amount of time inside and outside the classroom required by the teacher and the students to plan, implement, and carry out these tasks (Hamp-Lyons, 1992, pp. 317–357). Time allocated to planning and implementing performance assessment tasks is necessary to insure validity and reliability checks for performance products (Damico, 1992; Hamp-Lyons, 1992). The usual criticisms of bias and subjectivity leveled at observation and portfolio methods are also leveled at all forms of performance assessments. This criticism can be reduced substantially by following rigorously Cohen and Spenciner's (1994) four guidelines for performance assessment tasks noted earlier.

In summary, alternative assessment methods provide viable windows for viewing the student's behaviors, products, processes, and environment in social context. Alternative assessment measures include portfolios and the observation tools of anecdotal records, rating scales, and checklists. Some helpful performance assessment methods used as alternatives to standardized and achievement testing are interviews, projects, demonstrations, and exhibitions. Used properly, alternative assessment methods can offer significant advantages over other evaluation methods when working with culturally and linguistically diverse students.

REFERENCES

Baker, E. L. (1992). Issues in policy, assessment, and equity. In *Proceedings of the Second National Research Symposium on Limited English Proficient Student Issues: Focus on Evaluation and Measurement* (Vol. 2, pp. 1–31). Washington, DC: U.S. Department of Education, Office of Bilingual Education and Minority Languages Affairs.

Ball, F. W., & Harry, B. (1993). Multicultural education and special education: Parallels, divergences, and intersections. *The Educational Forum, 57,* 430–437.

Baron, J. B. (1992). SEA usage of alternative assessments: The Connecticut experience. In *Proceedings of the Second National Research Symposium on Limited English Proficient Student Issues: Focus on Evaluation and Measurement* (Vol. 2, pp. 187–233). Washington, DC: U.S. Department of Education, Office of Bilingual Education and Minority Languages Affairs.

Burstall, C. (1990, June). *Update on a new national assessment in Great Britain.* Paper presented at the Large-Scale Assessment Conference sponsored by the Education Commission of the States and the Colorado State Department of Education, Boulder.

Chalfant, J. C., & Van Dusen Pysch, M. (1989, November). Teacher assistance teams: A model for within-building problem solving. *Counterpoint,* pp. 16–21.

Cohen, L. G., & Spenciner, L. J. (1994). *Assessment of young children.* New York: Longman.

Cummins, J. (1984). *Bilingualism and special education: Issues in assessment and pedagogy.* Clevedon, Avon, England: Multilingual Matters.

Damico, J. S. (1992). Performance assessment of language minority students. In *Proceedings of the Second National Research Symposium on Limited English Proficient Student Issues: Focus on Evaluation and Measurement* (Vol. 1, pp. 137–171). Washington, DC: U.S. Department of Education, Office of Bilingual Education and Minority Languages Affairs.

Diaz, M. E., & Moon, C. J. (1992). What do we want students to know?...and other important questions. *Educational Leadership, 49*(8), 38–41.

Duckworth, E. (1987). *The having of wonderful ideas and other essays on teaching and learning.* New York: Teachers College Press.

French, R. L. (1992). Portfolio assessment and LEP students. In *Proceedings of the Second National Research Symposium on Limited English Proficient Student Issues: Focus on Evaluation and Measurement* (Vol. 1, pp. 249–272). Washington, DC: U.S. Department of Education, Office of Bilingual Education and Minority Languages Affairs.

Gallagher, J. J., & Kirk, S. A. (1989). *Educating exceptional children.* Boston: Houghton Mifflin.

Gardner, H. (1991). *The unschooled mind.* New York: Basic.

Gonzalez, V. (1991). *A model of cognitive, cultural, and linguistic variables affecting bilingual Spanish/English children's development of concepts and language.* Doctoral dissertation, The University of Texas at Austin. (ERIC Document Reproduction Service No. ED 345 562).

Gonzalez, V. (1994a). A model of cognitive, cultural, and linguistic variables affecting bilingual Spanish/English children's development of concepts and language. *Hispanic Journal of Behavioral Sciences, 16*(4), 396–421.

Gonzalez, V. (1994b). Taking the risk to use critical thinking for stimulating in-service teachers' cognitive growth in multicultural education. In V. Gonzalez (Chair), *Restructuring schools from within: Promoting change in educators' cognition about multiculturalism.* Symposium conducted at the annual meeting of the American Educational Research Association, New Orleans.

Gonzalez, V., & Yawkey, T. D. (1993). The assessment of culturally and linguistically different students: Celebrating change. *Educational Horizons, 72*(1), 41–49.

Gonzalez, V., & Yawkey, T. D. (Winter 1994). Influence of cognitive, linguistic, and sociocultural factors on literacy and biliteracy in young bilinguals. *Education, 30*(10), 230–239.

Hakuta, K. (1992). *Transfer of basic reading skills across two languages in bilinguals.* Discussant and Chair at Symposium Presented at the American Educational Research Association (AERA) annual meeting, San Francisco.

Hamp-Lyons, L. (1992). Holistic writing assessment of LEP students. In *Proceedings of the Second National Research Symposium on Limited English Proficient Student Issues: Focus on Evaluation and Measurement* (Vol. 2, pp. 317–357). Washington, DC: U.S. Department of Education, Office of Bilingual Education and Minority Languages Affairs.

Herbert, M. (1994). *Title VII Academic Excellence Program Project P.I.A.G.E.T.: Summary evaluation report 1990–1993.* Pittsburgh: CHEC Point Systems.

Holtzman, W. H., Jr., & Wilkinson, C. Y. (1991). Assessment of cognitive ability. In E. V. Hamayan & J. S. Damico (Eds.), *Limiting bias in the assessment of bilingual students* (pp. 248–280). Austin, TX: Pro-Ed.

Jasmine, J. (1992). *Portfolio assessment for your whole language classroom.* Huntington Beach, CA: Teacher Created Materials.

Lloyd, J. W., Kauffman, J. M., Landrum, T. J., & Roe, D. L. (1991). Why do teachers refer pupils for special education?: An analysis of referral records. *Exceptionality, 2*, 115–126.

Ortiz, A. A. (1992). Assessing appropriate and inappropriate referral systems for LEP special education students. In *Proceedings of the Second National Research Symposium on Limited English Proficient Student Issues: Focus on Evaluation and Measurement* (Vol. 1, pp. 315–342). Washington, DC: U.S. Department of Education, Office of Bilingual Education and Minority Languages Affairs.

Ortiz, A. A., García, S. B., Wheeler, D., & Maldonado-Colón, E. (1986). *Characteristics of limited English proficient students served in programs for the speech- and language-handicapped: Implications for policy, practice, and research.* Austin: The University of Texas, Handicapped Minority Research Institute on Language Proficiency.

Peters, D. L., Neisworth, J. T., & Yawkey, T. D. (1985). *Early childhood education: From theory to practice.* Monterey, CA: Brooks/Cole.

Piaget, J. (1962). *Play, dreams, and imitation in childhood.* New York: Norton.

Piaget, J. (1965). *Mental imagery in the child: A study of the development of imaginal representation.* New York: Oxford University Press.

Piaget, J. (1967). Piaget's theory. In P. H. Mussen (Ed.), *Carmichael's manual of child psychology* (Vol. 1, pp. 703–732). New York: John Wiley & Sons.

Puckett, M. B., & Black, J. K. (1994). *Authentic assessment of the young child: Celebrating development and learning.* New York: Macmillan.

Salkind, N. J., & Ambron, S. R. (1987). *Child development.* New York: Holt, Rinehart and Winston.

U.S. Department of Education. *Reading framework for the 1992 national assessment of educational progress.* (1992). Washington, DC: U.S. Government Printing Office, Superintendent of Documents.

Walters, J. (1992). Application of multiple intelligence research in alternative assessment. In *Proceedings of the Second National Research Symposium on Limited English Proficient Student Issues: Focus on Evaluation and Measurement* (Vol. 1, pp. 1–18). Washington, DC: U.S. Department of Education, Office of Bilingual Education and Minority Languages Affairs.

Wilkinson, C., & Ortiz, A. (1986). Reevaluation of learning disabled Hispanic students: Changes over three years. *Bilingual Special Education Newsletter, 5*(1), 3–6.

Willig, A., & Ortiz, A. (1991). The nonbiased individualized educational program: Linking assessment to instruction. In E. V. Hamayan & J. S. Damico (Eds.), *Limiting bias in assessment of bilingual students* (pp. 282–302). Austin, TX: Pro-Ed.

Yawkey, T. D. (1992a). *Evaluation report on the Grand Rapids Family English Literacy Program (FELP): 1991–1992.* Unpublished manuscript. The Pennsylvania State University, University Park.

Yawkey, T. D. (1992b). *1987–1990 Three-year report of Title VII Academic Excellence Project P.I.A.G.E.T. Cycle I* (Technical Report 295). University Park: The Pennsylvania State University.

Yawkey, T. D. (1992c). *Final evaluative report on the Grand Rapids Family English Literacy Program (FELP): 1988–1991.* Unpublished manuscript. The Pennsylvania State University, University Park.

Yawkey, T. D. (1993). *P.I.A.G.E.T. Observation and Training.* Unpublished guidelines for staff development. The Pennsylvania State University, University Park.

Yawkey, T. D. (1994). *Final report on the Grand Rapids Family English Literacy Program (FELP): 1991–1994.* Unpublished manuscript. The Pennsylvania State University, University Park.

Yawkey, T. D., Gonzalez, V., & Juan, Y. (1994). Literacy and biliteracy strategies and approaches for young culturally and linguistically diverse children: Academic Excellence P.I.A.G.E.T. comes alive. *Journal of Reading Improvement, 31*(3), 130–141.

Yawkey, T. D., & Juan, Y. (1993). Linking assessment and instruction with language minority students: Extending the match. *NABE News, 17*(3), 9, 18, 34.

5

SEPARATING MILD DISABILITIES FROM CULTURAL AND LINGUISTIC DIFFERENCES: THE QUALITATIVE USE OF ENGLISH AND SPANISH TASKS (QUEST)

This chapter relates to this book's vision because the recommended alternative assessment method, the Qualitative Use of English and Spanish Tasks, or QUEST (Gonzalez, 1991, 1994, 1995), exemplifies the application of the "ethnic educator" constructivistic, developmental model to an educational problem (i.e., the identification of gifted bilingual Hispanic children). Thus, in this chapter, we will continue with the presentation of recommended alternative assessment procedures, initiated in Chapter 4, by explaining the implementation of QUEST for shedding some light on current educational problems. The first section includes a discussion of the robust psycholinguistic model on which QUEST was developed by Gonzalez (1991, 1994, 1995). The second section includes a brief description of the objectives, tasks administration and scoring procedures, and stimuli of QUEST. For the purpose of illustrating the implementation of QUEST, one case study of a bilingual Hispanic kindergarten girl, identified as gifted, has been selected. Other qualitative assessment methods included in this case study are a home language survey, and parents' and teachers' surveys of the child's cognitive and linguistic abilities.

THE QUALITATIVE USE OF ENGLISH
AND SPANISH TASKS (QUEST)

Model

This recommended assessment method is based on a new model (see Gonzalez, 1991, 1994, 1995) that explains the influence of linguistic and cultural factors on conceptual and language development in bilingual children. This model states that concepts are represented in three ways: (1) nonverbally, by abstract categories (i.e., basic semantic categories—daily life labels for objects—and nonbasic semantic categories—labels for categories and subcategories of objects); (2) symbolically, by meanings of sociocultural conventions (i.e., animate object referents as animals and inanimate object referents as food, natural and arbitrary linguistic gender, respectively); and (3) linguistically, by structures and markers (i.e., familiar and unfamiliar words, and similar and different linguistic structures between first and second languages).

According to this model, the cognitive process of mapping verbal onto nonverbal meanings involves the categorization and transformation of concepts that can be universal or culturally and linguistically bound. Then, one way of showing the interaction between cognitive, cultural, and linguistic factors is by assessing children's verbal and nonverbal classifications of objects representing nonverbal concepts, symbolic sociocultural meanings, and linguistic gender markers. Gender was selected as the first linguistic structure to study because of major differences between English and Spanish in the three ways of representing concepts (nonverbal, symbolic, and verbal) for animate and inanimate objects. Gonzalez (1991, 1994, 1995) found that bilingual children constructed: (1) one universal representational system common to Spanish and English for knowledge of nonverbal, symbolic, and verbal conceptual categories; and (2) a second representational system for symbolic and verbal conceptual categories unique to a specific language and culture. Gonzalez concluded that conceptual development in bilingual children is represented through abstract (nonverbal) and semantic (verbal) categories. Moreover, this new model that integrates cognitive, cultural, and linguistic factors has direct practical implications. The tasks created for developing the model have been used as an alternative qualitative assessment method for identifying successfully gifted bilingual Hispanic kindergartens in a large school district in the southwestern region of the United States (see Gonzalez, Bauerle, & Felix-Holt, 1994, 1995).

Gonzalez (1991, 1994, 1995) created five verbal (labeling, defining, and verbal justification for sorting) and nonverbal (sorting and category clue) classification tasks. Children were given manipulative objects representing animate (animals) and inanimate (food) items, corresponding to fourteen experimental stimuli groupings reflecting cognitive, cultural, and linguistic factors. Two parallel sets of stimuli, both representing animals and food, were designed to avoid the transference of learning when administering the tasks in both English and Spanish in a counterbalanced order. The classification tasks included in QUEST are based on developmental theories that focus on cognitive and linguistic processes that bilingual children use for verbal and nonverbal concept formation. Classification tasks tap verbal and nonverbal concept formation processes and represent the interface between the model proposed and two theoretical approaches, the traditional Piagetian theory (e.g., Piaget, 1965, 1967; Sinclair-de-Zwart, 1969) and the constraint approach (e.g., Markman & Hutchinson, 1984; Waxman, 1990). These two theoretical approaches were included because previous research has yielded different results in the level of semantic categories formed by children depending on the type of task used. Then, verbal and nonverbal classification tasks were used to compare how linguistic and cultural factors influence concept formation in Piagetian and constraint approach studies. A description of the implementation of QUEST using a case study with some genuine examples of responses and its categorization and scoring is included in this chapter.

Objectives of QUEST

This qualitative assessment method has four objectives: (1) to describe how bilingual children think nonverbally and construct concepts with language; (2) to identify the developmental stages at which bilingual children are functioning and have the potential to achieve with the scaffolding role of the evaluator; (3) to provide information for the differential diagnosis of second-language learning from giftedness and disabilities (e.g., mental retardation, learning disabilities); and (4) to link assessment with instruction by involving educators in the assessment process.

Moreover, QUEST needs to be used as part of a battery of standardized and other qualitative measurements because assessment is a sample of behavior that needs to consider that different informants have observed the child repeatedly in real-life contexts. Thus, the participation of teachers and parents is central for an accurate diagnostic process, as their feedback and information comes from "experts who have observed the child repeatedly in real-life contexts." QUEST can be used by teachers, school psychologists, educational diagnosticians, and counselors, resulting in the direct application of the qualitative information gathered in the diagnostic process to educational practices. Thus, the involvement of educators in the assessment process results in linking assessment with instruction.

QUEST Instructions for Administration and Scoring

Gonzalez (1991, 1994, 1995) created five classification tasks, three verbal (labeling, defining, and verbal justification for sorting) and two nonverbal (sorting and category clue). These five tasks are administered in the same

sequence in Spanish and English. Below we will explain the operational definitions of each task, specifically referring to the construct level measured in
each (see Table 5.1, in which the constructs and levels for each task are
listed).

The labeling task is operationally defined as measuring language development at two levels: (1) the object level, which reflects word knowledge;
and (2) the gender level, which indicates knowledge of the linguistic structures and markers for gender assignment. Thus, labeling is a verbal task at
the production level. The child was given one item at a time and asked,
"What do you call this?" The defining task is operationally defined as measuring verbal conceptual development, and thus it is a verbal task at the production and comprehension levels. That is, answers given by the child for
the defining task give information to assess the ability to produce and to
understand basic (i.e., nouns used for naming objects in daily life) and nonbasic (i.e., nouns used for naming the categories and subcategories of
objects) definitions of objects. Immediately after the child had labeled the
item, the examiner asked, "What is a _____?"; "What is a _____ like?";
"Tell me something about a _____"; and "What does it look like?" After,
to tap the comprehension level, the child was given a definition that pointed

TABLE 5.1   Constructs and Levels for Each Task

Task	Construct/Level
Labeling task	Language development Verbal task Production level
Defining task	Verbal conceptual development Verbal task Production and comprehension levels
Sorting task	Nonverbal conceptual development Nonverbal task Production level
Verbal justification for sorting task	Verbal conceptual development Verbal task Production level
Category clue task	Nonverbal and verbal potential for conceptual learning Nonverbal and verbal task Comprehension level

to verbal and nonverbal clues for class-inclusion categories of nonbasic objects (i.e., superordinate, intermediate, and subcategories). This definition was repeated three times, and each time the child was asked to define one different kind of item from the fourteen stimuli presented in each set. The ability measured by the sorting task is operationally defined as nonverbal conceptual development at the production level. In this latter task, the child is asked to sort manipulative objects into two groups that reflect feminine and male linguistic genders for animals and food in the Spanish administration and for animals in the English administration. For food items in the English administration, the child is asked to form two groups. The reason for these different instructions is because linguistic gender exists for both animate and inanimate referents in the Spanish language and exists only sometimes for animate referents in the English language. Thus, the linguistic structures of both languages reflect cultural and linguistic differences in the underlying symbolic and abstract representations. Then, the child is asked to explain verbally the underlying criteria for the groupings in the verbal justification for sorting task, which is operationally defined as measuring verbal conceptual development at the production level.

Finally, the ability measured by the category clue task is operationally defined as nonverbal and verbal potential for conceptual learning at a comprehension level. In this last task, the child is given an example of linguistic gender sorting and asked to follow the categorization explained. The examiner shows the child three basic and three nonbasic level instances of each superordinate category (animals and food), at a verbal and nonverbal level, as clues. Two pictures of identical dolls are selected, each doll identified with one linguistic gender assignment (feminine or masculine) in reference to the Spanish language for the food items, and in reference to the Spanish and English languages for the animal items. Then, the child is prompted to finish classifying the items by following the linguistic gender assignment criterion explained by the examiner. After, the child is asked some counterexample questions for changing the order she imposed on the objects and for changing the gender of the labels. In both verbal justification of sorting and category clue tasks, the child is asked to explain the criteria for her nonverbal classification of the stimuli as gender or general groups, and also to answer questions and metalinguistic counterexamples that tried to change the order imposed by the child on the items and the gender of the labels.

The final scoring system is divided into five areas of point assignments, based on which children are diagnosed on developmental levels of the formation of verbal (defining, and verbal justification for sorting tasks), nonverbal (sorting and category clue tasks), and language development (labeling task) areas according to general and gender-based levels. Thus, the child's responses to the five tasks that are administered once per language are scored twice, based on these five general and gender-based areas of point assignments. General areas include any valid criteria that the child uses for classification (e.g., color, functions, subcategories); and gender-based areas include classification criteria referring to physical gender for animates, linguistic gender assignment for inanimates, or functional use for animates and inanimates.

Moreover, for the verbal and nonverbal general and gender-based areas of points assignments, the child's responses are categorized into five developmental stages based partially in Piaget's (1965) theory: (1) no classification (1 point for affective responses, juxtaposed groupings, and graphic collections); (2) preconceptual: perceptual (2 points for extralinguistic features—color, size, and parts of the items—at the basic level); (3) pre-conceptual/functional (3 points for functional characteristics or thematic relations at the basic level); (4) concrete (4 points for organized hierarchical categories linking extralinguistic and intralinguistic features at the basic and nonbasic levels); and (5) metalinguistic (5 points for intralinguistic abstract clues and social conventions of symbolic meanings). The language development area is categorized into three levels—(1) low (0–2 points); (2) moderate (3–5 points); and (3) high (6–8 points)—according to the number of labels produced by the child.

Stimuli of QUEST

Concrete manipulative objects represented by toys are used as stimuli that are divided in two groups of animate object referents (animals) and inanimate object referents (food). Animal stimuli are scale plastic toys, and food stimuli are real-size plastic toys, both portraying realistically animals and food in full color. Two sets of each animate and inanimate object referents are used to avoid transfer of learning from administrations in English and Spanish. Stimuli correspond to fourteen stimuli groupings that represent cognitive, cultural, and linguistic factors included in the model. Linguistic variables include familiar or unfamiliar words and translation or no translation conditions. Cognitive variables include basic (i.e., daily life words for objects) and nonbasic labels (i.e., hierarchical terms including superordinate, intermediate, and subordinate categories). Cultural variables include inanimate (food) and animate (animals) objects. Different objects corresponding to these fourteen stimuli groupings can be selected as representative of any first and second language and culture, which means that QUEST can be adapted for use with any ethnic, cultural, or linguistic group.

Each set of stimuli includes only eight stimuli selected at random, so that time for administration could be reduced and the information gathered could still be representative of the child's performance, resulting in a more efficient assessment method. More than one object of each kind is given to the child in order to offer the opportunity to classify objects of the same basic level together (e.g., to sort two bears together or six sheep together). The number of objects required varies from six to one of each kind. Moreover, objects provided in each set can be categorized at the basic, superordinate (classes of objects as animals, mammals, or reptiles), and subordinate levels (objects that differ in color, as sheep of different colors, or in kind, as breeds of dogs). In addition, two full-color pictures of identical dolls are used for the category clue task. QUEST uses feminine dolls that are presented in two letter-size pieces of cardboard with the names *Pili* and *Mili* written at the bottom of the boards.

CASE STUDY

The following real-life case study of a bilingual Hispanic kindergarten girl is included as an illustration of how to implement QUEST. Information was collected for this case study as part of an applied research project conducted in a large metropolitan school district in the southwestern United States (other case studies that illustrate the assessment process are included in Gonzalez et al., 1994, 1995).

The Implementation of QUEST: Applied Problem

Presently, there is an applied need for developing qualitative assessment methods to make decisions related to placement of bilingual children in regular or special education classrooms (Oller & Perkins, 1978; Zirkel, 1976). This need for qualitative assessment methods is also present when the purpose is to identify gifted bilingual Hispanic children. The current reality is that minority children are underrepresented in the gifted classes of major school districts across the United States. This underrepresentation is due to the use of standardized instruments that do not take into consideration cultural and linguistic factors affecting cognitive development in bilingual children.

At the request of the school district, which had a large percentage of Hispanic children (close to 48% of the school population), QUEST was adopted experimentally as an individualized procedure for selecting and placing bilingual Hispanic kindergartners in gifted classrooms. These students were referred for further individualized testing based on four measurements: (1) a qualitative group screening procedure using observations of spatial, linguistic, and mathematical/logical abilities based on Gardner's theories of multiple intelligences developed by Maker (1991); (2) a home language survey (HLS) developed by Gonzalez (1991, 1994, 1995) for measuring language use reported by parents; (3) teachers' and parents' ratings of students' creative behaviors, gathered using a locally designed open-ended survey; and

(4) students' samples of classwork selected by classroom teachers. Referred children were tested individually using QUEST in both Spanish and English by two different bilingual evaluators and a standardized test for nonverbal intelligence, Raven Coloured Progressive Matrices (Raven, 1976). Dual language assessment is important because verbal performance in the first language will be higher than in the second language. Results of this prereferral information and individual testing were examined by an interdisciplinary placement committee formed by teachers, administrators, parents, school psychologists, graduate students, and university faculty.

Bilingual Family Home Language Survey

The background information was obtained using HLS (Gonzalez, 1991, 1994, 1995), which consists of open-ended, closed, and multiple-choice questions. Four areas are measured by HLS: (1) the language used at home by parents, siblings, and extended family members; (2) parents' self-ratings of their language proficiency in both Spanish and English; (3) parents' ratings of the child's Spanish and English proficiency; and (4) some information on the educational level of parents, and number and age of siblings. Information released by parents on this survey for the case study is included below.

Patricia (a pseudonym) is a bilingual English/Spanish child who was six years and two months old at the time of the assessment. She was assessed during the middle of the academic year, while she was in a regular kindergarten class with a monolingual English teacher in an elementary school in a low socioeconomic Hispanic neighborhood. Patricia is the oldest of four siblings, who were five years, three years, and seventeen months old by the time of the assessment. Patricia's mother is originally from a border Mexican town, but she had been living in the United States for twenty-two years by the time of the assessment. Patricia's father is originally from the same United States town in which the family was residing at the time of the assessment. Her parents reported that they both had a complete high school education, and that the mother is a housewife and the father is a construction worker. In addition, they reported that both English and Spanish were used at home, but that Patricia, her parents, and siblings used English more frequently to speak with family members and friends. However, Patricia's parents reported that the child's grandparents preferred to speak in Spanish with her, and that the child responded to her grandparents by using code-switching (i.e., used Spanish for one full sentence, followed by a full sentence in English) and code mixing (i.e., used both Spanish and English in the same sentence). Patricia's mother and father self-rated their Spanish and English proficiency as above average. They rated Patricia's Spanish proficiency as adequate for her age and her English proficiency as above average for her age.

Parents' and Teacher's Surveys

Patricia's parents and her teacher were asked to respond to an open-ended survey about her talents and abilities that were relevant for identifying children for gifted classrooms. This survey was constructed in a collaborative effort with the coordinator of the gifted education program, with professors and graduate students serving as consultants. Her parents reported that Patricia was very eager to learn, as she enjoyed reading nursery rhymes and being read to, asked how to spell words, and had watched educational programs such as "Sesame Street" since she was a baby. They felt that she had always being ahead of other children her age, and that her teacher and parents had had a positive impact in her life as role models who stimulated her interests. When her parents were asked about her special talents and abilities, they included singing, drawing very detailed pictures, and being very fast at learning new concepts such as telling the time. When they were asked about her language abilities, they considered Patricia ahead of others for her age. They reported that she had a vast repertoire of words, that she liked to create and illustrate stories, and that she liked to dance and make up songs with words that rhyme. The parents said that Patricia liked to do puzzles and to attend to details in shapes, colors, and sizes in order to match the puzzle pieces. They described her as a child who liked to share her toys but got angry when people took her belongings without asking. When playing with others, Patricia liked to be in command, but she also enjoyed working alone, as she had an imaginary friend called "Cindy" to whom she talked when playing. She liked to ask questions of her parents, because she was very curious to get to know her environment. Patricia was also very collaborative at home, as she helped with chores around the house and took care of her siblings. In general, her parents described her as a caring, sensitive, persistent, friendly, observant, talkative, energetic, independent, and creative child who was developmentally advanced for her age.

Patricia's kindergarten teacher was an experienced, monolingual Anglo educator who taught a regular class. The teacher described her as a serious, cooperative, hard-working child, who was always pointing out similarities among objects and activities. When Patricia's teacher was asked to point out the child's special talents and abilities, she described her as a child who drew with a great deal of detail and creativity, and who liked to write many words and complete sentences in her journal. Patricia was described by her teacher as a verbal child who liked to ask questions, who preferred to interact in small groups rather than in large ones, and who was willing to help adults and children in need of her assistance once she was done with her work. Patricia was also described as a cautious and focused problem-solver who liked to observe details carefully before she started. The teacher reported that she did her homework carefully and methodically, taking great pride in her work because she was an independent worker who found answers on her own. In general, Patricia's teacher described her as a caring, sensitive, persistent, friendly, observant, thoughtful, independent, cautious, and cooperative child who was far ahead of others in her class in written language.

QUEST in English

QUEST was used to diagnose Patricia's ability to label, define, sort, and justify her reasons for sorting animals and food into general and gender-based categories. She was assessed in English by a bilingual English/Spanish graduate student in educational psychology. The evaluator observed that Patricia seemed to be enthusiastic in her own quiet way about the activities. This, in addition to her cooperative spirit, made it easy for the examiner to establish a good rapport with her. The girl seemed to be quite verbal when given the opportunity to express herself.

Throughout the assessment procedure, Patricia seemed to display abstract reasoning. She examined the small plastic animals, classified them all, and then explained their functions while giving explanations or proofs. For instance, when she was presented with two brown sheep, two black sheep, and two white sheep, she at first said that she did not know what they were called, but then she quickly explained that she knew "one of them" (one pair, the white sheep). Then, she continued to explain, while holding the white sheep, that "it [the white sheep] was a sheep or lamb." After additional probes of the evaluator, the child explained that "it is soft, it likes to eat grass, and that they [she now began pointing at all of them regardless of their colors] look like bears, because they have furs like bears." For the lion, she defined them as "animals, but that it [the lion] could also be a tiger because it looks a little like a tiger, but it does not have the stripes." For the armadillo, although she did not know what it was, she guessed that it was a dinosaur. Then, when she was told that it was not a dinosaur, she said that it was "a wild animal because it looks real mean." Then, with additional probes, Patricia explained that "it [the armadillo] looks like a dinosaur because of its long tail." Thus, she demonstrated her ability to state her definitions based on her initial observations, and also her ability to make revisions. She also appropriately categorized every animal and then explained each animal's functions. When additional probes were given to her, she always compared animals using perceptual features.

Patricia further demonstrated her abstract reasoning by supporting her statements with evidence. When she compared animals, she illustrated her explanation by touching the perceptual feature to which she was referring to. Then, she explained functions that were not observable with these toy animals, followed by her explanations of how she knew about those functions. For instance, in reference to the horses, she explained, "They smell bad because I live somewhere and across the street there is a man and a lady and they have a horse and it always smells bad because it stinks." She gave examples from television to show how she knew rhinoceros like mud and dogs like to chase cats. Patricia demonstrated to perform at the metalinguistic level when she explained how a dog could be referred to as a "doggie," a pet, "Because it does not destroy nothing," and an animal. Likewise, she explained how a gorilla could be called a monkey or an animal, and then commented, "I cannot think of anything else," which may imply that she knew there may be other names for it. Likewise, for the food items, Patricia defined all of the objects as either food, fruits, or vegetables, and when prompted explained how each resembled another, similar type of food. These different labels show the presence of categories and subcategories and a flexibility of thinking that demonstrated her potential to perform at the metalinguistic level.

In sum, Patricia showed in her responses different developmental levels for verbal concept formation, including perceptual (e.g., attributes of objects as color, parts, or shapes), functional (e.g., the use of objects and activities), concrete (e.g., the presence of categories and subcategories), and metalinguistic levels (e.g., her understanding that a referent can have several labels). Thus, Patricia's performance at the concrete and metalinguistic levels was very advanced for her chronological age.

For the sorting and category clue tasks, when Patricia was asked how she had grouped objects, she explained that she had grouped them "standing up because they are supposed to be so a person can see them." Similarly, for the food items, she explained that she had grouped them "on top of each other because they cannot stand up." Thus, Patricia demonstrated social awareness of an audience she had evoked. For the verbal justification and category clue tasks, when probed Patricia explained how she had grouped the objects according to gender for the animals and according to food group for the food items. Then, when she was asked if certain items could be moved to another group, she always agreed and, without any probing, could justify her answer using different criteria. For instance, she explained that the pie could be grouped with the fruit because "it had fruit in it" and that the pizza could be grouped with the meat because "it had meat on it." At other times, Patricia would justify her answers according to the shapes of the objects or the shapes they could form if they were cut or made whole. Thus, she seemed to demonstrate cognitive flexibility by being able to justify any grouping the evaluator created and used her abstract reasoning to provide justifications quite easily and quickly. Thus, Patricia performed at the concrete level for both animals and food items, as she was using categories and subcategories with flexibility.

QUEST in Spanish

QUEST was administered to Patricia in Spanish using a parallel set of stimuli and again, after two weeks, by another bilingual Spanish/English graduate student from an educational psychology department. Even though the evaluator administered the assessment method entirely in Spanish, Patricia mainly used English for her answers, speaking Spanish only occasionally. However, she demonstrated a full understanding of the questions posed to her in Spanish. Administering the assessment method in Spanish was considered important to give the child the opportunity to express her verbal and nonverbal thoughts using two cultures and languages. The evaluator observed that Patricia was very quiet and cooperative during the assessment. She was very soft-spoken and gentle with the objects. Patricia responded to all probes asked, taking her time to think about the answers as she manipulated the objects.

Patricia performed at the concrete and metalinguistic levels in the definition task, showing abstract thinking abilities. For instance, when she was describing the cow in the defining task, she said, "They are animals, they make milk, and it looks like a pig because of their face." When Patricia was describing the orange she said, "It's a fruit, a food, looks like a cherry, and it tastes like sugar." In addition, in the verbal justification for sorting task, she was able to separate the animals into "mamas" and "papas." She was consistent about her justification of how she had grouped the animals and would not allow changes across gender groups. When changes were allowed between categories, she explained that "they were the same because they were still in their same [gender] group." Patricia also allowed changes to occur with subcategories, as she would say, "It is okay because it has one of its kind in the same category group." With the food items, she separated the items into *"los"* and *"las,"* and formed subcategories of objects according to shape and types of food simultaneously (e.g., breads according to shape). She did not allow any changes within the particular subcategories. Patricia allowed changing the linguistic gender of labels of objects, which was a metalinguistic task. For instance, when she was asked if *"el tigre"* (the tiger) could be changed to *"la tigresa"* (the tigress), she said "Yes, because it looks like the mom, and it [the label *"la tigresa"*] sounds like it [the mom]." Thus, Patricia described and justified her responses using perceptual features of the objects and the sound of the label in relation to gender assignments. When Patricia was asked if *"el tomate"* could be called *"la tomate,"* she said "Yes, because it [the label *"la tomate"*] sounds like it [feminine]." Although she allowed the names to be changed, she was able to conceptualize that despite certain linguistic changes, the intrinsic properties of the objects remained the same.

The Ravens Coloured Progressive Matrices

In the Ravens Coloured Progressive Matrices (Ravens, 1976), a standardized test of nonverbal intelligence assessing spatiotemporal abilities, Patricia received a total score of 128 and performed at the 95th percentile. Yet despite her high score, she would not have qualified for placement in a gifted education program if the strict standard of scoring in the 97th percentile had been used. In this particular case, the standardized test supports the diagnosis based on QUEST. Diagnostic decisions are more reliable and have concurrent validity by putting together samples of behaviors gathered by qualitative and standardized sources of information. Even though in most cases diagnostic conclusions based on standardized and qualitative assessment methods are contradictory, information gathered using qualitative instruments always coincides.

Diagnosis

Information gathered with QUEST is considered to be a sample of behavior that needs to be interpreted with a battery of qualitative and standardized instruments in order to be a valid and reliable psychoeducational evaluation. QUEST can show evidence of children's learning potential even when they are not proficient in English and/or Spanish. Both qualitative and standardized assessment instruments point to the conclusion that Patricia is developing cognitively and linguistically at above-average levels for her chronological age. Moreover, different informants who knew her in formal and informal contexts also pointed to similarities in the description of the child's personality, talents, and abilities.

Information reported by the teacher is extremely important, as the teacher knows the child from extensive, daily, real-life observations of behavior and performance in an academic and formal environment. The teacher's report also gives information about academic expectations and about attributions and perceptions regarding the girl's behaviors. In addition, the teacher could qualitatively compare the child's behavior with a cohort of children of about the same chronological age. Information from the parents is also extremely important, as it describes the child's behavior in a daily real-life environment that represents an informal context of social interaction with her culture and languages. Because the parents can acknowledge the child's bilingual and bicultural personalities, they add a complementary window to the teacher's view of the child's personality in the mainstream language and culture.

Evaluators contribute certain technical and professional skills for observing a sample of the child's behavior in specifically designed tasks that measure a particular construct, such as cognitive and language develop-ment. It is important to include more than one evaluator because their cul-tural and linguistic backgrounds, philosophies, belief systems, and prior academic knowledge of bilingual children's development may influence their diagnostic decisions. Moreover, internal validity is enhanced when these three sources of information—the teachers', parents', and evaluators' perspectives and conclusions—coincide. Diagnostic decisions are more reli-able and have concurrent validity if reached by putting together samples of behaviors in testing situations with normal performance in real-life social contexts.

Thus, after all information obtained from different informants and from qualitative and standardized sources has been analyzed, the diagnosis is that Patricia's cognitive and language development is above average. She was described by all informants as very advanced in her verbal reasoning, and thus achieved at abstract and even metalinguistic levels in QUEST. Patricia was described by both evaluators as a cooperative, motivated, socially ori-ented girl, and a good problem-solver who thought ahead, planned, and jus-tified her responses.

Recommendations

A multidisciplinary placement committee of five persons, including univer-sity professors and graduate students as consultants, bilingual and gifted education teachers, and parents from the community, was appointed. After reviewing her file, which included qualitative and standardized measures as well as the best products of her journal (such as the stories she had narrated and illustrated), the committee recommended that Patricia be placed in a gifted and talented first-grade classroom the following academic year.

Discussion

We can observe that Patricia's parents and her teacher coincided in their descriptions of her talents, abilities, personality, and above-average develop-mental characteristics. Patricia was described by both her parents and teacher as a well-adapted child with high self-esteem and intrinsic motiva-tion for learning, who has been supported by the scaffolding role of the mod-els that she saw in her parents and teacher. However, her parents and her teacher could open different dimensions for the evaluator. Patricia devel-oped and interacted in a bilingual environment at home with adults and younger siblings. In addition, she was exposed to a monolingual environ-ment at school with a cohort of children of about her same chronological age and a monolingual adult. Patricia's parents revealed that indeed she pre-ferred to interact verbally at home by asking questions about her environment. Moreover, her teacher confirmed that she preferred to interact verbally with smaller rather than larger groups and that she preferred to work independently without asking questions. Based on all the information provided by Patricia's parents and her teacher, it seems that she was stimulated by her parents at home for getting new information and that she used this newly acquired knowledge at school. As a result, she felt proud of her display of independence when she was working away from her parents at school. Thus, the child was certainly receiving support as her interest for learning was being stimulated by her parents and teacher. Patricia excels in verbal abilities, such as reading and writing, but she also has talents for nonverbal spatiotemporal abilities, as revealed by her high score on the Ravens Coloured Progressive Matrices and in her complex drawings. In sum, Patricia was portrayed by both her parents and her teacher as a well adjusted, above-average child who enjoyed learning in a social environment.

It is important to point out that Patricia was recommended for placement in a gifted classroom mainly because of the consistency in the qualitative sources of information, including different informants and instruments. For language-minority children, the standard assessment and diagnostic procedures need to be complemented with alternative methods of assessment. That is, we need to include a broader view of intelligence to acknowledge cultural and linguistic differences and thus to identify genuine giftedness in language-minority children. I do not believe that standards need to be lowered in order to place language-minority children in gifted classes. Instead, we need to improve, replace, and complement the models and instruments that we are currently using in order to portray accurately the genuine potentials and high abilities that language-minority children indeed have.

In sum, the "ethnic researcher" perspective should be endorsed when alternative assessment methods are implemented in school districts serving a high percentage of language-minority children. As a result, real progress can occur in solving the present problem across the nation of the underrepresentation of language-minority children in gifted educational programs.

Conclusions

A number of CLD students have language-minority backgrounds and therefore are bilingual. Even though some bilingual children have a functional command of English, assessing them through a qualitative method that encompasses cultural and linguistic factors gives them the opportunity to show their genuine potentials and high abilities. Due to the number of external factors (e.g., cultural and linguistic differences, socioeconomic level) that need to be taken into control when developing instruments for measuring accurately cognitive and language development in language-minority children, they may not qualify for gifted educational programs. An accurate assessment and diagnostic process needs to include standardized and qualitative assessments that encompass different informants and contexts, such as the child's behaviors and performance in formal academic settings as well as in daily home environments and in testing situations using problem-solving tasks. The traditional psychometric assessment approach is being replaced presently by multidimensional qualitative assessment methods derived from an "ethnic researcher" approach that includes social, cultural, and linguistic factors that contribute to the development of the bilingual child's personality (see Chapter 4). In sum, by including qualitative assessment instruments based on robust psycholinguistic models, such as QUEST, we are acknowledging the complexity of becoming bilingual, bicognitive, and bicultural in diverse sociocultural contexts.

THEORETICAL AND PRACTICAL IMPLICATIONS OF IMPLEMENTING QUEST

The implementation of QUEST has important implications for the education of CLD students. First, the model underlying QUEST includes two languages and two cultures as multidimensional factors influencing the cognitive development in CLD students. Second, QUEST can provide information for accurately diagnosing cognitive and language development in bilingual children. Third, the implementation of QUEST addresses the important educational issue of the underrepresentation of language-minority children in programs for gifted students. Moreover, QUEST can be adapted for use with children from other culturally and linguistically diverse groups across the United States.

REFERENCES

Gonzalez, V. (1991). *A model of cognitive, cultural, and linguistic variables affecting bilingual Spanish/English children's development of concepts and language.* Doctoral dissertation, The University of Texas at Austin. (ERIC Document Reproduction Service No. ED 345 562)
Gonzalez, V. (1994). A model of cognitive, cultural, and linguistic variables affecting bilingual Spanish/English children's development of concepts and language. *Hispanic Journal of Behavioral Sciences 16* (4), 396–421.
Gonzalez, V. (1995). *Cognition, culture, and language in bilingual children: Conceptual and semantic development.* Bethesda, MD: Austin & Winfield.
Gonzalez, V., Bauerle, P., & Felix-Holt, M. (1994). A qualitative assessment method for accurately diagnosing bilingual gifted children. *NABE '92–'93 Annual Conference Journal*, 37–52. Washington, DC: NABE.

Gonzalez, V., Bauerle, P., & Felix-Holt, M. (1995). *Theoretical and practical implications of assessing cognitive and language development in bilingual children with qualitative methods.* Manuscript submitted for publication.

Maker, C. J. (1991). Problem solving: A process approach to identifying giftedness in special populations. *AAGT Potential 22* (4), 1–2.

Markman, E. M., & Hutchinson, J. E. (1984). Children's sensitivity to constraints on word meaning: Taxonomic vs. thematic relations. *Cognitive Psychology, 16* 1–27.

Oller, J. W., Jr., & Perkins, K. (1978). *Language in education: Testing the tests.* Rowley, MA: Newbury House.

Piaget, J. (1965). *Mental imagery in the child: A study of the development of imaginal representation.* New York: Oxford University Press.

Piaget, J. (1967). Piaget's theory. In P. H. Mussen (Ed.), *Carmichael's manual of child psychology:* Vol. 7 (pp. 703–732). New York: John Wiley.

Raven, J. C. (1976). *Coloured Progressive Matrices.* London: H. K. Lewis.

Sinclair-de-Zwart, H. (1969). Language acquisition and cognitive development. In T. E. Moore (Ed.), *Cognitive development and the acquisition of language* (pp. 78–134). New York: Academic Press.

Waxman, S. R. (1990). Linking language and conceptual development: Linguistic cues and the construction of conceptual hierarchies. *The Genetic Epistemologist 17,* 13–20.

Zirkel, P. A. (1976). "The whys" and ways of testing bilinguality before teaching bilingually? *The Elementary School Journal 3,* 323–330.

6

HOW TO LINK ASSESSMENT WITH INSTRUCTION FOR CLD STUDENTS

This chapter focuses on how information collected using qualitative assessment methods can be used in the development of instructional programs that are culturally and linguistically appropriate. Linking assessment and instructional needs and objectives will be discussed in relation to guidelines for implementing qualitative assessment approaches such as summative and formative measures, and instructional strategies for literacy. This sixth chapter relates to the vision statement of this book because one of the features of the "ethnic researcher" approach is to highlight the importance of implementing qualitative assessments that can link assessment with instruction.

LINKING ASSESSMENT AND INSTRUCTIONAL NEEDS AND OBJECTIVES

At present, there is evidence in the literature of the need for valid and reliable instruments for the assessment of cognitive and language development in CLD students that can lead to accurate diagnosis, placement, and educational decisions (see, e.g., De Avila & Havassy, 1974; Erickson & Iglesias, 1986; Healey, Ackerman, Chappell, Perrin, & Stormer, 1981; Mercer, 1973, 1980). This need exists at two levels:

1. To describe accurately children's language dominance and proficiency (Gillmore & Dickerson, 1980; Russell & Ortiz, 1989) to make decisions related to the placement of CLD students in bilingual, regular, or special education classrooms (Oller & Perkins, 1978; Zirkel, 1976)

2. To develop bilingual educational programs that optimize the cognitive, linguistic, affective, and social development of CLD students

According to Srihdar (1980), there are four criteria for tests to be used in bilingual educational programs. Such tests should:

1. Include guidelines or specific directions for the use of test results in planning instruction
2. Separate linguistic from cognitive competence
3. Incorporate pragmatic factors
4. Avoid cultural and linguistic biases, taking them as control variables in the studies

The existing standardized assessment instruments are neither valid nor reliable with reference to these four issues.

As discussed in Chapter 2, the Individuals with Disabilities Education Act (IDEA) required, among other directives, that procedures used for the evaluation and placement of children with disabilities be selected and administered so as not to be racially or culturally discriminatory. This mandate also indicated that the administration of these procedures be in the native language or mode of communication of the child. "Native language," as defined by the Bilingual Education Act of 1968, means the language normally used by an individual, or in the case of a young child, the language used by the parents of the child. The goal of the aforementioned legislation is to provide adequate assessment and thus educational and remediation services. In addition, the Bilingual Education Act speaks to the importance of determining the dominant language of the child (see Chapter 2 for an extended discussion of this topic).

However, given the state of assessment instruments and the difficulty of measuring the complex construct of language proficiency, which includes academic and functional language skills, it is hard to comply with current laws and mandates. Wong-Fillmore (1986) pointed out that it is common for students of low socioeconomic status to experience difficulty with academic language because their language skills, although adequate for communicating in their homes and communities, do not match the type of language spoken by teachers. Thus, prior to assessing their proficiency levels in both languages, these CLD students require a language development program in order to develop the academic language needed in the classroom.

In addition, Commins and Miramontes (1989) indicated that teachers frequently underestimate students' linguistic and academic abilities in both English and Spanish based on their classroom performance. This happens because teachers mistake a lack of vocabulary in Spanish and a lack of English structural proficiency for the absence of underlying conceptual ability. As a result, teachers provide CLD students with basic skills tasks that lack meaning and context, as they perceive these students as not possessing adequate concepts to handle higher level activities. However, Commins and Miramontes's study offered data on the language use and abilities of CLD students in a variety of school and nonschool settings that, after a qualitative analysis, demonstrated that they had the ability to use language as a vehicle for self-expression both socially and cognitively.

It is proposed that to help alleviate current problems in the assessment of CLD students, the comprehensive assessment of cognitive and language development must be done. Moreover, the assessment of the conceptual development of CLD students is extremely important, as it taps the interaction between cognitive and linguistic processes, and should be conducted using nonverbal and verbal procedures in both the first and second languages.

This nonverbal and verbal assessment should shed light on the most important and pragmatic educational needs at present:

1. Differential diagnosis between the normal process of learning a second language and disabilities, such as learning problems, speech handicaps, and language disorders
2. Normal patterns of errors for CLD students in both the first and second languages
3. Normal and abnormal developmental stages in the process of first- and second-language acquisition in CLD students
4. The influence of linguistic and cultural factors on the cognitive development of CLD students

To conduct a differential diagnosis, nonverbal cognitive processes must be assessed. If CLD students are not able to form abstract nonverbal conceptual categories at a normal developmental level for their age, then there is the need to explore possible learning problems related to cognitive and language development. There is also the need to differentiate between speech and language disorders. Speech disorders involve perceptual problems (i.e., auditory discrimination) or articulatory problems (i.e., difficulty in coordinating motor schemes for the accomplishment of points and manners of articulation). In this latter case, language problems are external, and do not have a deeper cognitive or neurological basis.

On the other hand, language disorders involve underlying cognitive and neurological problems. For example, learning disabled students have problems with reading and writing, and with using language for knowledge acquisition. Moreover, the use of nonverbal tasks for the assessment of linguistic, cognitive, and affective processes is an important source of qualitative information, as the optimal potential learning developmental levels of CLD students can be observed. This nonverbal approach can be used as a screening and diagnosis procedure, because linguistic and cultural biases are diminished when cognitive and affective processes are discussed. For example, nonverbal classification tasks can be used for diminishing assessment biases (as proposed in Chapter 5), if careful consideration is given to the selection of the stimuli (e.g., familiar, unambiguous stimuli to the first and second language and culture of the student).

Furthermore, for the purpose of linking assessment with instruction, it is proposed that informal assessment, such as natural observations of the student's behavior in the classroom, teachers' ratings, and actual classroom work (e.g., workbook, graded work, drawings), should be used. The analysis of a sample of linguistic, cognitive, and affective performance should be based on a qualitative assessment approach that examines learning strategies, patterns of errors, strengths and weaknesses, developmental levels, cultural and linguistic background, and motivational levels of CLD students. In addition, a comprehensive qualitative method should also include the measurement of teachers' and evaluators' attitudes toward the first and second language and culture of CLD students.

In relation to the goal of linking assessment with instruction, Yawkey and Juan (1993) have proposed several strategies, including observation, determination of the student's level of development, individualization, developmental language, directed dialogue, and family potential. These strategies have been applied when disseminating Title VII Academic Excellence Project P.I.A.G.E.T., directed by Dr. Thomas D. Yawkey. By using structured and natural observations, educators are able to identify strengths and weaknesses, interests, and conceptual and problem-solving levels of understanding and performance of students across many contexts and along an extended period of time. It is also important to identify the students' developmental levels, taking into consideration their linguistic and cultural backgrounds, and using verbal and nonverbal measures. Educators should also individualize education in order to match the varied cultural and linguistic backgrounds of CLD students by using multiple alternative assessment methods. For example, portfolios provide a multidimensional way of connecting assessment with instruction based on students' performance in the classroom.

In addition, according to Yawkey and Juan (1993), holistic developmental language programs that focus on a sequence of activities for mastering academic tasks naturally link assessment with instruction, as they provide the student with a context for communicative processes that respects their cultural and linguistic experiences. Directive dialogue, oral dialogue between teacher and student, or dialogue journals can also be used as strategies for naturally linking assessment with instruction, as students' communication skills and language functioning levels can be analyzed as a structure formed by several related abilities (i.e., articulation, voice, fluency, phonology, morphology, syntax, semantics, and pragmatics; see Damico, 1991, p. 160). Finally, family potential can also be used as a strategy for linking assessment with instruction, as parents serve as their children's role models for learning social values and behaviors. When communication is established between the home and the school, parents and teachers can collaborate as partners for stimulating children's learning and development, while using congruent values and reward systems. P.I.A.G.E.T. home programs (Yawkey, 1992b), offer effective ways of training parents that include demonstrating, modeling, and playing back, as family members imitate various problem-solving actions, routines, and activities that use cooperative patterning with home visitors and their children.

Developmentally based assessments also include the adaptation of standardized tests to qualitative assessment methods by using a technique called "testing the limits" that is very useful and effective for linking assessment with instruction. To obtain qualitative information for diagnostic purposes that is compatible with the "ethnic researcher" approach, the examiner explores students' abilities beyond those exhibited during a standard test administration. Five procedures are used by the "testing the limits" approach:

1. *Provide additional clues:* The examiner can return to failed items and let the student attempt them again with additional help, such as providing the first step in problem-solving or increasing structure.
2. *Change modality:* The examiner can change the modality (i.e., from written to oral language, from English to the student's first language, from verbal to nonverbal forms) that is involved in problem-solving.
3. *Establish methods used by the student:* Focus on the process that the student used for solving the problem (i.e., strategies, styles, learning).
4. *Eliminate time limits:* This can give the examiner needed information about the student's ability to accomplish specific tasks.
5. *Ask probing questions:* If a student gives responses that the examiner wants to explore further but cannot while following a standardized testing procedure, she or he might want to return to those items upon completion of the test.

In conclusion, we can link assessment with instruction by incorporating a qualitative assessment approach, by implementing assessment and instructional strategies in bilingual classrooms, and by using a technique called "testing the limits" when assessing CLD students.

Gonzalez (1993) calls the realization of the links between assessment and instruction an "awakening experience." Indeed, it *is* an awakening experience and a developmental encounter, as teachers, administrators, and parents explore the interrelations within an "ethnic researcher" approach for CLD students. Linking assessing and instructing is a needed and a definite reality relative to CLD students. However, since CLD students demonstrate unitary and multiple traits, actions, and interactions that reflect the sum totals of their development and learning, matching assessment and instruction is not enough. This match must be extended to nurture learning potential. Thus regardless of CLD students' positive or negative susceptibilities to situations derived from past experiences (i.e., the principle of canalization), extending the match better develops their potentials (Gonzalez, 1993). In addition, this extension based on the principle of canalization affects teachers, because we realize the severe impacts and interrelations that culture, race, and ethnicity have on CLD students (Gonzalez, 1993). As students come to understand their own developmental and learning progress and their variable degrees of performance, depending on the task, they begin to exercise more control over themselves and their potentials. Accordingly, and in context of the "ethnic researcher" approach, we are stressing multiple links between assessment and instruction for potential growth and for self-realization and self-actualization. Whether in good developmental bilingual programs or any of the federal bilingual Academic Excellence models (Yawkey, 1992a), multiple links are viewed as strategies that extend matches between assessment and instruction (Yawkey & Juan, 1993). Each of these strategies, used as multiple links between assessment and instruction, is described in the following sections.

SUMMATIVE AND FORMATIVE MEASURES

Observational measures include instruments such as anecdotal records, rating scales, and checklists. Measures such as these record observational behaviors, processes, products, and relevant aspects occurring in the environment. They record what students do and say through note-taking or in other written forms. Performance assessment focuses on various products, stories, narrative interviews, and other assessment standards that evolve from students' and teachers' input.

Within the "ethnic researcher" approach, teachers' decisions rest on many observational and performance assessment measures in either summative or formative ways, both of which link instruction by providing different types of information to teachers and students. This information then enables them to make decisions about assessment and instruction. Here, the important question becomes, "What types of information do summative and formative measures provide to students and teachers?" Within assessment and instruction interaction, a related question focuses on uses of the information: "How is summative and formative information used in instruction?" In the following sections, both questions are answered for summative and then formative evaluation.

Summative measures are usually administered in pre- and post-test fashion. Several weeks or months may intervene between the first and second administrations of the same test. However, in observational and performance assessments, summative information can be gathered at more than two points in time. These markers across time might appear as: point 1 (end of October), point 2 (mid-January), point 3 (end of March), and point 4 (end of May). Summative measures gathered at more than two intervals show growth at various points in the observed and performance streams of students. These points separated by time:

1. *Show* measurement taken at different, successively established intervals.
2. *Demonstrate* growth and learning on relevant dimensions that are characterized by each of these particular measures used for data collection.
3. *Provide* broad indexes of growth showing either descriptive or quantitative changes.
4. *Are summarized* in narrative form (Puckett & Black, 1994).
5. *Mark and document* significant changes in individual students' growth and the growth of students as classroom groups across these designated time points.

Especially in contemporary classrooms following the "ethnic researcher" approach, sound evaluation with summative measures respects the students and their growth, learning, and performance (Hopkins & Stanley, 1981). This respect for students means illustrating the students' contributions to their learning, growth, and performance. Sound evaluation also respects teachers by documenting clearly the progress of all students. Sound evaluation within an "ethnic researcher" approach shows what teachers have done previously and what they are doing currently to understand realistically what students are learning. In this sense, summative evaluation attempts to encourage CLD students' progress without ruining it through aggregates of achievement test totals plotted along "normal" curve distributions.

Along with respecting the students, teachers and clinicians must also understand very well each instrument, including what it sets as its goals, how it is administered and scored, how its standards are to be used as criteria in making decisions about quality, and how observed and performance results can be reported accurately and reliably. All instruments require examiner understanding. In our opinion, is even more important and imperative for summative (and formative) measures than for achievement and intelligence tests because of the continuing criticisms of the former (for detailed discussions of these criticisms, see Cohen & Spenciner, 1994; Puckett & Black, 1994).

In answer to the question of how summative assessment is to be used in instruction, data are generated and need to be analyzed for instructional decision-making, regardless of whether there is one pretest referent and one posttest marker, or a series of four or five continuous markers across, for example, ten successive months. Puckett and Black's (1994, pp. 200–201) discussion of classroom summative measurement uses implies two tiers of usage: one focusing on one student (tier one), and another targeting a group of students (tier two). Using the one-tier summative data gathering procedures yields ongoing information on one student. Understandably, this procedure provides detailed, in-depth data at predetermined periods across time. Puckett and Black suggest that items assessed should be summarized and their quality assessed according to previously developed standards. The description of quality is a narrative one, and like Puckett and Black, we see *no* reason why some actual items cannot accompany the summative narration. Since "summative" refers to a totality, we recommend that the teacher write as many summative narratives as necessary to accomplish both the classroom goals and the student's personal and/or self-perceived goals across time in the development of these items. Summary narratives written in this manner provide ongoing, developmental glimpses of individual student growth.

This idea also refers to summative narratives of groups of students as well as to formative assessment descriptions. Summative narratives for groups of students (tier two) share several similarities with tier one. Given a summative orientation, tier two, like tier one, uses established points in time as markers for systematically collecting information. Items from all students need to be included in tier-two summative evaluation. If there are multiple examples of items at the same time period, such as three interviews of book authors, we recommend asking the students which one they want included in the evaluation. The same procedure for producing summative narratives in tier one can be followed in tier-two narratives.

These items represent a sample of items to include in summative narratives in the classroom. The same concerns for developing reliability and consistency and for using standards for quality that are applicable for making observations and performance-based measures are applicable to summative narratives. In addition, other items to consider in summative (as well as formative) evaluation include multiple measures, student involvement in establishing evaluation criteria, provisions for making the genuinely important decisions needed in authentic assessment, and the freedom for self-growth and auto-evaluation to occur (Cohen & Spenciner, 1994).

Formative assessment, the second type of evaluation, is repeated continuously. All types of observation and performance assessment measures can be used in an ongoing formative sense. As with all forms of testing (including achievement and intelligence instruments), decision-making here rests on both long- and short-term school and teacher objectives and school and teacher views on development and learning in CLD and mainstream students. Formative assessment opens additional windows through which to view the contributions and potentials of culturally and linguistically different children. Here, formative data are compiled on a day-to-day, week-to-week, or month-to-month basis. These smaller intervals of time over which formative assessment is systematically conducted provides teachers and administrators with much data. In addition, other types of information provided by formative evaluation give ample evidence of ongoing growth. In P.I.A.G.E.T. Programs, formative assessment of individual children occurs week to week (Yawkey, 1992a). P.I.A.G.E.T., like other good bilingual/ESL programs, focuses on nurturing and then assessing concepts such as problem-solving and critical thinking. In social-environmental contexts, the Daily Observation Cards (Peters, Neisworth, & Yawkey, 1985), used as a formative index, track the ongoing acquisition of critical thinking processes such as observing, predicting, sorting, and generalizing.

Using formative assessment results for instructional purposes focuses first on the nature of this assessment and second on the teacher's and clinician's goals. For example, the short-term nature of formative assessment excludes using portfolios, which are long-term projects. However, a teacher or clinician who wants to determine a student's progress in contributing work products to the portfolio on a weekly basis could make easily an observation record. Here, the teacher or clinician would write down the products contributed each week. This observational record would be an ongoing evaluation of contributions that would be invaluable in documenting the type and/or quality of these contributions. So, under certain conditions a long-term project, such as a portfolio, might be applicable to a short-term formative evaluation as developed by a teacher or clinician. In similar fashion, other long-term projects such as story and essay writing, interviewing, and exhibiting can be evaluated formatively. Likewise, the various processes and steps that make up the long-term project can be identified and then assessed using formative evaluation.

Anecdotal records, like observations, can be used in a formative ongoing basis. Such records and observations made, for example, of students working in small groups or individually, produce an ongoing data trail of work group activity along such possible dimensions of interest as cooperativeness, work group choices, and leadership. In a formative manner, rating forms are also extremely handy and usable.

Summative and formative measures become real, valuable strategies that bridge assessment and instruction. Here, multiple measures are ideal sources, and the joint use of summative and formative evaluation provides much utility in instruction.

LITERACY

Gonzalez and Yawkey (1994) and Yawkey, Gonzalez, and Juan (1994), in related papers, address literacy development in CLD students. Literacy development is viewed as the interaction of cognitive, linguistic, and socio-cultural factors that provide several strategies that crystallize links from assessment to instruction. In the context of literacy and biliteracy, these links are identified by Yawkey, Gonzalez, and Juan (1994) on "language experience approach, story telling and story-book reading. All of these strategies are part of 'whole language' because they focus on language production and meaning and are easily suited to authentic assessment, materials and activities.

The Language Experience Approach

The language experience approach (LEA) is a dynamic process of utilizing actual experiences to initiate and develop reading and other literacy processes. Developed shortly after World War I, LEA is now a great link to the instruction of CLD students. Writing of its contemporary uses, Tinajero and Calderon (1988) note that "the approach is particularly appropriate for use with this [CLD] student population because it capitalizes on the student's own interests, experiences and oral language faculty as a basis for teaching them to read....Thus, learning to read becomes easier and more enjoyable because reading materials match the language patterns and speaking vocabulary of LEP [limited English proficiency] students." (p. 31).

LEA is explained elsewhere in detail (see Goodman, 1986; Stauffer, 1986; Tinajero & Calderon, 1988). However, in the context of bilingual education programs, the LEA as an instruction and assessment link is briefly described (see Yawkey, Gonzalez, & Juan, 1994).

Classrooms with an "ethnic educator" perspective using the P.I.A.G.E.T. (*Promoting Intellectual Adaption Given Experiential Transforming*) Programs generally format the LEA by exploring and interacting, composing the narrative, and clarifying messages in the narrative. However, any format can be used. In exploring and interacting, the bases of language generation are real experiences in which the students are actively engaged. After having had the experiential bases, students collect their thinking by discussing their experiences; they may also draw them and talk about them. At this initial level, teachers can quickly assess to see the quantity and quality of informational data that the students have acquired. Through questioning, redirecting, refocusing, and reexperiencing, as necessary, instruction and assessment are continuous.

In composing the narrative written content, the students' spoken words, phrases, and expressions and written sentences are written by the teacher.

With beginnings, midpoints, and endings, the written narratives evolve. The teacher usually writes the content as it is generated by the students. After the narratives are written, the students then discuss, clarify, reorder, correct, rethink, and agree generally on their content and flow. At these points, the teacher assesses, guides, and instructs as the students read the narratives. After practicing reading the literary compositions, the students may do "extensions" (Yawkey, 1992b; Yawkey, Gonzalez, & Juan, 1994). These extensions, or extended experiences, add to the core narratives in diverse ways. For example, the students may make up and act out the narratives, they may add more literary content, or they may type them into the computer. Other examples of extenders are framing sight-word vocabulary and making word banks (Tinajero & Calderon, 1988).

Storytelling

Culturally and linguistically different children learn the art of storytelling by direct involvement in these family and peer experiences. Henry and Pepper (1990) note that "in such situations, verbal instruction is neither offered nor required because the close proximity to the observable action makes instruction giving quite redundant" (p. 90). Yawkey, Gonzalez, and Juan (1994) feel that the establishment of this learning in peer-adult, adult-adult, and peer-peer endeavors greatly affects a student's literary development. In bilingual education classrooms, storytelling is a genuinely motivating endeavor because it involves home lives, families, and communities. In classroom situations, other sources of storytelling might include myths, fables, children's literature (Maldonado-Colón, 1991), and fantasy.

The need for storytelling as a basis for literacy development and as an opportunity for assessment and instruction revolves around three general understandings (Yawkey, Gonzalez, & Juan, 1994; Yawkey, Askov, Cartwright, Dupuis, Fairchild, & Yawkey, 1981).

1. The desire and interest of children to tell cultural-ethnic stories
2. Composites of experiences
3. Oral forms of communication

Based on the interests, desires, and needs of students, storytelling can become part of their reading and literary growth. Students want to talk about themselves, their families, their communities, and their activities. As they tell stories, Maldonado-Colón (1991) recommends inviting students to join in the narrative and extend it. This procedure can also be used by professionals when they question students for clarification of main ideas, sequential information, and other relevant contextual items as they are storytelling (Maldonado-Colón, 1991). Examples of such questions include

1. What do you think might happen next?
2. Why do you think the main character made that statement?
3. How long do you think it might take for the alien to get well?

Storytelling represents the reservoir of the students' experiences, which help direct thought and provide needed description to the storytelling. Whether these experiences are from the immediate family, the nearby community, or the world at large, storytelling offers students opportunities to communicate with others. They also share their cultural and ethnic identities and linguistic traits as they show understandings of their experiences. Storytelling becomes an asset, and professionals must make every effort to nurture and encourage storytelling experiences, and support their use and the students who present them.

Storytelling in classrooms is also motivating because cultural and linguistic talk is

1. Self-motivating
2. Not graded or assessed
3. Part of the students' daily reading and literacy efforts
4. A positive contribution to an individual's well-being and self-esteem
5. Appropriate to interactive, complementary behaviors of modeling, gesturing, convincing, and negotiating, which are elements of social relations

Oral histories of the family are most appropriate for storytelling. These oral histories are handed down across generations. Their beauty is their cultural, ethnic, and family relevance, which spells out the individual's interrelations from past to present.

Whether storytelling takes the form of oral histories, the retelling of favorite stories students have read, the dramatization of events, and so forth, Lapp and Flood (1993) recommend several uses. For example, they suggest students use flannel boards, complete with cutouts, to tell a story. From a fantasy or pretend perspective, children can project their thoughts and actions through these cutouts and thus better express themselves. This projection onto objects by using flannel board cutouts or puppets is an ideal form of emotional release (Piaget, 1964), as students can divest their emotion, anxiety, and frustration in the characters in the episodes. In addition, they come to understand better their own thoughts, expressions, and emotions.

Lastly, storytelling routines are largely oral expressions in which students generate the dialogues that present situations for language learning and communicative interchanges (Blank & Franklin, 1980). With young children, oral expression and body movements go hand in hand. As children express themselves, they show physically what they are saying and thinking. Words, phrases, and monologues are repeated endlessly, and children

150 Chapter 6

play with language and invent new words to say. With increasing age, they are able to put words and oral expressions together into novel-sounding patterns that produce variability in oral language and learning. Through trial and error, oral expression and phonological development approximations to more mature, logical, and adult-like language are made. Here, oral expression is intentional and planned, with a beginning, midpoint, and ending, and greater group pleasure is derived from oral interchanges. It becomes a mode for storytelling and a way for students to make statements about their cultural and linguistic selves. Acquiring and sharing ideas through storytelling are effective means of developing language variety for use in classrooms and among individuals (Lapp & Flood, 1993).

Story Reading

For many of our CLD students in "ethnic-educator" classrooms, reading storybooks may be a novel, unfamiliar experience in schools in their native countries or for that matter in their homes. As Faltis (1989) explains, in many Latin American countries reading storybooks is not common in either homes or schools because of high adult illiteracy and a general dearth of reading materials and activities. Thus, the potential of story reading in the "ethnic educator" classroom is tremendous.

In providing a rationale for the use of storybooks, Faltis (1989), citing the ideas of literacy advocates (e.g., Au, 1979; Moustafa, 1980; Shannon, 1986), strongly supports the use of print media for CLD students. First, Faltis notes that reading storybooks increases the conceptual and linguistic growth of students. Gonzalez and Yawkey (1994) see storybook reading especially significant in promoting the microtransfer and macrotransfer of linguistic competence from lower to high levels. Another benefit of reading storybooks in the classrooms is the promotion of the development and use of metalinguistic precursors and generalizations in literacy. Yawkey, Gonzalez, and Juan (1994) cite several precursors to metalinguistic development in storybook reading, including:

1. Opening, closing, and caring for books
2. Turning the pages of a book from left to right
3. Reading from the top to the bottom of the page
4. Understanding that words and pictures, as printed symbols, carry meaning

Examples of extensions of storybook reading are (Yawkey, Gonzalez, & Juan, 1994):

1. Learning that individuals write books, as shown by their names on the title pages

2. Understanding that storybooks contribute to the readers' vicarious experiences
3. Developing and writing narratives for storybooks
4. Employing methods of citing, paraphrasing, and quoting to represent ideas and use exact words from storybooks as resources

A third value of storybook reading is developing and using social cognitive relationships among individuals (Faltis, 1989; Gonzalez & Yawkey, 1994). The traits that make up social cognitive relationships are culture-derived and culture-bound. That is, these traits vary across cultures and develop from situational learning, modeling, initiation, and feedback (Peters, Neisworth, & Yawkey, 1985). Among the examples of these social traits cited by Peters, Neisworth, and Yawkey (1985) are

1. Showing emotion
2. Understanding and sharing feelings and frustrations
3. Naming objects, situations, events, and people
4. Interacting among children, family members, and other adults, including police officials, teachers, and medical personnel
5. Interrelating abilities such as cooperation, independence, and helping

Since these social relations and values are culturally variable and sensitive, they can be nurtured through social group experiences such as reading stories (Faltis, 1989; Shannon, 1986). Interestingly, Faltis (1989), in citing Dale (1985) and Shannon (1986), states that cooperation may be a core social trait that can be encouraged by story reading in schools. Relatedly, certain culturally and linguistically different populations may stress similar traits, covertly and overtly. For example, Faltis (1989), says that "collaboration and cooperation are values that are generally familiar to Spanish-speaking children from Mexico and Central America...[and that]...cooperation-fostering storybooks provide support for the norm of cooperation required for successful peer interaction in the classroom" (p. 48). Thus, Faltis implies that story reading is an ideal situation where both the culturally and linguistically different families and schools can work together in nurturing cooperation and collaboration.

In operationalizing the rationale for utilizing story reading, there are common core themes between culturally and linguistically diverse families and schools. Faltis (1989) recommends developing a criteria for selecting classroom storybooks that contain cooperation, collaboration, and/or other culturally relevant family variables (e.g., sharing, working). (For details of the application of cooperation criteria to storybooks, see Faltis, 1989, pp. 49–50.) Within this context, story reading becomes a social-family-school approach to literacy growth. Hernandez (1991) says that this approach to literacy helps students nurture their literacy abilities because they are able to move conceptually and linguistically from their familiar social worlds to their individual, self-oriented worlds. Moving from the social group "known" to the individual "known" is meaningful interactive conceptual and linguistic learning, because the students can see, touch, and taste these thoughts—they are real.

Based on the "ethnic educator" approach, linking assessment with instruction is straightforward, natural, and observable. Here, for example, vocabulary words from storybooks and dictated stories derived from oral histories using the LEA approach become the professional's curricular and instructional procedures. As the students follow through with the activities to implement these procedures, the professional utilizing authentic assessment may evaluate by:

1. Using vocabulary words in speaking and role-playing the stories
2. Reading the stories that were dictated by the students
3. Choosing storybooks with themes related to the dictated stories

Within the students' literacy learning, Tinajero and Calderon (1989) view this whole, interactive literacy area for culturally and linguistically different children as "a process of selection, prediction, confirmation, and self-correction in an effort to gain meaning" (p. 42).

Representation

Representation as a strategy of linking assessment with instruction is also called representational thinking, representational knowledge, and mediated learning modes (Peters, Neisworth, & Yawkey, 1985). As thinking and knowledge processes, representation is viewed by constructivists such as Piaget (1965) as modes students use conceptually to socially and physically internalize and mentally structure, encode, or integratively file developmental activities and experiential encounters. In this sense, representational thought occurs as students act upon their social group and physical environments and react to them as they come to learn more about them.

Professionals using this linking strategy between assessment and instruction understand that representational thinking focuses on developmental knowledge of:

1. Objects (e.g., dog, cup, car's rate of speed) from a part that stands for the whole (i.e., index)
2. These objects and object relationships, even though they are physically absent from the setting (i.e., symbols)
3. Written, higher-order, abstract symbols for these absent objects and relationships, such as written names, mathematical numerals, scientific symbols, and other marks (i.e., signs)

Hwambo and Yawkey (1995) note that "these modes of learning are critical to constructivist schooling for they are ways young and older children mentally construct objects, actions, and situations and at an operative level interrelate them logically to solve problems." Implicit within the construct of representational knowing is the critical idea, often overlooked in schools, that knowledge of the spoken word and the written word are developmental acquisitions. The representational knowledge of signs in the form of writing and recognizing words in print is *not* the beginning and ending of classroom instruction, diagnosis, or prescription. If the classroom does not provide index- and symbol-level experiences and encounters prior to sign-level teaching, how can we expect our CLD students to recognize and represent automatically their experience through spoken and written words in either their native language or English?

In using the strategy of representation to link instruction and assessment, several procedures emerge. First, word speaking and word writing are the end results of a *long, meaningful* developmental learning process. Here, index and symbol learning activities must be used *first,* before sign-level criterion learning is utilized with students. Second, index learning focuses on having real, meaningful experiences with the objects, ideas, and situations present in the learning encounter. After encountering the objects and so forth, index learning also includes understandings that basic symbols can be used to represent these objects. As an example, we use a commonly known idea-sample of a duck from Weikart, Rogers, Adcock, and McClelland (1971). A duck print (i.e., a graphic outline of a duck or its beak or feet) is recognized by young students as representing the real bird, the duck. Older students recognize the outline or imprint of a bell to represent freedom—a higher order abstraction than the duck. All these index experiences build toward the printed and spoken word—"duck," "freedom", and so forth. (For superb, practical descriptions of representational levels of learning, see Weikart, Rogers, Adcock, & McClelland, 1971.)

From index learning, the students proceed to symbols and then lastly to sign learning. From the instruction and assessment perspectives, there are several elements that make up a student's symbol growth (i.e., symbolization). In development and learning, these elements are integrated, and affect and nurture conceptualization objects, situations, and events not present in the immediate setting. These interactive elements are the bases for linguistic growth of students and adults. The first element is three-dimensional models (Peters, Neisworth, & Yawkey, 1985). Here, individuals develop conceptual understandings of objects, situations, and events by actually building them. In other words, these constructions represent those objects not present. For example, children may use dough, mud, or blocks to build garages, airplanes, or "A Visit to Uncle Juan's House." Students and adults can also represent absent objects and events by building three-dimensional models of them.

A second element is the representation of absent objects, situations, and events using two-dimensional media (Peters, Neisworth, & Yawkey, 1985). This representational form focuses on flat-surface media such as paper, easels, watercolors, and finger paints. Here, individuals sketch, draw, and create other two-dimensional aids to conceptualizations.

The third interactive element is imitation (Peters, Neisworth, & Yawkey, 1985). As examples, we think immediately about pantomime and modeling actions that represent that which is not physically present. Other examples include imitating "Aunt Sally telephoning," "Mother washing her car," and "Winnie the dog walking" as well as using physical movements to show favorite movie and television characters. Without using oral expressions, body movements, actions, and their coordinations come to represent and show things not present.

A fourth interactive element is make-believe, fantasy, sociodramatic play, and drama (Peters, Neisworth, & Yawkey, 1985). Through dramatizing plays, movies, chapters from books, and so forth, students gain much ability in linguistical conceptualization. Here, children take on roles and pretend to be someone or something other than themselves. With make-believe, children gain in understanding and internalizing roles as they continue to practice and extend them. By becoming lost in a sea of phrases and other oral expressions and movements, children extend their conceptual abilities and develop related capacities such as concentration.

A final element is onomatopoeia or the use of sounds to represent objects, events, and situations (Peters, Neisworth, & Yawkey, 1985). As a part of auditory conceptualization and a sensory learning channel, onomatopoeia is critical to representational thinking. Sounds of birds, dogs, horses, parrots, cars, trucks, and other means of transportation provide ample opportunities for students to advance their development and learning linguistically.

These elements present professionals with significant opportunities to assess for their uses in activities at any time and as appropriate. In turn, these same elements can be turned into teaching strategies that help develop and extend the students' cognitive and linguistic competencies.

Massed Experiences

This particular link between assessment and instruction is a critical key that supports the "ethnic educator" approach and authentic learning for students. Massed experiences focus on core concepts that are actualized with students in many ways and using many different materials. Peters, Neisworth, and Yawkey (1985), and Hwambo and Yawkey (1995) think of massed experiences as keystones for developmental generalizations. For our students to understand the color blue or any other concept in native and English languages, the concept is taught with one set of materials and in one situation. This strategy of mass experiences requires this same concept to be extended with different materials and in many other situations so students can generalize it from numerous perspectives. For CLD students to realize and achieve their linguistic and cognitive potentials, professionals need to be aware of several procedures fundamental to massed experiences and developmental generalizations.

We have all heard or made the following comments:

1. "The material was covered!"
2. "We did a short review of fractions because they had it last year!"
3. "We couldn't spend more than one class period on it! At least they were exposed to it!"
4. "No matter how many times I teach it, they just simply don't get it!"

Implied within these statements is the notion that once a concept is taught or written on the board, our students "have" it. We often think that teaching or stating the concept is equivalent to the student automatically writing it mentally on a blank file card in the brain and putting it in a long-term storage folder or in a cabinet. However, the massed experience link between instruction and assessment calls this notion and the above comments into serious question.

In using this link, continual, different experiences with the same concept are mandated *if* we:

1. *Believe* in authentic education
2. *Believe* in the relevance of the "ethnic educator" classrooms
3. *Believe* in teaching for generalization

These continual, different experiences permit students to understand that even though a concept may be presented using different objects, events, and situations, it is usable and functional across these other learning opportunities.

Professionals working with CLD students can illuminate their learning and developmental potential with this linking strategy. Regardless of the students' ages and conceptual and linguistic abilities, massed experiences can be readily and easily used in both teaching and assessing situations. We regard massed experiences as increased opportunities to learn authentically and to develop understandings, skills, and attitudes meaningfully.

Family Involvement

The family must be genuinely seen and utilized as a link between instruction and assessment as well as a significant institution. Even though one of the nation's educational goals for the year 2000 is family involvement in schools and schooling activities, and even though the family involvement is part of all new paradigms in educational reform, the concept is neither understood nor utilized well in our schools and communities.

Under current and traditional educational paradigms, the family and parents are regarded as part of education because families supply the "kids"—the raw materials for our schooling factories, which mill and mold their brains and bodies. Education goals and objectives of the new educational reform paradigms require family involvement (see Chapter 9). Indeed, the new bilingual provisions and amendments of the Elementary and Secondary Education Act require partnerships between schools and homes. In fact, the words "family literacy" have crept into titles of Even Start and Migrant Education programs, and have solidified and crystallized the position on family significance taken by Head Start since its beginning in the mid-1960s.

Family involvement is extremely critical to our CLD students and families. Title VII Project P.I.A.G.E.T. and other good bilingual/ESL programs have components that focus on family involvement. From instruction and assessment perspectives, family involvement becomes a viable, functional link that strengthens our classroom program, the school's programs, and those of our local educational agency.

Families understanding classroom goals for their children can be instrumental in making sure that students are "on target," that homework is done, and that related school obligations and responsibilities are met. Results of classic narrative description (e.g., Berger, 1981) and numerous contemporary investigations show students' increased academic behaviors as parent involvement is instituted in school programs and in homes.

For example, one of P.I.A.G.E.T.'s (Yawkey, 1991) ongoing "side effects" after children graduate from the program is that parents continue to be involved in their children's education by:

1. Volunteering in their children's classrooms and lunch halls
2. Attending school board meetings to discuss and support particular interests
3. Chaperoning field trips and helping in the school office
4. Attending and participating in parent-teacher meetings and conferences

As family members continue to become empowered and learn more about schooling processes, students and families will benefit. Since the family and the classroom have the same focus—the betterment of the student—the much needed greater working relationships between both groups is increasing.

Interactive Dialogue

Interactive dialogue, also called directed dialogue, is a teaching and assessing strategy used in the P.I.A.G.E.T. Program and other bilingual/ESL programs (Blank & Franklin, 1980; Petrykowski, 1992). Directed dialogue is an actual replay or playback of student activity or action. Directed dialogue requires: (1) experiences completed by the student; (2) verbal descriptions and explanations of what happened and what occurred in these experiences; and (3) a sequencing of events in the description.

This particular link between instruction and assessment rests on experiences and activities. They are authentic and real, and provide the foundation for linguistic and conceptual growth and development. They can be common, day-to-day activities such as riding the school bus. For younger children, using commonly repeated activities is advantageous because they are familiar, and content ideas can be easily used for directed dialogue. For older students, experiences such as field trips and other one-time classroom activities can serve as foundations for interactive dialogue. These real activities in which students participate are conceptually and linguistically more appropriate and better to use than those activities about which they hear. Here, the students experience background, content, and knowledge and understandings they can use in interactive dialogue. Community and cultural contexts as well as resource speakers are ideal experiences to use with this link to literacy development.

Second, verbal descriptions are used in interactive dialogue. After experiencing the activities firsthand, the students are asked to tell what they saw and heard. Here, the description of events and details in narration can be emphasized. Students collect their understandings and thoughts, and interactively develop a narrative. These personal and group experiences become natural and spontaneous vehicles for eliciting and developing descriptive content. If a group of students experienced the activity, they can assist each other in retelling the actions through dialogue. For example, as students listen to each other, they see and hear their mutual experiences come alive. With each student who adds verbal contributions, professionals can understand better their students' ideas, skills, and attitudes.

Lastly, directed dialogue provides sequencing experiences. As students verbally play back their activities, they can determine whether the events are described in appropriate order. The orally expressed activities are organized in base-line statements, midpoint expressions, and ending statements. The students, in using directed dialogue, gain many linguistic and conceptual opportunities for development. There is sequential, seriational learning occurring as the students begin and end their experiences in proper order. In addition, other experiential metalinguistic learning includes telling stories for understanding and cooperating in group settings for problem-solving.

Because directed dialogue utilizes experiences that have actually happened, it is part of authentic learning and performance-based assessment.

Activity and Object Uses

To implement education reforms in the classroom, tactics or strategies are required to anchor them for use both functionally and meaningfully. Generally, these reform movements focus on two common strategies that are also related to linking assessment and instruction: active learning and object utilization. They, in turn, become bases for instruction and assessment. Active learning is necessary for students to construct their learning. In active learning, students must interact or come in contact with their environments in some fashion. Didactic telling or rote learning therefore plays little role in authentic learning. In actively constructing their knowledge, students must be provided with critical ingredients for active learning, which include an emphasis on process and concrete object manipulation. Emphasis on process means that ways, avenues, and encounters experienced along the paths to learning and development are more critical than the end points of learning— or what was learned. We have made this point many times before, both implicitly and explicitly. Given that active learning provides processes in operation to solve problems experientially encountered, processes in context, such as generalizing, predicting outcomes, observing, and many others, provide the challenges found in constructing meaningful understandings, skills, and attitudes.

With the press of educational reform for active learning with process rather than product outcomes, the use of concrete bases for activities is mandated. Here, concrete objects provide students with the potentials to probe, classify, seriate, order, and so forth, through trial and error, to reach active, planned solution sets. As they use the objects, students in peer group settings discuss options and techniques and test predictions. The peer-peer interaction adds additional insight into the meaningful testing of ideas as the students expand their representational and deductive thinking capacities. Their daily experiences and activities take on new meaning as they tackle situations that extend their learnings. Having many kinds of materials is important to active learners. It is also imperative to have multiple objects of the same material, for this promotes their multiple uses at the same time (Peters, Neisworth, & Yawkey, 1985).

There are many types of materials available for use in active, authentic learning episodes. As suggested by Johnson, Christie, and Yawkey (1987) and Yawkey and Trostle (1982), several types of such objects include construction, instruction, real, and toy materials. Constructional materials are used by students in many ways. They have *no* exact, convergent outcome. Examples for young children are blocks. Instructional materials have specific outcomes for learning and are built by manufacturers to be convergent in nature. Examples for older students are geography games and cubes for exponential equations. Toys are small-sized realia that represent objects in the actual world. These include miniature cars, trucks, and other objects that represent transportation. There are also animal sets, those that represent housekeeping, and so forth. The last type of objects found in and out of classrooms are real materials—actual objects made for adults' use that students can use in their learning activities. For the young child, these include cardboard boxes, pans, and pots. For older students, numerous examples include small, one-cylinder lawn mower engines that are dismantled and put back together in home, personal care, and industrial education classes. Hammers and nails are also used (for detailed explanations and examples, see Trostle & Yawkey, 1990; Yawkey & Trostle, 1982).

Critical Thinking

An especially important link between instruction and assessment for CLD students is critical thinking. This link is also called problem-solving, thinking skills, critical analysis, and higher-order thought processes. In Piaget's (1965) terms, we also see critical thinking as inventing or understanding how to discover, or how to reconstruct by rediscovery. Critical thinking stresses the hows of mental processes of thought rather than the whats of factual, recognitory memory (Vygotsky, 1978). Here, knowledge becomes secondary, and understanding and knowing is primary (Walsh & Paul, 1968). The students will think critically at their own levels if given the opportunity. This critical thinking comprises the ability to examine a situation or problem from a global as well as a segmented or piecemeal perspective. In turn, this leads to the ability to apply and test possible solutions from a global as well as a segmented perspective to see which works best. This continual application and reapplication of understandings continually combines ideas from each of the previous attempts until a best solution is found.

In addition, as students develop and use problem-solving, they express their attempts and ideas verbally. In such situations, we have observed students using high verbal thinking, complete with analogies. In these problem-solving situations, students also use readily syllogistic and other more abstract forms of verbal logic and reasoning. As students express verbally their ideas, they experience discrepancies between their reasoning and their experiences that differences produce cognitive conflicts. These conceptual conflicts arise especially in peer settings, as each student verbally and intellectually reasons and shares this critical thinking segment. This peer-group sharing of problem-solving ideas encourages additional dialogue and alternate solutions. As a part of the problem-solving process, the peer-peer interaction fans solutions, encourages the motivation to test these solutions, and decreases students' egocentric thinking. As a part of the process, the cognitive conflict in peer-peer interaction helps students see things more logically, objectively, and from more of a group rather than an individual perspective.

Lastly, critical thinking also involves demonstrating flexibility and the ability to keep on track. Flexibility is the analytic ability to view situations from varying perspectives and to use the insights gained through these perspectives to solve the problems. Keeping on track is the capacity to reduce or eliminate distractions that are irrelevant to the problem-solving and to develop the persistence to try.

With the nurturing and developing of critical thinking, students use current understandings and develop new ones as they cooperatively problem solve in group settings. The use of thinking and verbal processes to develop new meaningful understandings has great advantage for developing higher, more complex thought in our CLD students.

Choices

For CLD students, choices present real learning opportunities for decision-making, social participation, and successes. Choices in classroom settings mean alternatives. In these classrooms, students select from among alternate activities, alternate channels of learning, and alternate assignments. Providing the students with choices enhances several learning options: making decisions, developing independence, and individualizing. In choosing among activities, students initiate choices and make decisions. Having to choose one activity over another encourages the ability to make up one's mind and to follow through in completing the activity, which are significant to learning and development. In making decisions among alternatives, Trawick-Smith (1994) recommends that professionals guide students who are not making decisions. Guiding students may range from strategies in which the professional is simply physically present to those in which they ask questions and make declarative suggestions to the students. Physical presence provides students with the needed reassurance that it is acceptable to make decisions. Examples of questions for guiding decision-making include:

1. Which one of the two choices do you prefer?
2. Would you like to complete a book report on this sport's hero?
3. Why do you think you would like to try this activity?

Relatedly, making decisions is also a classroom teaching strategy used systematically by professionals with CLD students in Title VII Project P.I.A.G.E.T.

(Petrykowski, 1990; Yawkey, 1992). This classroom strategy focuses on nurturing persistence in task completion. Here, students are guided to finish the tasks they have chosen. This guiding for task completion supports self-esteem development and provides successes in decision-making.

Second, independence is fostered through making choices. Here, student-chosen activities provide them with ample opportunities to initiate and follow through with their decisions. Independent thinking comes from doing tasks well. In developing independence, students could begin making decisions by choosing among two or three alternates. Later, as their ability to choose responsibly expands, students' options and choices can be increased in quality and in number.

Lastly, choices mean individualizing. Here, students make choices and decisions that are especially tailored to their developmental and learning levels. From perspectives of individualization, choices meet needs. As students opt for one activity over another, it becomes apparent that they are cognitively and emotionally involved with their decisions and abilities to complete them. This focus on individualization through choices provides much practice for generalizing understandings across settings. Individualization gives students the necessary freedom to pursue activities that they feel are important for them. Sound judgment and personal initiatives are practiced and encouraged. Through appropriate amount of guidance and independence in making choices, students better understand their potentials as productive individuals.

GUIDELINES FOR LINKING ASSESSMENT AND INSTRUCTION USING QUALITATIVE ASSESSMENT METHODS

As discussed in Chapter 2, according to the recommendations of the IDEA, an individualized educational program (IEP) needs to be developed within thirty days of the placement of a student with disabilities, and should be reviewed prior to the beginning of the school year and at least once during the school year. For meeting with the IDEA requirements, an ideal IEP should include a description of the student's present level of functioning, annual and short-term instructional objectives, specific educational services to be provided (e.g., parent training, counseling), projected dates for the initiation and duration of services, and criteria for evaluating annual progress.

According to Collier and Kalk (1989), teachers, parents and specialists need to collaborate in developing the IEP, which should be based not only in results in standardized tests but also on qualitative assessment procedures that will help teachers to link assessment and instruction. Collier and Kalk recommended four steps for developing the IEP: identification of needs, objectives, methods, and evaluation. Objectives should be described very clearly in lesson plans, detailing what the student needs to learn and what the student will be able to do when the objectives of the lessons are met. Broader goals within the educational program that will serve as an umbrella for the more specific objectives of each lesson plan also need to be described. The sequence of the lessons, the scope of the curriculum, and realistic time lines for the units also need to be developed. The student needs to be given developmental time for acquiring the preskills needed for the sequence of lesson plans in the curriculum, the teaching and reteaching, and the reevaluation of the student's skills. Appropriate instructional methods and strategies for CLD students for meeting the objectives of the educational program and individual lesson plans also need to be carefully planned.

Six specific considerations for selecting instructional strategies and methods have been suggested by Collier and Kalk (1989):

1. Careful selection of language(s) of instruction based on results on language proficiency and dominance testing (ideally using qualitative assessment methods, as recommended in Chapter 5)
2. Choice of the teachers who are responsible for the accomplishment of specific objectives within the educational program and lesson plans (in the case of regular classroom teachers who are team teaching with special education, resource, or ESL teachers)
3. Assignment of responsibility of different phases of instruction (i.e., initiation, application, remediation, and maintenance) to various team teachers
4. Consideration of the students' strengths and weaknesses in relation to their cognitive styles
5. Selection of an optimal time for the accomplishment of each objective within the educational program and specific lesson plans
6. Integration of all the specific considerations listed above, especially centered around the students' cultural and linguistic background

In addition, according to Collier and Kalk (1989), evaluation is also an important component of the IEP and must be part of each lesson. In order to link assessment and instruction, the use of qualitative assessment methods by the classroom teacher should be emphasized (see Chapter 5). In the next chapter, a recommended educational program with its corresponding instructional model, program, and objectives will be explained. In addition, specific lesson plans that follow the guidelines for linking assessment and instruction presented in this chapter will also be given as examples.

REFERENCES

Au, K. H. (1979). Using the experience-text relationship with minority children. *Reading Teacher, 28* (8), 102–108.

Berger, E. H. (1981). *Parents as partners in education—The school and home working together.* St. Louis: Mosby.

Blank, M., & Franklin, E. (1980). Dialogue with preschoolers: A cognitively based system of assessment. *Applied Psycholinguistics, 1,* 127–150.

Cohen, L. G., & Spenciner, L. J. (1995). *Assessment of young children.* New York: Longman.

Collier, C., & Kalk, M. (1989). Bilingual special education curriculum development. In L. M. Baca & H. T. Cervantes (Eds.), *The bilingual special education interface* (2nd ed., pp. 205–229). Columbus, OH: Merrill.

Commins, N. L., & Miramontes, O. F. (1989). Perceived and actual linguistic competence: A descriptive study of four low-achieving Hispanic bilingual students. *American Educational Research Journal, 26* (4), 443–472.

Dale, D. C. (1985). *Bilingual books in Spanish and English for children.* Littlewood, CO: Libraries Unlimited.

Damico, J. S. (1991). Descriptive assessment of communicative ability in limited English proficient students. In E. V. Hamayan & J. S. Damico (Eds.), *Limiting bias in the assessment of bilingual students* (pp. 157–218). Austin, TX: Pro-Ed.

De Avila, E., & Havassy, B. (1974, November-December). The testing of minority children—A neopiagetian approach. *Today's Education, 4,* 133–145.

Education for all Handicapped Children Act of 1975. P.L. 94–142, 89 Stat. 773.

Erickson, J. G., & Iglesias, A. (1986). Assessment of communication disorders in non-English proficient children. In O. L. Taylor (Ed). *Nature of communication disorders in culturally and linguistically diverse populations.* (pp. 176–201). San Diego: College Hill Press.

Faltis, C. (1989). Spanish language cooperation-fostering storybooks for language-minority children in bilingual programs. *Journal of Educational Issues of Language-Minority Students, 5,* 46–55.

Gillmore, G., & Dickerson, A. D. (1980). The relationship between instruments used for identifying children of limited English proficiency (LEP) in Texas. *Bilingual Resources, 3,* 16–29.

Gonzalez, V. (1993). Assessment of language-minority students: An awakening experience. *NABE News, 17* (3), 9–10, 26.

Gonzalez, V., & Yawkey, T. D. (1993). The assessment of culturally and linguistically different students: Celebrating change. *Educational Horizons, 72*(1), 41–49.

Gonzalez, V., & Yawkey, T. D. (1994). Influence of cognitive linguistic and sociocultural factors on literacy and biliteracy in young bilingual children. *Education Journal, 30*(10), 230–239.

Goodman, K. (1986). *What's whole in whole language.* Portsmouth, NH: Heinemann.

Healey, W. C., Ackerman, B. L., Chappell, C. R., Perrin, K. L., & Stormer, J. (1981). *The prevalence of communication disorders: A review of the literature.* Rockville, MD: American Speech, Language, and Hearing Association.

Hernandez, J. S. (1991). Assisted performance in reading comprehension strategies with non-English proficient students. *Journal of Educational Issues of Language Minority Students, 8,* 91–112.

Hopkins, K. D., & Stanley, J. C. (1981). *Educational and psychological measurement and evaluation* (6th ed.). Englewood Cliffs, NJ: Prentice-Hall.

Hwambo, Y., & Yawkey, T. D. (1995). Constructivist schooling at early and middle grades: Some key elements that work. *Contemporary Education.*

Improving America's Schools Act of 1994, P.L. 103-382, 108 Stat. 3518.

Individuals with Disabilities Education Act of 1990, P.L. 101-476, 104 Stat. 1103.

Johnson, J. E., Christie, J., & Yawkey, T. D. (1987). *Play and early childhood development.* Glenview, IL: Scott, Foresman.

Kuhlman, W. A., Bastian, M., Bartolome, L., & Barrios, M. (1993). Emerging literacy in a two-way bilingual first grade classroom. In L. M. Malave (Ed.), *Annual Conference Journal: NABE '90–'91* (pp. 45–59). Washington, DC: National Association for Bilingual Education.

Lapp, D., & Flood, J. (1993). *Teaching reading to every child.* New York: Macmillan.

Maldonado-Colón, E. (1991). Development of second learners' linguistic and cognitive abilities. *Journal of Educational Issues of Language Minority Students, 9,* 37–48.

Mercer, J. (1973). *Labeling the mentally retarded.* Berkeley: University of California Press.

Mercer, J. (1980). Testing and assessment practices in multiethnic education. In J. Banks & B. Shin (Eds.), *Education in the 80's: Multiethnic education,* (pp. 177–199). Washington, DC: National Education Association.

Moustafa, M. (1980). Picture books for oral language development for non-English speaking students. *Reading Teacher, 33* (9), 914–919.

Oller, J. W. Jr., & Perkins, K. (1978). *Language in education: Testing the tests.* Rowley, MA: Newbury House.

Peters, D. L., Neisworth, J. T. & Yawkey, T. D. (1985). *Early childhood education: From theory to practice.* Monterey, CA: Brooks-Cole.

Petrykowski, J. (1990). *Twenty-two major teaching/learning strategies from Title VII Project P.I.A.G.E.T. for use with young bilingual children.* University Park: The Pennsylvania State University.

Petrykowski, J. (1992). *Twenty-two major teaching/learning strategies from Title VII Project P.I.A.G.E.T. for use with young bilingual children* (Technical Paper No. 280). University Park: The Pennsylvania State University.

Piaget, J. (1964). *The early growth of logic in the child: Classification and seriation.* New York: Columbia University Press.

Piaget, J. (1965). *Play, dreams, and imitiation in childhood.* New York: Norton.

Puckett, M. B., & Black, T. K. (1994). *Authentic assessment of the young child: Celebrating development and learning.* New York: Macmillan.

Russell, N. L., & Ortiz, A. A. (1989). Assessment and instruction within a dialogue model of communication (Part II). *Bilingual Special Education Newsletter, 5,* 1–3.

Shannon, P. (1986). Hidden within the pages: A study of social perspective in young children's favorite books. *Reading Teacher, 39* (7), 656–663.

Srihdar, K. K. (1980). Language testing in bilingual education: A critical analysis. *Bilingual Resources, 3,* 30–36.

Stauffer, R. G. (1986). *The language-experience approach to the teaching of reading.* New York: Harper & Row.

Tinajero, J. V., & Calderon, M. E. (1988). Language-experience approach plus. *Educational Issues of Language Minority Students, 2,* 3–45.

Trawick-Smith, J. (1994). *Interactions in the classroom: Facilitating play in the early years.* New York: Macmillan.

Trostle, S., & Yawkey, T. D. (1990). *Integrated learning activities for young children.* Boston: Allyn and Bacon.

Vygotsky, L. S. (1978). *Mind in society: The development of psychological processes.* Cambridge, MA: Harvard University Press.

Walsh, D., & Paul, R. W. (1968). *The goal of critical thinking: From educational ideal to educational reality.* Washington, DC: American Federation of Teachers.

Weikart, D. P., Rogers, L., Adcock, C., & McClelland, D. (1971). *The cognitively oriented curriculum.* Urbana: University of Illinois Press.

Wong-Fillmore, L. (1986). Teaching bilingual learners. In M. C. Wittrock (Ed.), *Handbook of research on teaching* (3rd ed., pp. 648–685). New York: Macmillan.

Yawkey, T. D. (1992a). *1987–1990 Three Year Report of Title VII Academic Excellence Project P.I.A.G.E.T. Cycle I* (Technical Report 295). University Park: The Pennsylvania State University.

Yawkey, T. D. (1992b). *Title VII Academic Excellence P.I.A.G.E.T.* Proposal submitted to the U.S. Department of Education, Office of Bilingual Education and Minority Languages Affairs, Washington, DC.

Yawkey, T. D., Askov, E. N., Cartwright, C. A., Dupuis, M. M., Fairchild, S. H., & Yawkey, M. L. (1981). *Language arts and the young child.* Itasca, IL: Peacock.

Yawkey, T. D., Gonzalez, V., & Juan, Y. (1994). Literacy and biliteracy strategies and approaches for young culturally and linguistically diverse children: Academic Excellence P.I.A.G.E.T. comes alive. *Journal of Reading Improvement, 31* (3), 130–141.

Yawkey, T. D., & Juan, Y. (1993). Linking assessment and instruction with language-minority students: Extending the match. *NABE News, 17*(3), 9, 18, 34.

Yawkey, T. D., & Trostle, S. (1982). *Learning is child's play.* Provo, UT: Brigham Young University Press.

Zirkel, P. A. (1976). "The why's" and ways of testing bilinguality before teaching bilingually. *The Elementary School Journal, 3,* 323–330.

7

HOW TO INSTRUCT CLD STUDENTS

In this chapter three current educational problems will be discussed: (1) the need for better educational programs for CLD students; (2) the lack of a common philosophy for the placement of CLD students across schools, school districts, states, and the nation; and (3) early inclusion of CLD students. In addition, a multidimensional bilingual educational program developed by Virginia Gonzalez for young CLD students will be presented, including the underlying theoretical model, assessment and instructional needs and objectives, instructional model and program, sample activities, educators' training, and parents' orientation. Emphasis will be given to planning and designing individual educational programs (IEPs), taking into account multidimensional and interacting factors stemming from cognitive, linguistic, sociocultural, and affective domains that affect the development of CLD students. Valuable characteristics of this multidimensional educational program are that it can be adapted for CLD students who have different native language and cultural backgrounds, and that it can be used with the qualitative assessment method described in Chapter 5 with the objective of linking assessment with instruction.

The multidimensional bilingual educational program proposed has as a major philosophical assumption that educators facilitate learning when they take into consideration the idiosyncratic cognitive, sociocultural, linguistic, and affective characteristics of CLD students. In this way educators are helping CLD students achieve at their maximum learning potentials. Thus, educators implementing multidimensional instructional programs need to be aware of linguistic and cultural minority issues, and need to have critical knowledge for developing educational procedures tailored to the needs of CLD students (see Chapter 3 for an extended discussion of this topic).

This chapter is related to the vision of this book because the "ethnic educator" model that we propose and endorse has as a major premise the use of

166

qualitative measurements for linking assessment with instruction. Moreover, providing educational programs that take into consideration the interaction between internal maturational and developmental factors of CLD students as well as the external context of formal and informal education is also endorsed by the "ethnic educator" model. Furthermore, the multidimensional developmental educational program presented in this chapter assumes, like the "ethnic educator" model, that there is a dynamic interaction across developmental domains, such as emotional/affective, social, moral, cognitive, linguistic, motor, and physical. Thus, this chapter is intimately connected to the "ethnic educator" philosophy endorsed in the vision for this book.

THE NEED FOR BETTER EDUCATIONAL PROGRAMS FOR CLD STUDENTS

Presently, a major educational problem is the need to develop better educational programs to stimulate the development of CLD students by linking assessment, diagnosis, and placement with instruction from a multidimensional perspective. Thus, we consider that the differential diagnosis between genuine disabilities, giftedness, and the normal process of learning English as a second language has to be conducted as a double and parallel process of assessment and instruction.

Several authors have pointed out current needs in the education of CLD students. For instance, as Rodríguez (1988) asserted, educational programs that take into account cognitive, linguistic, personality, and sociocultural factors have not been developed or proven effective for CLD students. Moreover, Rodriguez suggested three factors that indicate major needs in the education of CLD students:

1. Overrepresentation of CLD students in the classes for the mildly handicapped and their underrepresentation in the gifted classes
2. Inappropriate policies and procedures for assessment and instruction
3. Lack of minority personnel

Sosa (1990) pointed out the need for community programs that prevent the high underachievement and dropout rates of CLD students in American public schools. These community programs begin at the preschool level by seeking the enrichment of young CLD students through exposure to experiences in multiple developmental areas (i.e., motor, linguistic, cognitive, emotional, moral, and social). Peers, adults, and parents counsel CLD students individually about setting goals, being responsible, and prioritizing demands. It is also very important that community programs validate the language and culture of students' homes, facilitate other support needed to assure school attendance (e.g., meals, transportation, and child care), and celebrate students' accomplishments publicly.

Moreover, as Sosa (1990) noted, community programs train parents and school personnel in how to stimulate competence in CLD students by enhancing their self-esteem, personal communication, and aspirations through

1. Making students feel valued and supported
2. Providing minority role models
3. Establishing support groups

Another need for CLD students is their engagement in science, mathematics, and engineering programs that are compatible with their home, community, and school environments. There is need for a culturally relevant curriculum for CLD students, because the materials available for the science curriculum taught in public schools reflect an ethnocentric Western orientation. CLD students will develop an interest in science as a career if they are presented with a wider diversity of examples from different cultures.

Furthermore, as mentioned in Chapter 3, the establishment of a curriculum that meets the needs of CLD students has been a difficult endeavor for the American educational system since its creation, despite the multicultural nature of this nation. As discussed in Chapter 2, an historic account of bilingual education programs in contemporary American society portrays a recent revitalization of bilingual education due to research studies conducted with CLD students and to the advocacy efforts of various immigrant groups.

In summary, there is need to develop instructional materials and curricula that meet the different cultural and linguistic individual characteristics of CLD students as reflected in their developmental and learning processes. At present, the curriculum methodologies and content being used for CLD students are not sensitive to their idiosyncratic needs, and therefore the external learning environment is not optimizing their internal learning potential.

THE LACK OF A COMMON PHILOSOPHY FOR THE PLACEMENT OF CLD STUDENTS ACROSS SCHOOLS, SCHOOL DISTRICTS, STATES, AND THE NATION

A second major educational problem at present is the existence of disparate underlying philosophies in educational programs that lead to different diagnostic and placement decisions for CLD students. As a result, contradictory educational outcomes and rates of success in different school districts and local schools are obtained. A number of studies have been conducted to evaluate how current educational programs serve CLD students in the public schools. One of the most important studies was conducted by Ramirez, Yuen, Ramey, and Pasta (1990), who compared the effectiveness of the structured English immersion and late-exit Transitional Bilingual Education (TBE) with the early-exit TBE. This longitudinal study included over 2,300 Spanish-speaking students in 554 classrooms from kindergarten to sixth grade in New York, New Jersey, Florida, Texas, and California. Findings were consistent and can be summarized in the following patterns:

1. Achievement in mathematics and in English language and reading skills was comparable in the English immersion and early-exit TBE.
2. Students in the late-exit TBE showed the greatest growth in mathematics, English language, and reading skills.

Thus, the Ramirez et al. (1990) report shows that a successful bilingual program would give the native language a much more important role than is typically done in TBE, which might enable CLD students to achieve at levels comparable to those of majority students. Even though some bilingual educational programs are more successful than others, mainstreaming is still one of the most important objectives of most educational programs for CLD students (De George, 1988). Moreover, educational programs have implicit as well as explicit curricula for serving CLD students in bilingual, special education, bilingual special education, and regular education classrooms. The implicit curriculum will be related to unstated attitudes, cultural values, belief systems, and philosophies held by educators toward CLD students. This implicit curriculum also has been called the "school culture," and can be considered the most important factor affecting the quality of bilingual, special, and mainstream programs serving CLD students. The explicit curriculum refers to the actual educational materials and programs selected as well as the overt messages conveyed by educators. In fact, a genuine school restructuring process that would lead to equality of education for CLD students involves a change in both the implicit and the explicit curriculum.

However, the definitions of language proficiency vary across districts and schools because they are based on different traditional and contemporary assessment and instructional approaches (see Chapter 3 for a discussion of assessment approaches), and a number of different standardized and qualitative assessment procedures are selected at the local level, which originate contradictory findings. As discussed in Chapter 3, the interpretation of these contradictory findings is related to theoretical and philosophical approaches, and to evaluators' attitudes and belief systems. At the same time, the criteria used for identifying and exiting CLD students from specialized academic programs varies across school districts. As discussed in Chapter 2, the expanded guidelines of the Title VI of the Civil Right Act of 1964, issued in the Department of Health, Education, and Welfare (HEW), prohibit placing students in special education on the basis of criteria that reflect English skills and grouping students based on their language abilities, which may result in permanent tracking.

Moreover, the Bilingual Education Act, amended most recently in the Improving America's Schools Act of 1994, provides several reasons for providing educational programs for students of limited English proficiency (LEP). Most important issues supported by this law relate to the value of developing students' first language *and* the English language to help them become productive members of society, develop self-esteem and content knowledge learning, reduce dropout rates and low median years of education, and involve parents and the community in the education process effectively.

In sum, of the many problems that were problematic back in the late 1960s and are still present today, we have discussed inappropriate assessment and instructional procedures for serving CLD students, and the disproportionate representation of CLD students who are still in the process of learning English as a second language in special education, including the categories of mentally retarded, gifted, and talented. (In this book, we prefer to use the label "in the process of learning English as a second language," rather than the term "limited English proficient," which is used in legislation, because of its negative connotation. See Chapter 1 for an expanded discussion of this topic.)

EARLY MAINSTREAMING OF CLD STUDENTS

Another major educational problem is that different educational programs serve their CLD students differently, and as a result the success rates and achievement outcomes of these students are different. For De George (1988), mainstreaming into English-only classes is a placement decision that includes a set of sequential procedures that may encompass:

1. Defining placement decisions
2. Determining student needs and other information required to make those decisions
3. Developing and implementing procedures and instruments for gathering the information
4. Collecting, analyzing, and interpreting the information

For CLD students, we need to consider that they simultaneously go through the stages of developing interpersonal communication skills, mastering subject-area content and skills, and acquiring academic language proficiency for each subject, all in their second language. Thus, CLD students need some time to develop their communicative abilities and basic literacy skills in English before they can start using English as a tool for learning subject matter or begin thinking in the English language. According to Cummins (1980, 1984), academic language proficiency involves using a specific language, such as English, as a medium of thought or construction of knowledge, rather than as a means of interpersonal communication. Academic language will become more decontextualized and thus more cognitively demanding as the student advances in grade level. Taking these factors of second-language learning into account helps schools develop appropriate instructional sequences that provide CLD students with the necessary opportunities for developing academic language proficiency in English without sacrificing the acquisition of content areas.

Many times deciding whether a student is ready to be mainstreamed in an all-English class is based solely on the level of oral English language proficiency. However, Chamot and O'Malley (1986) have argued that the students' placement should be decided on the basis of the demands that will be made upon them in mainstream subject classes in terms of cognitive and linguistic skills. Chamot and O'Malley suggest developing a "bridge" curriculum to facilitate the transition from an ESL or bilingual program to the mainstream. This "bridge" curriculum would include ESL instruction with a focus on the content areas and training in learning strategies for study and learning skills improvement.

According to De George (1988), the framework for determining the language demands made by the mainstream classroom encompasses:

1. The selection of subject areas to be taught
2. The analysis of each subject area by content
3. The identification of prerequisite cognitive skills needed to allow CLD students to benefit from instruction in each subject
4. The analysis of each mainstream subject area for linguistic components (e.g., technical vocabulary, language structures and functions, and discourse features)

In sum, the criteria for identifying which CLD students should be included in regular education classrooms refer to the following issues:

1. A multiple instrument approach
2. A common conceptualization of language proficiency in assessment methods that will match the educational programs used
3. A revision of the cognitive and English linguistic abilities that will be demanded upon the CLD students in order to succeed in mainstream subject-area classrooms

In summary, as Wong-Fillmore (1986) has pointed out, it is common for CLD students coming from low socioeconomic status to experience difficulty with academic language. The language skills of these CLD students, although adequate for communicating in their homes and communities, do not match the type of language spoken by teachers. Thus, before any attempt is made for mainstreaming these students, they require a language development program in order to develop the academic language needed in the classroom context. The educational program proposed in this chapter has a developmental philosophy that aims to develop both languages as a method for teaching and stimulating multidimensional developmental areas in CLD students. Mainstreaming, if at all necessary, can be made possible by developing higher thinking skills in both languages.

A MULTIDIMENSIONAL BILINGUAL EDUCATIONAL PROGRAM FOR YOUNG CLD STUDENTS

Model

Presently, the referral and placement procedures legally required by federal and state laws across the United States have not resolved assessment and instructional issues affecting CLD students (see Chapter 2). These students continue to be misdiagnosed and misplaced in special education classes in public schools. The current problem may be attributed to educational programs that focus only on the linguistic aspects of the developmental process. These educational programs typically underemphasize or ignore the influence of cognitive, affective, and sociocultural factors in the process of first- and second-language learning. When these educational programs that focus only on the linguistic aspects of the developmental process are used, the learning problems that have been identified in CLD students need not arise. Many CLD students are mislabeled as having a learning disability, mental retardation, or another disability due to lack of models and assessment methods that represent their linguistic and cultural backgrounds. In addition, evaluators' and educators' attitudes, beliefs, values, and cultural and linguistic knowledge also affect current mislabeling and misdiagnosis practices (see Chapter 3).

The multidimensional bilingual educational program proposed here considers that cognitive and linguistic development in the first language is needed to acquire the second language and be able to use both languages as methods for teaching and learning. Moreover, this multidimensional educational program is based on a model developed by Gonzalez (1991, 1994, 1995) that has a strong theoretical foundation and that can be adapted for any language-minority group. In the model, it is assumed that bilingual educational programs should include the influence of linguistic, cultural, and affective factors on cognitive development when serving CLD students. Thus, this multidimensional bilingual educational program assumes that the essence of learning a language is the construction of concepts that correspond to the interaction of cognitive, affective, linguistic, and sociocultural factors. This multidimensional interaction leads to the formation of nonverbal or abstract concepts, sociocultural symbolic meanings, and verbal concepts in first and second language. Conceptual learning occurs through verbal and nonverbal representations of concepts that stand as mediational symbols of cognitive-linguistic processes. Verbal and nonverbal instructional activities are used for designing the content areas, stimuli, and responses of the educational program. Then, conceptual learning is emphasized as first- and second-language learning is considered an active process in which cognitive, affective, and sociocultural factors have an influence. In the model underlying the proposed multidimensional educational program, conceptual learning is considered the central language learning process that shows a double interaction between language and cognition:

1. The acquisition of new verbal knowledge can influence the formation of new nonverbal concepts.
2. The acquisition of new nonverbal knowledge can influence the formation of new verbal concepts.

In the model, affective and cognitive processes are described in part in adaptations from Piagetian theory terms (Piaget, 1965, 1967; Sinclair-de-Zwart, 1969). Specifically the cognitive operations, the affective processes, the emphasis on the generation of new knowledge through assimilation and accommodation processes, and the nonverbal assessment approach are borrowed from neo-Piagetian adaptations. However, the proposed educational program also departs from traditional and from neo-Piagetian views because it proposes a multidimensional interaction between language, cognition, and culture that influences conceptual learning. That is, this bilingual educational program includes the influence of linguistic, affective, and sociocultural factors on language and conceptual learning. It holds that language can be used for the generation of new knowledge, a major difference with the traditional Piagetian theory, in which cognitive development is considered to be the basis for language development and language is seen only as a tool for the crystallization of cognitive processes. Thus, in the traditional Piagetian theory, language cannot be used for the generation of new knowledge.

Even though neo-Piagetian views acknowledge the influence of language on cognition, the model proposed departs from this view by arguing that language represents linguistic structures and sociocultural symbolic meanings that are sometimes common or different between languages, as Spanish and English. That is, the process of concept formation in the first and second languages will vary depending on the conceptual complexity and sociocultural context of the use of the linguistic structures. Any language carries with it sociocultural symbolic meanings that can be reflected or absent in its linguistic structures. Languages differ in which aspects of meaning they represent directly in their structures, and this fact influences the formation of symbolic meanings and semantic categories. Learning a language means learning a new underlying concept that is related to the sociocultural symbolic meanings of the community. Whether a specific concept will be represented with a linguistic structure and marker and its corresponding symbolic meanings will depend on its cultural value. This process is reflected in the historical social development of linguistic structures. The semantic categories that a child constructs may develop better in one language than in the other because of the duplicity of the symbolic meanings of linguistic conventions made by the sociocultural communities. This means that:

1. If the linguistic structure and markers and/or symbolic meanings of linguistic conventions exist in both languages, children will instantiate the representation of their first into their second language.
2. If the linguistic structure and markers and/or symbolic meanings of linguistic conventions exist only in the second language, children will have to construct new abstract representations that constitute new semantic categories.

These two complementary processes—the instantiation of a concept already constructed in one language to the other and the construction of a new concept for the unique sociocultural symbolic meanings of one of the languages of bilingual children—have to be taken into consideration in the development of bilingual programs. It is important to stimulate the formation of new concepts and not only the acquisition of new labels in the language. If children have constructed new concepts, they can access and use these symbolic representations for achieving further levels of cognitive development. Children can use language for the acquisition of new knowledge when the language learning process has stimulated conceptual learning.

In summary, this new model that integrates cognitive, cultural, and linguistic variables has direct practical implications for improving current assessment practices with CLD students and for linking assessment with instruction. Furthermore, as explained in Chapter 5, the tasks created for developing the conceptual learning model have been used as an alternative qualitative assessment method for accurately identifying gifted bilingual Hispanic children in a large school district in the southwestern United States (see, e.g., Gonzalez, Bauerle, & Felix-Holt, 1994).

AN INSTRUCTIONAL PROGRAM PROPOSED

In the multidimensional bilingual educational program, students are immersed in a cognitive and affective stimulating environment that will lead them to high levels of achievement. They are encouraged to develop a positive attitude toward speaking both languages, and a high motivational level for using both the first and second language for learning. Furthermore, students are taught how to learn through the use of cognitive, linguistic, and affective strategies. The focus of instruction is on concept development through discovery and problem-solving activities that lead to flexibility of thinking and creativity. In addition, learning through metaphor is emphasized as a mechanism for the construction of new nonverbal and verbal sociocultural symbolic representations of both languages. Cognitive (perception, memory, and operations), linguistic (phonology, lexicon, morphosyntaxis, semantics), affective (intentionality, realism), and social (reciprocity, social adaptation) processes are stimulated simultaneously through holistic activities at different levels (e.g., perception, motor abilities, labeling, defining, peer work, interiorization of social values). Figure 7.1 (on p. 176) describes the model of the multidimensional bilingual educational program.

Thus, the model has an epistemological cognitive orientation that considers learning as an active process in which concepts are constructed through cognitive, affective, and symbolic processes that represent sociocultural factors reflected in the language. That is, in this model it is considered important to generate new concepts so that not only the assimilation of concepts but also the accommodation of concepts for the generation of new knowledge is stimulated. The model thus has a developmental perspective, as both languages are used as a method of instruction, with competency in both languages and the mastery of subject matter being pursued at the same time. The philosophy underlying this model also views bilingualism as an enrichment that can benefit minority and majority students (see the definition of developmental bilingual education programs in Chapter 2). Moreover, the multidimensional bilingual education program assures equal educational opportunity by providing meaningful education in the native language as well as appropriate education across the curriculum areas.

There are two main categories of materials and responses, nonverbal and verbal (see Figure 7.2 on p. 177). Each category includes two types of materials:

1. Auditory, which are primarily sounds and phonemes for stimulating the cognitive process of auditory discrimination as well as linguistic processes and contents
2. Visual, which are primarily manipulative concrete objects, graphic symbols, pictures, and graphemes for stimulating operational cognitive processes as perception and memory as well as linguistic processes and content

FIGURE 7.1   The Instructional Model of the Multidimensional Bilingual Educational Method

Cognitive Processes	Levels of Cognitive Processes
Perception	Acquisition of voluntary motor abilities
Memory	Automatization of motor abilities
Operations	Kinesthetic perception
	Auditory discrimination of sounds
	Auditory discrimination of phonemes
	Visual discrimination of graphemes and figure ground
	Body image
	Automatic memory of nonverbal and verbal information
	Constructive memory of nonverbal information and analysis/synthesis
	Concept construction (classification, seriation, space and time, number, causality, conservation, reversibility, assimilation, and accommodation)
Linguistic Processes	**Levels of Linguistic Processes**
Phonology	Verbal concept formation
Lexicon	Labeling
Morphosyntaxis	Defining
Semantics	Semantic concepts
Affective Processes	**Levels of Affective Processes**
Cooperation	Peer work
Intentionality and realism	Understanding internal and external factors of social behaviors
	Understanding causes and intention of social behaviors
Reciprocity	Mutual respect
Social adaptation (self-help skills, socialization, communication)	Responsibility for social roles
	Interiorization of social values

All the materials selected should represent familiar content in the first and second language of the student. Familiar and unambiguous stimuli are useful for assessing learning and for stimulating overlearning when instructing CLD students. Novel stimuli and ambiguous problem-solving tasks are useful for assessing potential for learning, and for enhancing conceptual learning, creativity, and learning transfer to real-life situations when instructing CLD students. The inclusion of verbal as well as nonverbal tasks and responses from students is very important, as some CLD students will

FIGURE 7.2   The Instructional Program of the Multidimensional Bilingual Educational Method

Content Areas	Stimuli	Responses
Linguistic listening	Verbal	Verbal
	Auditory	
Speaking	Nonverbal	Nonverbal
Reading	Visual	
Writing	Tactile	
	Kinesthetic	

be in the process of developing proficiency in both languages, and they will be more familiar with one of the two cultural systems.

Specific Objectives and Sample Activities

The proposed multidimensional bilingual educational program tries to link appropriate and accurate assessment procedures with instructional objectives for better serving CLD students' wholistic needs. The multidimensional bilingual educational program includes as its objectives:

1. To set the developmental prerequisites for accomplishing tasks in order to maximize success and minimize failure in the educational process
2. To use qualitative assessment procedures, such as nonverbal classification tasks, for the planning of teaching activities and the development of instructional materials
3. To develop cognitive and affective processes through the use of the first and second language and culture as a method of teaching
4. To consider cognitive, affective, and linguistic development as parallel processes
5. To improve first- and second-language proficiency through conceptual learning
6. To develop an individualized educational program (IEP) according to the strengths and weaknesses of the students in terms of cognitive, affective, and language development
7. To select instructional materials and teaching strategies according to students' cognitive and linguistic developmental levels
8. To use instructional materials and teaching strategies that encompass a holistic view of the students' channels for stimuli perception (visual, auditory, kinesthetic, etc.)
9. To pace instruction according to the students' learning needs

10. To allow overlearning through extended periods of practice for the assimilation of new content
11. To emphasize the formation of new concepts through discovery and exploration for the stimulation of accommodation processes
12. To develop students' awareness of their characteristics as learners so that they can learn how to use appropriate metacognitive, cognitive, and affective strategies for enhancing the learning process
13. To adapt instruction according to the symbolic sociocultural representations that are part of the students' sociocultural background in their first and second language
14. To stimulate the formation of positive attitudes, high motivation, high self-expectations, and high self-esteem toward learning both languages and cultures through instructional activities
15. To stimulate affective processes as important sources of energy and motivation for accomplishing cognitive tasks
16. To involve parents in the educational process by planned home orientation and support for getting to know their children's needs better

Specific objectives for implementing the multidimensional bilingual educational program involve cognitive, linguistic, sociocultural, and affective processes that interact in holistic instructional activities:

1. Cognitive processes include perception, memory, and concept formation processes (i.e., the acquisition of voluntary motor abilities; automatization and generalization of motor abilities; auditory discrimination of sounds and phonemes; concept construction of assimilation and accommodation, problem-solving, classification, seriation, number, and space)
2. Language processes include verbal concept formation, labeling, defining, and describing abilities performed using listening, speaking, reading, and writing abilities
3. Affective processes include intentionality, realism, and reciprocity, processes that are stimulated simultaneously through holistic activities at different levels (e.g., peer work, cooperation). Sociocultural processes include social adaptation and the interiorization of social values and rules

Most of the time, cognitive and linguistic processes interact when performing instructional activities such as the classification of objects based on their shape, color, size, texture, and weight. Classification tasks give children the opportunity to use language for describing objects based on their similarities and/or differences. Furthermore, classification tasks are also associated with prereading skills, such as the recognition and clustering of letters based on similarities and/or differences in their shapes and orientation in relation to spatial relations. In fact, cognitive processes underlying the concepts of body image and topological space are related to prereading skills. For example, children need to develop kinesthetic perception by performing movements associated with the position of their body in relation to a referent in space (right/left and up/down). Another interactive activity in which children use cognitive and linguistic processes is ordering objects in a sequence by developing the concept of seriation. For instance, given stimuli in a sequential order, children have to identify the elements and the total unit to which they belong (part-whole relationships) through motor, graphic, and verbal responses. By using different kinds of responses, children are using their nonverbal cognitive skills (e.g., sorting objects based on a sequential order) and verbal skills (e.g., writing, reading, speaking, listening) in both languages. The use of different symbols for representing concepts allows children to assimilate concepts in both languages at a higher developmental level, as they can understand the presence of arbitrary cultural labels for otherwise similar concepts. This latter ability is called metalinguistic awareness, a positive outcome of becoming bilingual and bicognitive through forming concepts in both languages that have deeper nonverbal conceptual foundations.

Other examples of activities in which cognitive and linguistic processes interact are the acquisition, automatization, and generalization of voluntary motor abilities; the development of language processes; and the acquisition of the concepts of number and space. For the case of voluntary motor abilities, children have to accomplish motor sequences for the representation of letters and numbers, and to practice the motor sequences already acquired in new contexts while receiving feedback. For the development of language processes, children have to identify the sounds of nature and the environment, label sounds of their body, and differentiate phonemes in meaningful words. For concept of number, children need to use their language abilities in order to count items that belong to sets and classes, to make comparisons and correspondences of sets of objects, to identify the order of sequences of objects, to order objects according to symmetrical and asymmetrical properties, to describe the relationships among objects, and to count groups and subgroups of objects. For the concept of space, children have to develop the topological concept (i.e., up/down, forward/backward, above/behind, near/far, in/out, first/last, between/among, across/along), to place themselves in their environment, to form spatial relationships through the perception and description of objects from different spatial perspectives, to move and to recognize people and objects in space, to identify the sequence of their daily activities (present, past, and future), and to establish relations in space and time simultaneously (i.e., slow/fast, short time/long time).

Examples of activities that involve the interaction of affective, sociocultural, cognitive, and linguistic processes include the development of cooperation and social adaptation abilities (i.e., socialization and communication).

By imitating the behavior of other children and adults, establishing interpersonal contacts, and developing feelings of affection and belonging, children integrate their behavior to the peer group, learn to understand different perspectives, acquire social values and flexibility in their social behavior, and develop a critical comprehension of the society's rules. Examples of activities directed at the development of intentionality and realism concepts include understanding the meaning of individual and team activities, trying to match the causes and interactions in the social group to the concrete consequences in the social context, evaluating the internal and external factors that cause behaviors, and taking into account the intentionality of the behavior. Examples of activities designed to stimulate the concepts of reciprocity and socialization include the self-control of behaviors according to social rules and values, the understanding of the meaning of censure as an important cue to behavior modification, and the acceptance of the responsibility for the consequences of one's tasks and social roles.

The first sample activity for illustrating the implementation of the multidimensional bilingual educational program includes:

1. Cognitive processes such as the auditory and visual discrimination of sounds and phonemes
2. Linguistic processes such as the development of new concepts through listening activities
3. Specific objectives involving the discrimination and representation of sounds of the natural environment by body movements and letters; the identification of the cause, origin, function, and context of sounds of the natural environment; the identification of words that rhyme; and the discrimination of phonemes and meanings in words

The second sample activity for the multidimensional bilingual educational program includes:

1. Cognitive processes such as the acquisition of voluntary motor abilities, automatization of motor abilities, body image, automatic memory, and concept construction (i.e., classification, seriation, space, and time)
2. Linguistic processes such as the formation of semantic categories through speaking, writing, and reading activities
3. Specific objectives, namely the discrimination of the characteristics of concrete manipulative objects (e.g., texture, size, shape, weight, color), the classification of objects according to their similarities and differences and the verbal explanation for the classification criteria, the association of written words with objects, the classification of written words according to similarities and differences in spelling, and the sequential ordering of actions according to space and time

The third sample activity for the multidimensional bilingual educational program includes:

1. Cognitive processes such as constructive memory for semantic categories and concept construction (i.e., classification, space, and reversibility).
2. Linguistic processes such as labeling, defining, and semantic categories formation through the use of listening, speaking, reading, and writing activities
3. Affective processes such as cooperation and communication
4. Specific objectives, namely the association of objects and first letters of written words, the reproduction of objects placed according to topological space relations, the formation of classes of objects, the description and definition of objects, and the generation of strategies for classifying objects in idiosyncratic ways

In sum, the specific objectives of the multidimensional bilingual educational program have as a major philosophy the multidimensional interaction of cognitive, linguistic, sociocultural, and affective processes. Some instructional activities showing these holistic processes were given above to illustrate the specific objectives of the proposed educational program.

Educators' Training

Educators of CLD students need to have knowledge of bilingual and special education principles, as these two areas are related to the cognitive, linguistic, sociocultural, and affective factors that influence the process of first- and second-language acquisition in CLD students. Thus, it is proposed that educators should be familiar with the following contents:

1. Second-language processes and models; and assumptions, and philosophies underlying the different models
2. Developmental norms for monolingual and bilingual normal children, and monolingual and bilingual handicapped children
3. Cognitive developmental theories applied to bilingual and special education
4. Affective processes (e.g., attitude towards the second language and culture of CLD students, motivation, interest) involved in the process of learning a second language
5. The development of conceptual learning through metalearning (learning how to learn), creativity (the use of techniques such as metaphor in learning), and learning strategies that students can generalize to other domain-content knowledge

6. Standardized and qualitative assessment methods in order to be familiar with the individual characteristics of students, such as preferred modality for learning (auditory, visual, etc.), strengths and weaknesses, patterns of behavior, and idiosyncratic learning interests

Thus, there is need to have a multidimensional perspective on the interface between cognitive and language development. Part of this multidimensional knowledge involves being aware of the influence of affective processes and sociocultural factors on this cognition-language interface in CLD students. Educators also need to be familiar with the theoretical constructs that underlie behaviors measured by standardized and qualitative assessment methods. These are just some of the most important areas in which educators should have knowledge in order to work successfully in a developmental bilingual program.

There is therefore the need to improve teacher training programs so that educators can provide a more active learning environment for language and cognitive skill development in CLD students (Ramirez, 1991). Tarone and Yule (1989) have pointed out that language teachers are constantly adapting language materials and methods because no two second-language classes are the same and because students have different needs. They concluded that teachers should:

1. Define their own teaching goals in relation to their students' needs
2. Develop practical methods to identify different aspects of their students' needs
3. Be assertive in their professional competence in order to be able to assess critically the claims of theories in the field of second-language acquisition by looking at their own data derived from their practical experiences with their particular group of learners

In relation to knowledge of the cultural and linguistic factors that affect learning, Thonis (1991) noted that teachers who work with CLD students should develop an:

1. Awareness of cultural differences
2. Recognition of language diversity and a view of diversity as a source of enrichment for all students
3. Understanding of the students' realities
4. Sensitivity to the values of families
5. Knowledge of the history and heritage of the group

In addition, Milk (1991) pointed out that the process of training educators should meaningfully reflect the way that teachers should teach to their own students, because teacher trainers function as role models that teacher trainees are interiorizing. Therefore, it is very important to provide educators with firsthand exposure to use the second language as a method of teaching, and to demonstrate relevant methodologies and strategies that teachers should use and adapt in their classrooms. Teachers should be introduced to an immersion experience for the attainment of language proficiency goals through the means of content area instruction from the bilingual curriculum in math, science, social studies, and language arts. Milk emphasized the need to achieve greater integration of theory and practice in teacher preparation. Milk suggested that this objective can be pursued through the development of method courses that stress the interrelationship of theory and practice, and, most importantly, thorough experiential activities including clinical supervision, demonstration, and field-based experiences to supplement course work and seminars.

Milk also pointed out that teacher training programs need to provide a research perspective to teaching so that teachers are stimulated to:

1. Ask relevant questions to solve their real-life problems in their classrooms
2. Use research-generated methods and approaches or guidelines
3. Be able to adapt methods and approaches in order to solve their practical problems

According to Milk, bilingual trainees in this immersion program realize how important is to get to know the specialized vocabulary for each content area as well as the academic language for developing concepts in each subject. In summary, Milk proposed to supplement competency-based goals of teacher training in isolated courses with an integrative model that encompasses methods, approaches, and guidelines developed by research studies with real-life problems in the bilingual classroom.

In addition, several authors have identified positive characteristics that effective teachers of CLD students use in the classroom. Tikunoff (1985) conducted a study that identified the most important features of the effective bilingual programs as:

1. Active teaching
2. Teachers' explicit and consistent communication of their objectives and high expectations to the students
3. Use of the first language and English as a second language for instruction
4. Integration of the development of the second language with ongoing instruction in the content areas
5. Use of the cultural and language background of the students as a method of teaching

Garcia (1988) studied successful bilingual teachers and concluded that they:

1. Provided students with high-level activities and tasks that demanded both creativity and a high degree of cognitive involvement
2. Emphasized the importance of substance and content in teaching, and deemphasized the mastery of specific skills
3. Provided students with a diversity of instructional activities integrating assessment and instruction as well as reading and writing in the context of actual learning activities
4. Strongly encouraged students to use their real-life experiences for learning purposes
5. Worked actively to accomplish autonomy in making curricular decisions within their classrooms and created support networks for implementing their general approach to education

In addition, classes and teachers have their own personalities that interact in a double process that modifies students' and teachers' behaviors in the classrooms. Teachers have to be able to observe and have insights about their own and their students' behaviors. As Brown (1983) stated, "successful teaching requires successful interaction with 'real learners,' and the personal human response that must occur between teacher and learner ultimately relies just as heavily on reflective intuition as it does on careful analysis of the classroom" (p. 56). As a result, teaching relies on a philosophical orientation toward the nature of human learning and as such is more an art rather than a technique. In relation to the need to adapt teaching strategies to the idiosyncratic characteristics of the learners, Merino and Coughran (1991) pointed out that the idea that one method or one educational program could be used for CLD students is no longer popular. Presently, second-language learning is conceptualized as a complex and multidimensional process.

As Politzer (1972) wrote, "pedagogy, research and linguistic theory could probably not deliver 'a general truth' about language teaching but rather [they] could provide a battery of possible procedures from which to choose in addressing the need of the learner'" (p. 152). Brown (1980) suggested that teachers should realize the multidimensionality of the second-language learning process, and that they must develop their own philosophy and theory of second-language acquisition and apply it to their own teaching situations. Thonis (1991) commented that good teachers are willing to modify and adapt current methodologies, approaches, and guidelines derived from research in second language to meet the needs of CLD students.

In sum, novel methods are needed as guidelines that can then be adapted by educators, who must make assertive decisions and have their own philosophy of teaching. Because diagnosis and good teaching are "arts" rather than techniques, educators need to be prepared to face the idiosyncratic personalities of their CLD students.

Parents' Orientation

The multidimensional bilingual educational program proposed in this chapter is developed on the premise that it is very important that parents participate in the educational process, because CLD students will spend most of the time at home. Parents (or guardians) can help when they guide their children at home, and share their experience and knowledge about their children with educators at school. In addition, it is the parents' right to have some information about their child's progress at school in order to help their children at home. Moreover, parents have important knowledge about child care that is transmitted culturally through social agents, such as parents and grandparents, from generation to generation. Thus, parents have an informally acquired knowledge of developmental norms, the importance of early stimulation while doing daily routines with their children (e.g., bathing, feeding, grocery shopping), the appropriateness of talking to their children even in the prelanguage stage, and the relevance of their behavior to their children's development because of imprinting, identification, and role model processes. After all, children spend the most important years of their lives at home, where the most important figures are the parents or other caregivers.

According to Rodríguez (1988), in order to train parents adequately it is necessary to offer workshops where instructional materials are explained and useful techniques that can be used for helping children practice new skills are taught. It is also very important that open communication exists between educators and parents, so that the socialization taking place at home and at school occurs in a parallel and complementary manner. Thus, what is needed is to give orientation, support, and clear guidelines to the parents of CLD students, who are at-risk because of the different cultural backgrounds that are transmitted by their families and the school system (mainstream culture). Many parents need emotional, social, and intellectual nourishment for themselves before they give these ingredients to their children. As Chilman (1968) has remarked, one cannot give what one does not have. Goals for the caregiver should include providing consistency of care, high-quality interactions, and diverse experiences for the child.

The parents' orientation will be provided by a teacher's aid appropriately trained in the model, methods, and techniques used in the multidimensional bilingual educational method. The aid will visit the child's home in order to inform the parents about the cognitive, affective, linguistic, cultural, and social stimulation the child is receiving in school. Training will be given in using daily routines for stimulating the child's development (e.g., peeling apples, sewing buttons, sorting silverware). It is expected that the benefits will reflect on both the parents' and the child's motivation, attitude, and expectations toward themselves. As a result, teamwork will arise among the teacher, the teacher's aid, the parents, and the child. The parents should also be continually informed of the child's performance, because development is a dynamic phenomenon with continuous changes over short periods. Feedback and suggestions in regard to the child's developmental needs should be given to the parents periodically, as the child passes through different stages.

In addition, as discussed in Chapter 2, according to the Individuals with Disabilities Education Act (IDEA), parents need to be informed in writing in their native language at every step in the special education process and need to give their consent to this process. Moreover, parents and their children who disagree with the educational agency decision about placement in special education can challenge the decision through a structured procedure called a due process hearing, as stated by the IDEA. Parents can also request another, independent evaluation. In sum, parents need to participate in the educational process of CLD students. Thus, they must be given orientation, support, and clear guidelines in order to coordinate the efforts toward reciprocal benefits for CLD students at school and at home.

In conclusion, in this chapter we have tried to present an alternative multidimensional educational program that illustrates the developmental principles and assumptions of the "ethnic educator" approach. This proposed program is representing the idiosyncratic needs of CLD students as the explicit educational objectives presented and instructional activities suggested take into consideration the influence of cognitive, cultural, and linguistic factors on their development and learning.

REFERENCES

Brown, H. D. (1980). *Principles of language learning and teaching.* Englewood Cliffs, NJ: Prentice Hall.

Brown, H. D. (1983). From ivory tower to real world: A search for relevance. In J. Alatis, H. Stern, & P. Stevens (Eds.), *Georgetown University Round Table on Language and Linguistics 1983* (pp. 53–58). Washington, DC: Georgetown University Press.

Civil Rights Act of 1964, 42 U.S.C. Section 2000d et seq. (Supp. 1984).

Chamot, A. U., & O'Malley, J. M. (1986). *A cognitive academic language learning approach: An ESL content-based curriculum.* Wheaton, MD: National Clearinghouse for Bilingual Education.

Chilman, C. S. (1968). Poor families and their patterns of child care: Some implications for service programs. In L. C. Dittman (Ed.), *Early childhood care: The new perspective* (57–89). New York: Altherton Press.

Cummins, J. (1980). The entry and exit fallacy. *NABE Journal* 4(3), 25–29.

Cummins, J. (1984). *Bilingualism and special education: Issues in assessment and pedagogy.* San Diego: College Hill Press.

De George, G. P. (1988). Assessment and placement of language minority students: Procedures for mainstreaming. *NEW Focus 3, Winter.* Washington, D.C.: The National Clearinghouse for Bilingual Education (NCBE).

Garcia, E. (1988, January). *Effective schools for Hispanic children: Making the connection.* Keynote address at the annual meeting of the San Antonio Area Association for Bilingual Education, San Antonio, Texas.

Gonzalez, V. (1991). *A model of cognitive, cultural, and linguistic variables affecting bilingual Spanish/English children's development of concepts and language.* Doctoral dissertation, The University of Texas at Austin. (ERIC Document Reproduction Service No. ED 345 562)

Gonzalez, V. (1994). A model of cognitive, cultural, and linguistic variables affecting bilingual Spanish/English children's development of concepts and language. *Hispanic Journal of Behavioral Sciences 16*(4), 396–421.

Gonzalez, V. (1995). Cognition, culture, and language in bilingual children: Conceptual and semantic development. Bethesda, MD: Austin & Winfield.

Gonzalez, V., Bauerle, P., & Felix-Holt, M. (1994). A qualitative assessment method for accurately diagnosing bilingual gifted children. *NABE '92–'93 Annual Conference Journal,* 37–52.

Individuals with Disabilities Education Act of 1990. P. L. 101-476, 104 Stat. 1103.

Improving America's Schools Act of 1994, P.L. 103-382, 108 Stat. 3518.

Merino, B. J., & Coughran, C. C. (1991). Lesson design for teachers of language-minority students: Insights from a case study of curriculum development. In M. E. McGroarty & C. J. Faltis (Eds.) *Languages in school and society: Policy and pedagogy* (67–96). Berlin, Germany: Mouton de Gruyer.

Milk, R. D. (1991). Preparing teachers for effective bilingual instruction. In M. E. McGroarty, & C. J. Faltis (Eds.) *Languages in school and society: Policy and pedagogy* (97–132). Berlin, Germany: Mouton de Gruyer.

Piaget, J. (1965). *Mental imagery in the child: A study of the development of imaginal representation.* New York: Oxford University Press.

Piaget, J. (1967). Piaget's theory. In P. H. Mussen (Ed.), *Carmichael's manual of child psychology:* Vol. 1 (pp. 703–732). New York: John Wiley & Sons.

Piaget, J. (1974). *The language and thought of the child.* New York: New York American Library.

Politzer, R. (1972). *Linguistics and applied linguistics: Aims and methods.* Philadelphia: Center for Curriculum Development.

Ramirez, J. D. (1991). Study finds native language instruction is a plus. *NABE News 14*(5).

Ramirez, J. D., Yuen, S. D., Ramey, D. R., & Pasta, D. J. (1990). *Final Report: Longitudinal study of structured English immersion strategy, early-exit, and late-exit transitional bilingual education programs for language-minority children.* (Submitted to U.S. Department of Education, Contract No. 800-87-0156). San Mateo, CA: Aguirre International.

Rodríguez, R. F. (1988, January). Bilingual special education is appropriate for Mexican-American children with mildly handicapping conditions. *ERIC Clearinghouse on Rural Education and Small Schools Digest.*

Sinclair-de-Zwart, H. (1969). Language acquisition and cognitive development. In T. E. Moore (Ed.), *Cognitive development and the acquisition of language* (pp. 78–134). New York: Academic Press.

Sosa, A. (1990). Making education work for Mexican-Americans: Promising community practices. *ERIC Digest 90.*

Tarone, E., & Yule, G. (1989). *Focus on the language learner.* New York: Oxford University Press.

Thonis, E. W. (1991). Competencies for teachers of language-minority students. In M. E. McGroarty & C. J. Faltis (Eds.) *Languages in school and society: Policy and pedagogy* (179–205). Berlin, Germany: Mouton de Gruyer.

Tikunoff, W. (1985). *Applying significant bilingual instructional features in the classroom.* Rosslyn, VA: National Clearinghouse for Bilingual Education.

Wong-Fillmore, L. (1986). Teaching bilingual learners. In M. C. Wittrock (Ed.), *Handbook of research on teaching* (3rd ed., pp. 648–685). New York: Macmillan.

8

WORKING WITH CLD FAMILIES

Assisting professionals in helping parents of culturally and linguistically diverse (CLD) students to become actively engaged in their children's schooling and learning processes is imperative. If schools are to respond to reform challenges and become more responsive to CLD students' learning and their potential, family involvement becomes the initial objective of every classroom and every school. This chapter relates to the vision statement of this book because the "ethnic researcher" perspective endorsed throughout includes as a major educational component the involvement of CLD students' families in the educational process.

These calls for family involvement in our schools are the increasingly natural outcomes of the decreasing tax dollars for schools and the decreasing achievement scores of American students (*Access to early childhood programs*, 1994). These decreasing scores ultimately imply increasing numbers dropping out or at least repeating grades because of the failure to acquire minimal competencies. Zill (1992a,b) feels that the students who are not succeeding because of these and related conditions are also the ones who are suspended from schools and enrolled in special education. Relatedly, a very high proportion of CLD students are at-risk for dropping out of school. These bleak scenarios of increasing numbers of dropouts, suspended students, and students with other school problems will continue to increase, especially with growing numbers of families immigrating and migrating to this country.

Calls for new paradigm shifts in schooling in the United States are exemplified by American 2000 Goals because they stress the need for family involvement in our schools. Moving from the old paradigm of disenfranchising of the parents to the new goal of empowering them, the American schools are riding the crest of a wave in which parents are now rightfully seen as their children's first and best teachers and as motivators for their children's achievement. This view of families as the initial and best teachers and sound motivators assumes that parents are involved in school activities (Bermudez & Padron, 1990).

With more changes occurring in schools as a response to reform movements and increasing responsibilities for learning and school encouragement falling on families, it is becoming imperative that professionals understand and begin to learn to work with families. This work must include an understanding of the "whys" and "hows" of the process, with a focus on CLD families. Accordingly, this chapter is divided into several major sections, discussing background information on CLD families, goals of family involvement, and family involvement strategies.

FAMILY DEVELOPMENT: SELECTED BACKGROUND

As reported by Hodgkinson (1992), the Census data of 1990 show that states with a higher growth rate tend to have a high minority population, especially minority youth. According to Hodgkinson, by the year 2010, "minorities" will encompass more than half of the population of twelve states and the District of Columbia. Thus, the American population has been changing dramatically during the 1980s and 1990s, especially among four states that have the highest proportion of minorities—New York, California, Texas, and Florida. Over half of the population in California, Texas, and Florida will be "minority" well before the year 2010. Moreover, projections of the U.S. population for the 1990–2010 period forecasts that the white, non-Hispanic youth will decrease by 3.8 million, while the Hispanic youth will increase by 2.6 million and the African American youth by 1.2 million (Hodgkinson, 1992). However, as more minority households enter the middle class, their fertility will decline. As Hodgkinson (1992) stated, "as the nonwhite youth majority moves through the age range in these four key states [New York, California, Texas, and Florida], we will see first a majority entry level workers, new households, new parents, promotions, voters, volunteers, semi-retirees, and finally minority Social Security recipients, in that order" (p. 7).

Several economic issues are used for developing a pragmatist argument for offering quality education to minority children, including the reality that these minority youth will be funding the American Social Security system after the year 2000. By the year 2030, the work force supporting the still-white, elderly population will be composed of approximately 40 percent white workers and 60 percent younger, "minority" female workers. Thus, as Hodgkinson (1992, p. 7) noted, "by about 2010, most Americans should come to see that as the number of children continue to decline as a percent of the U.S. population, we cannot afford to throw any child away."

Presently, only 36 percent of African American families and 40 percent of Hispanic families are middle class (Hodgkinson, 1992). Asian American families tend to have a large middle-income group due to having several workers in each family as as well as higher educational levels. Moreover, we have come to realize that one of the most important predictors for educational success is the socioeconomic background of the student. Hodgkinson (1992) said, "Show me a minority child raised in a suburb and whose parents are college graduates, and I will show you a child whose educational performance is roughly the same as the white child raised in a suburb by parents who are college graduates" (p. 7).

The American family has also changed dramatically during the 1980s in comparison to the stereotyped nuclear family of the 1950s with a working father, a housewife, and two school-age children. According to Hodgkinson (1989, 1992), the contemporary family of the 1990s has multiple and diverse characteristics:

1. Of the children under age eighteen, 82 percent have working mothers, and 60 percent of preschoolers' mothers work outside the home at least part-time.
2. Single women are raising 13.7 million children in low-income households.
3. Families now compose more than 50 percent of the homeless population, and are headed by women with two or three children under age five.
4. At some point in their lives, 60 percent of today's children will be exposed to a single-parent household before they reach age eighteen.
5. Single men who are raising children are becoming more numerous (their number rose 87.2 percent in 1980–90).
6. Over half of all of today's new marriages end in divorce.
7. Of the children born in 1989, 23 percent were born outside of marriage.
8. Children comprise 40 percent of the poor population.

Furthermore, Hodgkinson (1989) identified two patterns of contemporary families: the short-cycled family and the multiple dependent family. Short-cycle families are primarily formed by minority individuals of low socioeconomic status who produce a new generation every fourteen years or so. In contrast, middle-class families of every ethnic group are cutting back on their birth rates. The multiple dependent family is formed by individuals who have divorced and have children living with their aging parents.

Thus, as the characteristics of both the American general population and the family are changing dramatically, it is also important to change the educational services provided for CLD families and their children. Major needs at present are improving the dramatic situation of inner-city and rural schools across the nation, which have a high percentage of minority students. If state and federal assistance is offered to these schools, then it may be possible for minority students to graduate from high school and take some community college training and secure a health technology job, or receive a college education and obtain a well-paid job. However, if no assistance is given to inner city and rural schools with a high proportion of minority students, then a more negative scenario can materialize, in which minority students drop out of high school and get a service job or become prisoners (in 1992, African American males were 3% of college enrollment and 47% of the prison population; see Hodgkinson, 1992). By the year 2010, available jobs will be two-tiered: 30–40 percent will require a college education and will pay well, and 30 percent will continue to be service jobs for high school dropouts (Hodgkinson, 1992).

Given this view of the new characteristics of the American population and family, we as educators need to provide appropriate educational and community services to the increasing number of CLD families and their children. Below are certain guidelines in the form of goals and strategies for improving these services.

GOALS OF FAMILY INVOLVEMENT

In moving from the literature on family development, including theories, statistical data, and demographics of immigrant and migrant families, to the literature on implementation, we shall introduce and describe major goals of family involvement. Our transition from theoretical and statistical perspectives to application paints a picture of the applicability, transportability, and functionality of this information for CLD families in educational, school, and home settings. Accordingly, the following section contains major overriding goals of family involvement. In turn, the final section continues the transition from theoretical and statistical perspectives to day-to-day and week-to-week strategies that anchor and implement these perspectives with CLD families.

Comprehensive Goals

All of the narrative and empirical articles we reviewed shared a major emphasis on parent involvement. In prior years, parent involvement was focused and localized. With articles, workshops, and courses entitled "Home-School-Community Relations" or "Working with Parents in Classroom Settings," the stress was on parents volunteering and working in classroom and preschool centers. Accordingly, professionals were shown various activities they might use to keep parents who came to school gainfully "employed," "busy," and productively focused. These activities ranged from watching the students to cutting out pictures for bulletin boards to telling about a particular experience to sharing a hobby with the students. This outmoded form of parent involvement was focused exclusively on the classroom and entailed assigning parents "bite-sized" tasks to complete. Parents' roles were accordingly static, marginalized, and highly specific (Morrison, 1983; Nieto, 1992).

Currently, the focus has changed from the specific to the comprehensive. The comprehensive here means a mix of services to families. These services are integrated emphasizing the complexity of family involvement and development (p. 370).

Relatedly, multicultural theorists such as Nieto (1992) have expanded upon and actually enlarged this notion of the comprehensiveness of a reciprocal process to the multiplicity of reciprocal processes. Here, the emphases are on decontextualizing these processes from school to family involvement and development as school, home, and community. In viewing the goal of comprehensiveness as the multiplicity of reciprocal processes, Nieto (1992), Smith and Ingoldsby (1992), and Sontag and Schacht (1994) stress this new perspective of family and school.

From these reciprocal perspectives, the comprehensiveness of family involvement in education in the school context means several things. In addition to the usual, traditional helping routines in classroom and school, family involvement means the observation of students in school settings. This also means identifying and sharing the services that the school and classroom can provide CLD family members. Since one of the biggest roadblocks preventing parents from coming to schools is the lack of native language support, it would be natural to offer family members bilingual support (Lynch & Stein, 1987).

Informal family visits and parent-professional conversations are very meaningful ways to initiate family involvement. Further, since each family has diverse needs, the professional must be able to respond to these needs in order to nurture family involvement (Sontag & Schacht, 1994). Another aspect of this new comprehensive view of family involvement is asking for ideas. In other words, professionals might telephone family members to get their thoughts, opinions, and ideas on any number of items (e.g., field trips, foods to be served, projects to be made). Relatedly, Sontag and Schacht (1994) see family involvement and development as a decision-making process. For example, after family members' ideas are surveyed, these same individuals might be involved in deciding collectively on courses of action (e.g., the site of a field trip). These types of informal surveys that nurture educational decision-making markedly increase family development and involvement. Sontag and Schacht (1994) feel that this involvement in decision-making is an excellent way of meeting family members' individual needs. If we are to fulfill the demands of the contemporary view of family involvement as comprehensiveness in school and classroom settings, then we need to expand our ideas of family in school contexts.

The concept of the comprehensiveness of family involvement, education, and development also has expanded into home contexts. Traditionally, we thought of home involvement as only helping the student with homework. Currently, the comprehensiveness of family involvement includes many aspects. Nieto (1992) feels strongly that in viewing family involvement in the home, "we are not just concerned with those activities traditionally equated with school success, that is, many books and toys in the home!" (p. 264). (For a detailed description of comprehensive parental involvement in home settings, see Nieto, 1992, pp. 254–268). For example, comprehensiveness means the motivation of family members to support school and classroom efforts at home. It means family members stressing that their children complete their homework and not be tardy or absent from school. Involvement of family members in education in home settings also means not being afraid to use the native language. Nieto (1992), for example, emphasizes the use of "the strengths and resources parents already have, especially their culture and language" (p. 264). Further, home involvement means showing family members how to work on school tasks with their children in home settings (Herbert, 1994).

For Title VII Academic Excellence P.I.A.G.E.T. Programs and other sound bilingual projects and programs, this comprehensibility concept means increasing the positive attitudes of family members toward their children and their schooling processes. This means that home-based family programs, like P.I.A.G.E.T. for example, focus on developing child development concepts (Herbert, 1994). It is important to understand the patterns of development and to recognize that children can do certain activities that can nurture family involvement and understanding of their children's growth patterns. Likewise, family involvement in education in home settings is expanded to increasing the routines that children and other family members do together. Whether it is going to the park, riding bicycles, or talking, family involvement in education now means finding ways of developing and expanding interaction (Herbert, 1994; Yawkey, 1992a). Here, as Nieto (1992, p. 264) says, there are no "top-down" approaches to family members' involvement, where they are showered with child and family development expertise. Instead, it is a "bottom-up" approach, where family members use their own children in a living family laboratory and recognize increasing growth patterns and the positive impacts they have on interaction, intellect, and other developmental areas. In summarizing this new expanded view of family involvement in home settings, Nieto (1992) writes that "what we mean ... are intangibles: consistent communications, high expectations, pride, understanding, and enthusiasm for their children's school experiences" (p. 264).

This goal of comprehensiveness of family involvement is imperative. It becomes especially critical when we consider that it now includes both school and home within a reciprocal setting of family involvement as development and education (Morrison, 1983; Nieto, 1992).

Expanded Goals

No longer do we have a "typical" (i.e., "Parsonian") family that is white, with a father, mother, two children (girl and boy), and a dog or cat, and that lives in a house surrounded by a white picket fence. In this Parsonian view of the family, the father works and the mother stays home and performs housework, takes care of the children, cooks meals, and so forth. Finally, the mother and father, in this Parsonian scenario, are called "parents." In its purist form, this family definition is based on race, economic status, gender, and occupational roles that are no longer the majority perspective. For example, two paragraph titles from a recent work tell us that family changes have occurred and are occurring: "Demographic Changes Will Increase the Extent of Family Diversity" and "Definitions of Family Have Important Implications and Are Inextricably Intertwined with Values" (Fine, 1993, p. 235).*

Given the dramatic changes in understanding concepts such as "parents," we are using the terms "family members" throughout this chapter. This demonstrates the expanded concept of the family as well as highlighting the goal of involvement of various family members in schooling rather than only parents.

As the goal of involvement expands to family members, professionals need to understand that "there is no single correct definition of what a family is" (Fine, 1993, p. 235). As we target bilingual "parents" in Title VII family-based programs, we soon come to realize that the term "parent" largely gives a false idea of whom we are targeting. In many instances, the targets of home-based Title VII programming are family members such as the grandmother or other extended family members who care regularly for the students before and after school. In many cases in P.I.A.G.E.T. home programs, we encounter older sisters, brothers, or neighborhood family friends who watch the students on a daily basis. These older sisters or brothers, for example, become those family members who are trained for school-home involvement. In this context, Fine (1993) clarifies this point by stating that family members are "all individuals who are involved in the nurturance and support of a child, regardless of where the child lives...[and]...may include nonrelatives and may have flexible boundaries" (p. 236). Thus, the involvement of family members means expanding the concept of family to include the single-male-headed family, the single-female-headed family, all types of stepfamilies, and the lesbian mother or gay father with children (Fine, 1993; Yawkey & Cornelius, 1990).

As a goal of involvement is to expand the concept of the family to include family members, it is of great interest to note the sociological maxim

---

* All Fine (1993, pp. 235–236) references are copyrighted by the National Council on Family Relations, 3989 Central Avenue NE, Suite 550, Minneapolis, MN 55421. Reprinted with permission.

that there is greater heterogeneity within CLD families than across various diverse family groups. This means that as we begin to involve family members from several families who are linguistically and culturally Hispanic, for example, there may be tremendous variability among them. This heterogeneity destroys stereotypes and motivates professionals to work individually with families. It also emphasizes the individual demands of family members in educational and developmental involvement and the need to meet them through different strategies.

In this dilemma of heterogeneity, we recommend using Allen and Farnsworth's (1993)* concept of reflexivity, which holds that professionals must increase their "self-awareness and sensitivity to the experiences of others...[which]...is a practice well-suited to...family diversity" (p. 351). As professionals, we realize continually in our work for educational involvement of all families that we cannot use ourselves as criteria. We must move outside ourselves and our own families, and view and work with family members from other perspectives. This process of decentering is what Allen and Farnsworth (1993) mean by the phrase "reflexivity as a pathway to multiple truths" (p. 352). In this context, London and Devore (1988) see reflexivity and decentering as "layers of understanding" (p. 310). In Table 8.1, they provide a sound scaffold for using reflexivity to involve family members and helping us focus on individual family needs toward involvement.

TABLE 8.1   Schematic Model of the Layers of Understanding Required of Practitioners Working with Ethnic Minority Families

Basic Skills Required of All Practitioners	Additional Layers of Understanding Required of Practitioners Working with Ethnic Minority Families
A basic knowledge of human behavior	Self-awareness; knowledge of one's own ethnicity and its influence on practice
Professional values	Understanding the impact of ethnicity on the daily lives of clients
	Modification and adaptation of skills in response to working with ethnic minority families

Note: From "Layers of Understanding: Counseling Ethnic Minority Families," by H. London and W. Devore, 1988, *Family Relations, 37*, p. 310. Copyrighted 1988 by the National Council on Family Relations, 3898 Central Avenue NE, Suite 550, Minneapolis, MN. Reprinted by permission.

*All Allen and Farnsworth (1993, pp. 351–352) references are copyrighted by the National Council on Family Relations, 3898 Central Avenue NE, Suite 550, Minneapolis, MN. Reproduced by permission.

Consequently, this goal of involvement as expanding the concept from parent to family members also adds to our task. Guiding for special family needs, using reflexivity, and applying understanding across several tiers provide a focus for professionals working toward this goal.

Communication

Communication is another major goal of involvement of family members in educational and developmental processes, as it encompasses visibility, greater explicitness, and applied description. Although implied within the other goals of family involvement, communication gives the basic framework to operationalizing all the strategies identified in this chapter. Sound communication and information sharing with CLD families are essential if we are to develop and implement any degree of family involvement (Lynch & Stein, 1987; Sontag & Schacht, 1994). More specifically, Lynch and Stein (1987) define "lack of bilingual communication and general communication" as two of the top barriers between schools and CLD families (p. 105).

As professionals, we all have heard that "communication is a two-way street" and that "we need to communicate more." Let us think about the CLD family whom we serve. Throughout this chapter and this book we have repeatedly pointed out the need for using native languages in schools with family members to develop ease and understanding in communication. Hendrick (1988) points out that criticism, real or imagined, becomes a barrier to communication between school and home. CLD families may see the professional as a source of criticism because of their lack of English, level of education, or countless other reasons. Not communicating with the school comes to mean receiving no perceived or stated criticism. That is, both "out-of-sight-out-of-mind" and ultimately "teachers-know-best" are perspectives that reduce and ultimately terminate communication.

Following the strategies recommended later in this chapter will lead to communication as a two-way approach. In addition, respecting the CLD family members as individuals with particular and personal contributions is another lever for increasing communication. Serving as a friendly listener concerned with the CLD family members is another practical suggestion for improving communication for family involvement.

Planning your contacts and conferences with CLD family members wisely and appropriately pays great dividends in improved communication (Hendrick, 1988). The professional will need to capitalize on the contacts that arise during the natural course of the week. For example, CLD family members dropping off and picking up their children at school become natural situations for friendly and respectful communication toward the goal of increasing involvement of the family at school and home. These occasions become informal meetings that demonstrate realistically your desire to understand individually that family member and his or her child. Communication and its quality can make or break present and future involvement of family members.

Partnerships

Partnerships are being recognized as another goal of involvement of CLD families. Here, developing and enhancing partnerships between home and school, professionals and family members, and family members and administrators are critical as new paradigms in education emerge and are implemented (Forsyth & Tallerica, 1993). These partnerships not only build cultural bridges but also provide expertise among groups. Here, expertise from one constituent group and expertise from another achieve successes. In a sense, these partnerships become the "best of two worlds," because partnership expertise strengthens the entire effort and endeavor. Through family member–professional partnerships, both the family and school are strengthened and the development of the student is enhanced (Herbert, 1994; Yawkey, 1992a.)

The goals of family involvement include:

1. Developing a comprehensive understanding of involvement as the education and development of the family
2. Expanding the concept of "parent" to family members and building avenues toward involvement based on individual needs
3. Increasing communication between school and home and between home and school
4. Nurturing partnerships based on the realization of the strengths of the expertise of both partners

In the next section, we apply these goals through strategies. These strategies become ideal two-way avenues for CLD family members to contribute actively and meaningfully to development, education—and ultimately genuine involvement.

RECOMMENDED STRATEGIES TO INCREASE PARENTAL INVOLVEMENT OF CLD FAMILIES

Without a slightest doubt, we know that parental involvement of CLD families in the schooling processes and in the education of their children is imperative. With a previous rationale for this position described in the beginning of this chapter, parental involvement should be a state-mandated objective for all agencies and providers of service to language-minority students and parents—including school districts.

A host of recommended strategies for parental involvement are usable with CLD families. Obviously, some will produce better results (e.g., home visitor programs) than others (e.g., community meetings). Our intent is to identify and describe a wide range of strategies for parental involvement that then can be used and/or modified by agencies to fit their different needs and diverse family populations.

Conferences

Of all parental involvement strategies, individual conferences between parent and teacher are the most common and most recognizable form. Theoretically, these conferences can be called by either teacher or parent and for any number of reasons. Practically, they are more often called by the teacher, who invites the parent to school to meet with the teacher and possibly the principal, depending on the topic to be addressed. Although conferences can be called for any number of reasons, our experiences suggest the following:

1. One of the major reasons for a teacher to call a parent-teacher conference focuses on the behavior, misbehavior, and discipline of a student in the classroom and school.
2. A related second major reason is poor or failing grades.
3. Parent-teacher conferences almost exclusively focus on information sharing and gathering (Peters, Neisworth, & Yawkey, 1985).
4. Parent-teacher conferences, for the most part, become one-way channels of communication, in which teachers give information to parents.
5. Often, too many conferences booked for the same time, resulting in a short period scheduled per parent; the result is a hurried conference, which gives the parent a feeling of being rushed.

If professionals are to use this strategy with families wisely, there are several basic understandings necessary for effective conferences. First, through our nonverbal mannerisms, verbal statements, and means of planning and carrying out the conferences, we must let families know that we value cultural and linguistic diversity. The signals that we send must show that we value them and their ideas, and support their use of native languages in home settings with their children. Feeling welcomed and becoming a genuine member of the conference make it evident to family members that they are respected. If family members detect any nonverbal mannerisms and hear verbal statements that are negative or show attitudinal stereotypes (Fields, 1993), trust relationships will be destroyed and difficult to rebuild.

Second, conferences between teacher and family members do not necessarily have to occur with calendar precision once every six or nine weeks, or last exactly fifteen to twenty minutes, or always be called by the professional.

The most effective conferences are those that occur as they are needed, that are relevant to current situations, and that are held in a friendly, frustration-less atmosphere (Hendricks, 1988). Family members can also call conferences based on their needs and perceptions of situations. There are many ways for professionals to insure that family members understand this role. One way is to write notes home periodically or call family members to see if they have thoughts about this idea or that and/or a desire to meet. The perceptions that family members can call conferences must be developed and reinforced from the beginning of the school year onward.

Third, to be effective conferences and meetings must be viewed as two-way communication. Family members must see that their ideas and statements are acknowledged, genuinely accepted, and acted upon. These two-way avenues of sending and receiving ideas show that family members are valuable partners in the professional–family member–student triad. They also ensure that family members will not always be responding to top-down communication, which can be viewed as directives. In addition, these two-way modes of communication show that both the professional and family members are visible and highly accessible. These conferences are critical to working effectively with CLD families. Additional ways of developing sound communication between professional and family members are detailed in Hendrick (1988, see pp. 451–461).

Home Visits

Home visits are very effective as a strategy to use as you work with CLD families (Peters, Neisworth, & Yawkey, 1985). Across current bilingual programs, home visits are very popular and functional modes in which to work with family members. Home visits to family members one or more times per year are required by some school districts and many other agencies providing services to CLD families (Yawkey, 1992b).

The benefits of home visits can be summarized briefly:

1. Professionals and family members can interact more readily and genuinely in homes than in classrooms.
2. Home visits are less threatening and intimidating than classroom visits because family members are in familiar environments (Peters, Neisworth, & Yawkey, 1985).
3. Home visits offer professionals opportunities to observe family-child interactions and effectively match, model, and use these positive interactional styles with their students for effective results (Martinez, 1988).
4. Home visit formats can be easily adapted to particular cultural and linguistic variations to include special components that mesh with and support these variations (Martinez, 1988).

5. Professionals come to know the home settings of their students, the values of their family, and the materials common to the home that might be used in the home training of family members.
6. Understandings, skills, and attitudes of students in the home can be identified and used as the bases for successful work in the school (Nieto, 1992).
7. Home programs provide firsthand observations of the effects of the educational programming on students and family members.
8. By developing and sharing common understandings and visions through home programs, family members and professionals realize that they are working toward the best results with the same individual—the student (Melaville & Blank, 1993).

Home visits can take many forms. They can be regular and systematic, such as weekly or monthly across the agency year. Less beneficial and successful are random home visits.

Regardless of their scheduling, all home visit programs with CLD families should implicitly or explicitly contain the following characteristics:

1. *Planning:* The home visit must be planned thoroughly and in advance. Many bilingual programs require detailed family activity plans on file one week in advance of the visit (Yawkey, 1992b).
2. *Structuring:* As Head Start family programming has shown, home visits are more successful if they are structured. In P.I.A.G.E.T. Academic Excellence, for example, every family activity training session begins with family members reviewing how last week's activity was used with the child, and then proceeds to setting new activity objectives, gathering home materials, role-playing the new activity, and finally showing how it can be generalized to other settings (Yawkey, 1992b).
3. *Practicing:* Peters, Neisworth, and Yawkey (1985) recommend that a "practice loop" be built into the home visit so that family members can practice with the visitor the new activity they have learned. In P.I.A.G.E.T. programs, this practice takes the form of role-playing, as the visitor first role-plays the activity and the family member then plays it back to the visitor.
4. *Setting the time:* P.I.A.G.E.T., like other good bilingual programs serving family members of CLD students, uses collaboration to set the time for the home visit. In other words, family members and the professional agree on a time for the next meeting, which can occur in the evening, on Saturday, and even on Sunday.
5. *Providing services:* Authorities involved with home visitor programs (e.g., Melaville & Blank, 1993; Nieto, 1992; Yawkey, 1992b) strongly recommend that these programs not restrict their focus to education or

nutrition. In other words, to be effective, home visitor programs must provide multiple services and resources—educational, nutritional, abuse referrals, and so forth. Comprehensiveness is the key to successful family-based programming.

Family-based home visitor programs are tremendous assets. They further the agency's objectives while benefiting the family as well as the CLD student.

Family Liaisons

Critical to all successful family-based home programs is the family liaison chosen to deliver this programming. Family members must be actively involved in home visitor programs if they are to be successful. In order to involve family members actively, the family liaison has many roles to play. Argondizza (1987) says that "critical to initiating parent involvement is a competent liaison who is well respected in the native community, and who has outstanding interpersonal skills" (p. 158). Interpersonal skills in this setting mean sensitivity to cultural routines and native languages and the ability to play a number of roles in the family member–professional dyad. These roles of the family liaison include discussant, teacher, guide, "sounding board," group leader, and sympathizer. The liaison must know intuitively which of these roles to play when. Interpersonal skills also include the use of native languages. Here, the family liaisons must understand how to speak, read, and write the native languages of the families they serve. Smith and Ryan (1987) feel that family providers who can do this are more likely to render higher levels of service than those who do not speak the same languages. In addition, family members' levels of satisfaction with these agencies increase as these family liaisons are able to speak their native languages (Smith & Ryan, 1987). These same aspects of interpersonal skills for Sen and Smith (1987, p. 195) become roles that family members need to acquire in working with their children. It is imperative that family liaisons role-play these different interpersonal skills in working with family members (e.g., family member as discussant with the child, family member as counselor, family member as teacher; (see Yawkey, 1987). This role diversification of family members with their children helps strengthen the positive interaction between family members and their abilities to cope effectively with daily and ongoing situations.

In the work of the family liaison, the demand for diversification appears from another perspective—as the means of providing a variety of services as needs arise in families. Whether it is sharing with family members their rights concerning the education of their children or helping them cope with substance abuse, the family liaison educates them. Relatedly, they also provide information and emotional and physical support to the family. This support includes genuinely listening to their concerns and problems, making referrals, and building on family strengths such as group cohesiveness, the desire to work together, and so forth.

Parent Advisory Committees

If used properly and genuinely, parent advisory committees are very effective strategies to employ with CLD families. Although federally funded Title VII bilingual projects require such committees, they can also be used at the school and classroom levels. Hendrick (1988) recommends that such committees *not* be used for merely "rubber stamping" policies and procedures about to be put into operation or already in operation. The parent advisory committee used in this way sends messages to families that their ideas are not really valued and that only those ideas given by the educational agency matter. Hendrick (1988) stresses that ideas brought to or arising from the committee must be considered and discussed. As these ideas are discussed, the committee must be able to modify them, table them for further study, and develop ways to implement those ideas that they consider of relevance to solving the problem, concern, or situation. Trusting in the deliberations and outcomes of the parent advisory committee is primary (Hendrick, 1988). As this trust increases, ownership and group collectiveness in decision-making also increase. According to Melaville and Blank (1993), the goal of developing ownership and trust is nurturing a common vision and a shared present and future among diverse constituent memberships. When these outcomes are generated by the parent advisory committee, the direct benefits are to the students and the CLD family members that they serve.

The parent advisory committee provides many significant responsibilities once it is functioning properly. For example, in Project P.I.A.G.E.T. Programs, this committee has many responsibilities. It helps to plan culturally relevant field trips and family community meetings (Yawkey, 1987), surveys the family community for their understandings, identifies some of the skills the families need, and determines their attitudes and perceptions about critical issues. As a result of this family needs assessment, P.I.A.G.E.T. Programs hold monthly meetings sponsored by the parent advisory committee. Some of these monthly meetings focused on:

1. Legal rights of parents in school
2. Drug abuse symptoms and treatments
3. Dental advice
4. Accessment of community support systems
5. Overcoming of road blocks in applying for and receiving services

There are many other legitimate and genuine responsibilities that parent advisory committees can identify, assume, and complete. Indeed, there are few limits to their responsibilities and roles. Other functions parent advisory committees might perform include:

1. Producing and distributing a monthly newsletter of community information
2. Holding discussion groups to share opinions about a common problem
3. Providing translation services for medical, job, and legal information
4. Giving ideas on the "whats," "whys," and "hows" of parent-teacher conferences, lateness and absence from school, report cards, and persons in the school family members can contact as questions or concerns arise
5. Writing and distributing a list of community resources
6. Finding adequate low-cost housing
7. Identifying low-cost nutritional foods
8. Visiting classrooms and attending school board meetings
9. Interviewing potential agency personnel
10. Implementing a hot line for helping with homework and latch-key students

Family Education Workshops

The increasing number of articles on workshops for CLD families testifies to the growing interest in this strategy (Bermudez & Padron, 1989; Ensle, 1992; Mau, 1989; Rosado & Aaron, 1991). This recommended strategy assumes that CLD families have played a critical role in helping plan these workshops and that the needs of these families were assessed and monitored. Without identifying these needs, no workshops can be delivered. One of the major reasons why few family members attend current agency activities is that the topics are not of genuine interest or relevance to them (Yawkey, 1987). In other words, the family members have no ownership in the workshop topics. These activity topics were identified without appropriately surveying families and requesting their assistance in planning them. Mau (1989), in stressing the need for involvement workshops for family members as well as school personnel, calls such workshops "home-school partnerships" (p. 64).

In further preparing to think about and implement this strategy effectively with family members Walberg (1984) provides some useful planning guidelines for workshop development:

1. Having the parents view the programs as an opportunity and not a requirement
2. Treating parents as interested members in the education of their children

3. Providing the parents with a clear idea of what is expected of them in the program
4. Giving the parents specific strategies and skills needed
5. Praising and recognizing the parents' participation
6. Allowing parents to use objects that they can manipulate
7. Providing materials that do not need much explanation (pp. 397–398)

Finally, in planning family education workshops, we recommend planning for communication and considering the participants comfort and any obstacles that may arise (Ensle, 1992). According to Ensle, communication occurs through the use of the native language as family members and professionals interact and do the "hands-on" activities in the workshop. The use of the native language provides greater understanding and ease in communicating, learning, and implementing these ideas. Ensle, like Bermudez and Padron (1989) and Walberg (1984), view comfort or comfortability as making family members feel welcome in the workshop where they can share fellowship and friendship.

The third element to become aware of in planning and implementing these workshops is to identify and minimize potential obstacles or blocks that have potential to reduce workshop effectiveness (Ensle, 1992). Some might be overcome by barriers providing transportation to and from the workshop and child care at the workshop. Ensle sees other potential problems arising as professionals do not understand how to encourage and facilitate the use of their learning in school settings. By inviting parents to classrooms to observe and/or help and by facilitating communication, for example, professionals will increase the likelihood that family members will be able to apply workshop outcomes to building home-school partnerships. These critical elements provide a solid foundation for the successes of the workshop and insure appropriate channels for using the understandings, skills, and attitudes gained in them.

There are a number of clear, useful examples of family education workshops (e.g., Ensle, 1992; Rosado & Aaron, 1991). Rosado and Aaron (1991) describe a series of family education workshops aimed at inner-city Hispanic parents that focused on "language, culture, self-identity and parental involvement" (p. 26). Delivered in three training sessions, each lasted a full day, and parents with young children were provided with child care. A complete, detailed description of the content delivered in each of these sessions is given by Rosado and Aaron (1991). Briefly, however, some of the themes covered include geographic origins of Hispanics and their educational attainment prior to their immigration or migration, appropriate learning modes in Hispanic children, ways parents can help their children in school, and signals of drug abuse and prevention. The themes related to drug abuse were given at the request of the parents. From the descriptions of the workshops and the number of family members who participated in them, they appeared to be successful.

Mau (1989) used the networking technique in which she asked parents to ask other parents in each of their networks to come to a series of workshops. The various titles of the workshop components follow (Mau, 1989, pp. 65–68):

"Get-Acquainted Activity"
"Discussion of Research Findings of Interest to Parents of LEP Students"
"Information on Community Resources and Parent Networking Centers"
"Handout to Parents at the End of the Workshop"

Each of these components is detailed in Mau (1989, pp. 64–71), but some of the major themes were using native languages in home settings, working with children on school tasks in home settings, and becoming more involved in the classroom and with school activities. These workshops were also highly successful, with 85 percent of the participants saying they would use the techniques learned. Other examples of very effective family education workshops are described in Bermudez and Padron (1988), who used practice with parents, and Haynes, Comer, and Hamilton-Lee (1989), who used parents as volunteers in schools.

The Print Media

Print media as a strategy for family involvement include newsletters, community notes, personal memos, drawings, newspaper clippings, and handouts. Print media can be effectively used to initiate and increase family members' involvement in school activities by letting them know what is occurring in school and by "pitching" its content of the needs of CLD families.

Newsletters should be printed in the native languages of the families. They thus not only are better able to understand the contents but, more importantly, will take pride in knowing that the newsletters are especially for them. This newsletter can be distributed either at the classroom level or across grade levels by the school. Peters, Neisworth, and Yawkey (1985) recommend regular, systematic printings (e.g., monthly or every two months). Monthly releases have the benefits of increasing communication with family members and sharing more current ideas. Nieto (1992) states that these classroom newsletters should be translated to native languages by the students and contain samples of the students' work. P.I.A.G.E.T. monthly newsletters from its various adoption site agencies contain interviews with families and share some of the activities they have done and those of the community. We have also found that putting students' pictures in the newsletters and identifying their accomplishments provides sound, positive feedback to family members. Newsletters can also carry nutritional food buying and preparation tips characteristic of the various language-minority cultures served by the agency. Other P.I.A.G.E.T. newsletters include games and parent activities as well as safety tips and tips on handling parent-child situations (e.g., children fighting).

A note sent home with students (or its equivalent, a telephone call or home visit) about their progress in school greatly increases family members' interest in schooling and classroom activities. These notes, calls, or visits can also be invitations asking family members to come in for visits and so forth. It is our experience that in the majority of cases, notes sent or mailed to family members are negative in character and focus on aggressive or inappropriate classroom behavior or on failing grades. In turn, these notes may request family members to come to school or to telephone the school, or state that the student is to be detained after school or suspended from school for a period of time. In the context we suggest, however, these home contacts using notes, calls, or visits bring attention to something positive the student has done. As noted elsewhere in this text, the P.I.A.G.E.T. home visitor is trained to share a positive note on the student's performance when these contacts are made.

Other forms of print media, including newspaper clippings and handouts, can also be shared with family members. Newspaper clippings can highlight certain events special to the classroom, community, or student. Handouts serve to accent particular points, such as disciplining children, working with students on homework assignments, and managing sibling rivalry. These related forms of print media let family members know about student and classroom activities while increasing positive channels of involvement of family members in school functions.

Volunteers

Volunteers in school agencies can take many forms. Some provide assistance in the classroom, largely as paraprofessionals. Other volunteers serve in lunch rooms or other areas as monitors and as aids who check equipment in and out of media centers and help with the books in the libraries. Morrison (1983) notes that CLD family members can help by "volunteering time and services...as clerks,...tutors...in advisory groups, task forces,...[and] helping organize and operate the school's volunteer program" (p. 376). They also can become resource persons who volunteer their expertise based on their occupations, cultures, hobbies, or other interests (Argondizza, 1987; Morrison, 1983).

Regardless of the roles they may play in school agencies, the CLD family members serving as volunteers are a vast reservoir that needs to be tapped.

As stated by Argondizza (1987) students "are delighted to have parent volunteers working with them" (p. 159).

Students actively seek out and enjoy working with volunteers from CLD populations because they [provide] "a connection between home and school and [offer] a sense of security otherwise not felt, [and increases] the child's respect for the parent, as the parent is recognized as an important part of the school community" (Argondizza, 1987, p. 159).

As a major unmet need, family involvement as volunteers has a "lasting effect on student achievement...[and]...on the parents...[because the volunteers are involved] actively in the education of their children" (LeGage, Studley, Argondizza, & Sen, 1987, p. 111). Volunteers can help classroom professionals contact parents through visiting or writing notes in native languages, and may, under certain circumstances, help in organizing carpools and offering child care (LeGage, Studley, Argondizza, & Sen, 1987).

The above ways of working with CLD family members take years to nurture and develop. Our prior and present experiences in working with various CLD populations tell us that these family members are largely reluctant to participate in school activities. Their reluctance is reflected in not attending parent-teacher open houses or conferences, or even visiting and observing the classroom. Since they view the school as an institution that is different from the home, many CLD families do not understand the school's functions, their responsibilities as part of the larger school community, or even the basic importance of students being on time for school.

In working with many thousands of CLD family members since 1981, P.I.A.G.E.T. emphasizes taking small steps, one at a time, toward school involvement. First, when they drop the student off, family members are welcomed and encouraged to remain in the classroom for a minute or two. This time in the classroom increases, and before long the family member becomes an observer and then an active volunteer who helps at snack time. In having family members serve as volunteers, we recommend taking several small, successive steps, and then, with encouragement, other avenues for volunteering will open. After time, and as the program develops, family members will understand the importance of volunteers and the expectation that they serve in this capacity.

Involvement of family members in educational activities is challenging. As noted, family members may not *want* to be involved and may not know *how* to be involved. This hesitation may also be related to personal dislikes of individuals currently working or volunteering in the classrooms. Sen and Smith (1987) state further that CLD family members may not wish to become involved because of "feelings of shyness, passiveness, or powerlessness at public meetings of large groups of people" (p. 197). In addition, Sen and Smith (1987) cite anxiety and potential embarrassment as reasons for family members not becoming involved in educational activities. It may be also that these CLD family members come from a background that does not encourage school community involvement within an open communication context. Thus collaborating with teachers as partners in the education of their children was not viewed by their original sociocultural environment as an appropriate way of communication that needed to be nurtured. Each of these and other reasons can be explored. With thoughtful planning, dedicated time to nurturing involvement, and the use of a small, step-by-step model to involvement, CLD family members will become involved.

REFERENCES

Access to early childhood programs for children at risk. Washington, DC: National Center for Educational Statistics.

Allen, K. R., & Farnsworth, E. B. (1993). Reflexivity in teaching about families. *Family Relations, 42*, 351–356.

Argondizza, M. (1987). Utilizing bilingual parents in classroom settings. In T. D. Yawkey (Ed.), *Bilingual early childhood, parent education, and family literacy: Curriculum development, programs, and evaluation* (pp. 156–163). University Park: The Pennsylvania State University.

Bermudez, A. B., & Padron, Y. N. (1988). University-school collaboration that increases minority parent involvement. *Educational Horizons, 66* (2), 83–86.

Bermudez, A. B., & Padron, Y. N. (1989). The effects of parent education programs on parent participation. In L. M. Malavé (Ed.), *Annual Conference Journal* (pp. 159–169). Washington, DC: National Association for Bilingual Education.

Bermudez, A. B., & Padron, Y. N. (1990). Improving language skills for Hispanic students through home-school partnerships. *Journal of Educational Issues of Language-Minority Students, 6*, 33–43.

Ensle, A. L. (1992). Teachers' insights: Critical elements in parental involvement of culturally and linguistically diverse parents. *Bilingual Research Journal, 16* (3–4), 141–143.

Fields, B. (1993). Teacher perceptions of the school adjustment of children from single parent families—The Australian experience. *Australian Journal of Early Childhood, 18* (2), 3–8.

Fine, M. A. (1993). Family diversity—Current approaches to understanding diversity: An overview of the special issue. *Family Relations, 42*, 235–237.

Fleischman, H. L., & Hopstock, P. J. (1993). *Descriptive study of services to limited English proficient students* (Vol. 1). Arlington, VA: Development Associates & U.S. Department of Education, Office of the Under Secretary.

Forsyth, P. B., & Tallerica, M. (Eds.). (1993). *City schools leading the way.* Newbury Park, CA: Corivia.

Haynes, R. M., Comer, J. P., & Hamilton-Lee, M. (1989). School climate enhancement through parental involvement. *Journal of School Psychology, 27*, 87–90.

Hendrick, J. (1988). *The whole child: Developmental education for the early years.* Columbus, OH: Merrill.

Herbert, M. W. (1994). *Bethlehem Area School District and The Pennsylvania State University Title VII Academic Excellence Program Project P.I.A.G.E.T.: Summary evaluation report 1990–1993.* Pittsburgh: CHECpoint Systems.

Hodgkinson, H. L. (1989). *The same client: The demographics of education and service delivery systems.* Washington, DC: Institute for Educational Leadership.

Hodgkinson, H. L. (1992). *A demographic look at tomorrow.* Washington, DC: Institute for Educational Leadership.

LeGage, D. N., Studley, G. E., Argondizza, M., & Sen, P. (1987). Title VII Project P.A.L.S.: A project benefiting from replicating a quality bilingual program. In T. D. Yawkey (Ed.), *Bilingual early childhood, parent education, and family literacy: Curriculum development, programs, and evaluation* (pp. 107–116). University Park: The Pennsylvania State University.

London, H., & Devore, W. (1988). Layers of understanding: Counseling ethnic minority families. *Family Relations, 37,* 310–314.

Lynch, E. W., & Stein, R. C. (1987). Parent participation by ethnicity: A comparison of Hispanic, Black, and Anglo families. *Exceptional Children, 54* (2), 105–11.

Martinez, E. A. (1988). Child behavior in Mexican American/Chicano families: Maternal teaching and child-rearing practices. *Family Relations, 37* (July), 275–280.

Mau, R. Y. (1989). Parent involvement workshop components. *Journal of Educational Issues of Language-Minority Students, 5,* 64–71.

Melaville, A. I., & Blank, M. J. (1993). *Together we can: A guide for crafting a profamily system of education and human services.* Washington, DC: U.S. Government Printing Office.

Nieto, S. (1992). *Affirming diversity: The sociopolitical context of multicultural education.* New York: Longman.

Peters, D. L., Neisworth, J. T., & Yawkey, T. D. (1985). *Early childhood education: From theory to practice.* Belmont, CA: Brooks/Cole.

Rosado, L. A., & Aaron, E. B. (1991). Parental involvement: Addressing the educational needs of Hispanic inner-city parents. *Journal of Educational Issues of Language-Minority Students, 8,* 23–30.

Sen, P., & Smith, J. M. (1987). Working with parents in bilingual education: The parent-involvement training model. In T. D. Yawkey (Ed.), *Bilingual early childhood, parent education, and family literacy: Curriculum development, programs, and evaluation* (pp. 193–200). University Park: The Pennsylvania State University.

Smith, M. J., & Ryan, A. S. (1987). Chinese-American families of children with developmental disabilities: An exploratory study of reactions to service providers. *Mental Retardation, 25* (6), 345–350.

Smith, S., & Ingoldsby, B. (1992). Multicultural family studies: Educating students for diversity. *Family Relations, 41,* 25–30.

Sontag, J. C., & Schacht, R. (1994). An ethnic comparison of parent participation and information needs in early intervention. *Exceptional Children, 60* (5), 422–433.

Teeney, S., Christensen, D., & Moravcik, E. (1991). *Who am I in the lives of children: An introduction to teaching young children.* New York: Merrill.

Walberg, H. (1984). Families as partners in educational productivity. *Phi Delta Kappan, 65,* 397–400.

Yawkey, T. D. (Ed.). (1987). *Bilingual early childhood, parent education, and family literacy: Curriculum development, programs, and evaluation.* University Park: The Pennsylvania State University.

Yawkey, T. D. (1992a). *Evaluation report on the Grand Rapids Family Literacy (FELP): 1991–1992.* University Park: The Pennsylvania State University.

Yawkey, T. D. (1992b). *1987–1990 Three-year report of Title VII Academic Excellence Project P.I.A.G.E.T. Cycle 1* (Technical Report No. 295). University Park: The Pennsylvania State University.

Yawkey, T. D., & Cornelius, G. M. (Eds.). (1990). *The single parent family: For helping professionals and parents.* Lancaster, PA: Technomic.

Zill, N. (1992a, August 22). "Trends in family life and children's school performance." Paper presented at the annual meeting of the American Sociological Association, Pittsburgh.

Zill, N. (1992b, January 17). What we know about school readiness of young children in the United States. Presentation at the National Education Goals Panel Meeting. Washington, DC.

9

ORGANIZING AND DELIVERING
SUPPORTIVE SERVICES
TO CLD STUDENTS

This chapter poses eight basic questions for examining the quality of our school policies and procedures regarding CLD students, especially those with or at-risk of learning problems, in the context of meeting the National Education Goals. The questions address the establishment of an overall plan for school improvement relative to CLD students, including educational philosophy, identification of and services to at-risk students, teaching based on best practices, protection of the legal rights of students in the special education process, models for inclusive instruction, parental involvement, professional development, and ongoing evaluation. The chapter also reiterates the need for teaching and learning to occur within a holistic service delivery system and for educators to engage in a self-evaluation of their attitudes and behavior.

CLD STUDENTS AND THE
NATIONAL EDUCATION GOALS

The National Education Goals consist of eight priority areas designed to help students meet world-class standards (see Table 9.1). Six of the eight goals were formulated by President George Bush and the nation's governors in 1989 and addressed school readiness; student achievement, especially in the areas of science and math; adult literacy and life-long learning; and safe schools. The remaining two goals, dealing with the professional development of educators and partnerships with parents, were added in 1994 when President Bill Clinton signed into law Goals 2000: Educate America Act.

TABLE 9.1 The National Education Goals

Goal 1 **School Readiness:** All children in America will start school ready to learn.

Objectives: Access to high quality, developmentally appropriate preschool programs; parental support; access to improved health services.

Goal 2 **School Completion:** The high school graduation rate will increase to at least 90%.

Objectives: Lowered dropout rate; increased percentage of degree completion among students who drop out; no difference in graduation rates by racial/ethnic status.

Goal 3 **Student Achievement and Citizenship:** All students will leave grades 4, 8, and 12 having demonstrated competency over challenging subject matter including English, mathematics, science, foreign languages, civics and government, economics, the arts, history, and geography, and every school in America will ensure that all students learn to use their minds well, so they may be prepared for responsible citizenship, further learning, and productive employment in our nation's modern economy.

Objectives: Increased academic performance of all students with decreased discrepancies in performance across racial/ethnic status; increased ability to reason, solve applied problems, and communicate; involvement in good citizenship activities; access to physical and health education; increased percentage of students competent in more than one language; increased knowledge of the nation's diverse cultural heritage and the world community.

Goal 4 **Teacher Education and Professional Development:** The nation's teaching force will have access to programs for the continued improvement of their professional skills and the opportunity to acquire the knowledge and skills needed to instruct and prepare all American students for the next century.

Objectives: Access to preservice and in-service education suitable for teaching diverse students with a variety of educational, social, and health needs; access to continuing opportunities for development; creation of integrated system by states and districts for teacher recruitment and retention; creation of partnerships among LEAs, higher education, business, parents, local labor, and associations to support professional development.

Goal 5 **Math and Science:** U. S. students will be the first in the world in mathematics and science achievement.

Objectives: Strengthening of math and science education throughout system, especially the early years; increased number of teachers with math and science background; increased number of graduates with math and science degrees, especially women and minorities.

Goal 6 **Adult Literacy and Life-Long Learning:** Every adult American will be literate and will possess the knowledge and skills necessary to compete in a global economy and exercise the rights and responsibilities of citizenship.

Continued

213

TABLE 9.1   *Continued*

Objectives: Involvement of all major businesses in strengthening connection between education and work; opportunities for workers to acquire knowledge and skills from basic to highly technical; increased number of programs for part-time and midcareer students; increased completion of at least 2-year programs by students, especially minorities; increased percentage of college graduates who exhibit advanced applied reasoning and communication abilities; implementation of comprehensive parent involvement programs by schools, including literacy and parent training.

Goal 7   **Safe, Disciplined, and Alcohol- and Drug-Free Schools:** Every school in the United States will be free of drugs, violence, and the unauthorized presence of firearms and alcohol and will offer a disciplined environment conducive to learning.

Objectives: Implementation of policy on drugs and violence at all schools; establishments of partnerships to ensure safe, secure environments and community-based teams to provide support to students and teachers; development of comprehensive curriculum on drugs and alcohol, integrated with health education; elimination of sexual harassment in schools.

Goal 8   **Parental Participation:** Every school will promote partnerships that will increase parental involvement and participation in promoting the social, emotional, and academic growth of children.

Objectives: Development of state policies that assist schools in establishing programs for parents, including parents of students who are disadvantaged, bilingual, or have disabilities; establishment of partnerships with parents at every school; parental support of schools and demand for accountability.

Note: From Goals 2000: Educate America Act of 1994. 108 Stat. 125.

Goals 2000 creates a national framework for education reform to ensure equitable educational opportunities for "all students." "All students" are defined as those coming from a broad range of backgrounds and circumstances, including students from disadvantaged circumstances; students from diverse racial, ethnic, and cultural backgrounds; students with disabilities; students with LEP (limited English proficiency); students who have dropped out; students who are migrants; and students who are academically gifted. Among other activities, Goals 2000 provides financial incentives to SEAs (state education agencies) and LEAs (local education agencies) for systematic reform efforts that are to be documented in a comprehensive state improvement plan. The plan must include strategies for meeting the National Education Goals; providing all students with an opportunity to learn; improving governance, accountability, and management; involving parents and the community; making the improvements statewide; and coordinating with work-to-school programs. Addressing the National Education Goals is also a priority under the recently enacted Improving America's Schools Act, or IASA (see Chapter 2), which requires SEAs and LEAs to submit plans that are coordinated with Goals 2000 in order to receive funding. As a result of this new philosophical framework, two major programs that benefit CLD students under the IASA—Title I: Helping Disadvantaged Children Meet High Standards, and Title VII: The Bilingual Education Act—are now designed to work collaboratively, giving schools enhanced options to provide supportive services.

The overall effect of the National Education Goals and related legislation is to persuade SEAs and LEAs through authoritative means and financial incentives to make dramatic reforms in assessing, teaching, and delivering services to all students. Meeting high academic standards, achieving collaboration and coordination, and including all students are three major reform themes. Another recurring concept is that education agencies have freedom in determining their specific goals and how to meet them, provided of course that the goals and methods are generally consistent with stated policy. Despite the inclusive language of these policies, the extent to which SEAs and LEAs will actually address the needs of students with LEP and students with disabilities in their overall reform efforts remains to be seen. Lyons (1995), for example, describes an incident shortly after the passage of the IASA in which representatives of these groups were excluded from participation in rule-making related to parts of the act and questions whether the phrase "all students" really means just that. In fact, whether and how well the entire school reform movement has considered diverse groups are areas of continuing controversy (e.g., Greico Jones, 1993; Hodgkinson, 1991; Lipsky & Gartner, 1989).

History tells us that without personal advocacy, the educational programs of CLD students and students with disabilities are not likely to improve. We should, therefore, view the National Education Goals and related legislation as an opportunity to include our students in the striving toward excellence and to insist that the needs of diverse student groups be consistently considered in the formation of policy at federal, state, and local levels. Garcia (1994, 1995), in his position as Director of the Office of Bilingual Education and Minority Languages Affairs at the U.S. Department of Education, calls for educators to accept the challenge of reform by acting with commitment, resolve, and *"ganas"*; by understanding, using, and sharing the new knowledge base; by displaying leadership and collaboration; and by showing affective engagement in this new era. Whether or not we are involved in the development of formal plans to meet specific federal initiatives, we can contribute to reform efforts by examining policies and procedures at our schools and by working to lessen the gap between reality and our ideals.

DEVELOPING PLANS FOR
SCHOOL IMPROVEMENT

Throughout this text, we have debunked the search for "panaceas"—singular solutions to complex problems of assessment and instruction—in favor of more comprehensive, flexible, and futuristic problem-solving. Nowhere is the search for a panacea more futile than in the area of delivering educational services to students, where a myriad of factors, including the economic base of the community, local political support, and the individual characteristics of students and their families, play a role in the potential success or failure of the policies and models chosen. We suggest that educators can avoid the trap of looking for the panacea in their efforts to meet the National Education Goals by focusing on long-term interrelated outcomes, as in the "all-one-system" approach advocated by Hodgkinson (1985), and by operating in consideration of diverse populations, as in the "ethnic educator" approach advocated in this text. The following questions and responses are presented with these suggestions in mind as an initial inquiry into how overall school policies can facilitate the national education agenda for CLD students who are at-risk for school failure or who are receiving special education services.

1. Does the school have a formal, positive philosophy of service to CLD students with or at-risk of learning problems?

The formation of a philosophy of service to CLD students with or at-risk of learning problems implies that the educational community has actively engaged in discussions of values, theoretical approaches, and applied research related to diversity and disability issues and has formally agreed upon and committed to a particular course of action. These actions involve examining and responding to hard questions, including:

How does our community treat people of color, people who are immigrants, and people with disabilities?

How do monolingual English-speaking classroom teachers feel about facilitating bilingualism in public schools?

Do the achievement levels of the student body vary by race and/or ethnic status?

What staff and curriculum changes need to be made to enhance the learning of CLD students?

Unfortunately, our experience with most schools is that formal philosophical statements are rarely discussed or written, especially when they deal with the controversial topics of race relations, linguistic differences, or disability policy. Individual educators as well as the community at large are often afraid to go on record with particular policy decisions because of potential negative reactions from various interest groups or because of a desire to avoid accountability over the long term. So, what exists instead is a compilation of formal and informal school policies and procedures, often contrived under a crisis management mode, that may or may not be actually implemented, monitored, or address the causes behind the troubling symptoms.

A fresh opportunity for administrators to enhance instruction to diverse student groups is through the development of school improvement plans designed to meet the National Education Goals and related legislation. The process of developing such plans should take place at both the conceptual and operational levels. At the conceptual level, a series of discussions in a town meeting format, with teachers, parents, community representatives, and students present, will help to frame the major educational issues of concern to the community. Here, tough and honest conversation about issues that have historically made us uncomfortable will have to take place. In particular, the positive and negative qualities of the school climate on diversity and disability issues will need to be analyzed, including past and present institutional practices, the attitudes and knowledge of professional staff, and the historical allocation of resources to diverse student groups. The following philosophical statement is presented as a possible outcome of these extended discussions:

> *We believe that all students in the school have a right to an education that challenges them to excellence, is culturally and linguistically appropriate, is provided in safe and secure environments, and will result in long-term benefits to the individual and the community. Such education involves curriculum and instruction that reflect awareness of and respect for students' racial and ethnic backgrounds and learning differences and that address the need to develop high levels of communicative competence and achievement in the content areas. When students come from language backgrounds other than English, our preferred means of serving them is a long-term bilingual/ bicultural program in which educators are fully qualified to provide instruction. When circumstances do not permit bilingual instruction, carefully executed programs of ESL, with attention to acculturation issues, are acceptable. When students have disabilities, their right to a challenging, culturally and linguistically appropriate education in the general education environment remains intact and will be addressed in their IEPs (individualized education programs) in accordance with established special education mandates.*

At the operational level, this general philosophy of service can translate into meeting the National Education Goals if the plans for meeting each goal include specific strategies relative to CLD students and students with disabilities. Using Goal 2 as an example, the improvement plan for a high school might call for incremental increases in graduation rates for all students over the next five years. Activities to meet Goal 2 might include increasing the opportunities for vocational internships, providing parents with information on college financial assistance, and establishing an after-school and weekend homework center. If certain groups of students, such as those with learning disabilities or visual impairments or from specific language backgrounds, are found to have lower rates of graduation than other groups, activities could be adapted or added to better suit group needs. In the case of students with disabilities, devoting more resources to developing and implementing "transition" IEPs is a possible additional strategy. For CLD students, hiring school counselors who can speak the language of the home and providing them with time for home visits could enhance the strategies already in place.

2. Does the school have a system of intervention for CLD students at-risk of learning problems?

Two major categories of activities can be undertaken by school personnel to prevent learning problems prior to academic failure. The first category relates primarily to Goals 1, 6, and 8, and may be viewed as child/family preparation activities. The second category relates primarily to Goals 2 and 3 and may be viewed as prevention activities. Concerning child/family preparation activities, school personnel can work to build a community supportive of learning by conceptualizing the school as one piece of a dynamic social and educational system and then making the appropriate connections with social service, business, and community organizations as well as other educational institutions. Possibilities include adult literacy classes, workshops for parents, preschool programs, preschool health and developmental screenings, integration of park district and school activities, in-house health care, and in-house family and vocational counselors. Although school personnel may at first be uncomfortable with these activities because they move schools beyond the realm of their traditional responsibilities, the long-term benefits of assisting entire families in a community context cannot be overlooked.

Concerning prevention activities, a model designed by Garcia and Ortiz (1988) provides an excellent example to schools in the process of building or evaluating their own "fail-safe" system (see Figure 9.1). The basis of the model is the establishment of Teacher Assistant Teams (TATs) (Chalfant & Pysh, 1981), comprised of classroom teachers elected by their peers, that engage in immediate problem-solving activities to help students and teachers.

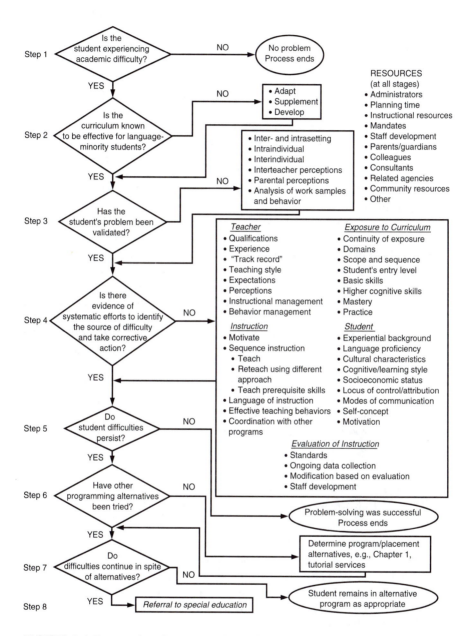

FIGURE 9.1 Preventing Inappropriate Placements of Language-Minority Students in Special Education: A Prereferral Model

From "Preventing Inappropriate Referrals of Language-Minority Students to Special Education" by S. B. Garcia and A. A. Ortiz, 1988 (June), *Focus*, p. 3.

The TAT differs from a typical special education prereferral team because it does not contain special education personnel and operates before any referral to special education is made. The TAT process reduces the number of CLD students inappropriately referred to special education by having general educators address learning and behavioral difficulties that may be caused by reasons other than disability, including poor choice of curriculum, inaccurate teacher perceptions, and inexperience of the student. Using an ecobehavioral approach, the model focuses on changing aspects of the environment to better suit the needs of CLD students. The common problem of blaming the student for failure is avoided while preventive actions are taken to help students succeed. Such a model may be conceptualized as the prevention component of a school's overall evaluation plan. Problems may be discovered at the system level or at the individual level. In some schools, large numbers of CLD students may be achieving at low levels because the standard curriculum provides insufficient time for students to develop their language skills, because the faculty lack qualifications related to teaching in CLD classrooms, or because the assessment measures used do not accurately reflect academic gains. In other cases, TATs may discover problems specific to individuals. Certain teachers may inaccurately represent the problems of students based on their own prejudices, may not take the time to evaluate for prerequisite skills, or may have poor skills in managing classroom behavior. Certain students may lack academic experience, be preoccupied with problems at home, or have learning styles at odds with the instructional modes used in the classroom. At both levels, intervention strategies are attempted to produce a better fit between the learning environment and the students, thereby decreasing the potential for failure.

3. Does the school plan instruction for CLD students with or at-risk of learning problems based on "best practice"?

Reaching high standards for all students requires that educators engage in instructional "best practice," an umbrella term used to refer to procedures that have been demonstrated to be effective in applied settings and to strategies based on current theoretical assumptions and philosophical orientations. Best practices are not infallible over time or across all instructional situations, but they do provide a framework for taking reasonable actions. Serving CLD students with or at-risk of learning problems requires educators to blend best practices from the fields of multicultural, bilingual/ESL, and special education and integrate them with current practices in the general education classroom. While best practices can be specific to subject areas like math or science and to disability areas like visual or hearing impairments, a number of general principles may be used as beginning criteria for self-evaluation. In multicultural education, best practice includes modifying the curriculum across subject areas to address issues including understanding of racism and prejudice, acceptance of differences, and the histories and contributions of various CLD groups; involving students in activities such as role-playing and decision-making, where they must examine their values about human difference; and teaching students to communicate effectively across cultures. In bilingual education, best practice includes using L1 (first language) as the base for building competence in L2 (second language), incorporating a whole language approach to teaching, promoting critical thinking skills, setting high standards for academic achievement, and developing bicultural skills. In special education, best practice includes planning instruction based on long-term career and life goals, providing peer role models for learning and behavior, promoting collaborative learning experiences, and adapting the typical curriculum based on individual needs. The willingness of educators to keep abreast of best practices and to implement changes that will keep the school current is an essential component of any serious school improvement effort. The National Education Goals and related legislation speak to the importance of professional development as a primary means by which high academic standards can be reached and maintained.

How to combine our knowledge of best practice with what is best for the individual student is especially important when learning problems are apparent. Cloud (1990) suggests that we make instructional decisions in these cases only after considering the characteristics of the student and the environment against two general categories of factors: (1) service delivery factors, including the philosophy of the school, staff expertise, and fiscal/logistical constraints; and (2) support factors, including the potential for reinforcement of skills at home and at school. Although Cloud's model is specific to making decisions about ESL instruction for students with disabilities, the concept may be expanded to consider instruction in L1 and L2 and to include students at-risk. The following are examples of characteristics that should be discussed prior to making service delivery, curriculum, and instructional choices on the IEP or as part of a prevention plan for students at-risk:

- *Stage of language development:* At what stage of language proficiency, oral and written, is the student in L1 and L2? What impact have past educational experiences had on language development? Will the environment facilitate further development?
- *Language skills:* What are the particular strengths and weaknesses of the student in oral and written L1 and L2 skills? What curriculum materials and instructional expertise are available to meet the student's needs? What skills are the parents able to work on at home?
- *Disability/at-risk status:* What impact does the student's specific disability or at-risk circumstances have on the acquisition of language skills in L1

and L2 and on other academic skills? Does the teacher have an adequate knowledge base to provide effective services? Does the school have access to community supports?

- *Age:* What impact does the student's age have on the ability to acquire L1 and L2 and to achieve in content areas? Is there a discrepancy between a child's age and emotional maturity? Is the curriculum developmentally appropriate?
- *Needs of the student:* What are the short-term and long-term needs of the student in academic, vocational, and community life? What are the needs of the student in relation to other students in the environment?
- *Amount of integration:* How much time will be spent in L1 and L2 environments? Will the student be able to interact with students who have various levels of ability?
- *Personal qualities:* How might the student's personality, learning style, and interests influence the acquisition of L1 and L2, achievement in content areas, and social/emotional growth? How might personal qualities of the student's peers and teacher influence learning?

4. Does the school have policies that protect the rights of CLD students in the multidisciplinary evaluation and staffing process?

There is less opportunity for error in the special education process if students are perceived first as members of a culturally and linguistically diverse school community with rights to an appropriate school program and then as students who may need specialized assistance within those programs as a result of a disability. A comprehensive prereferral system such as the one shown in Figure 9.1 should work to decrease the number of CLD students inappropriately referred for special education evaluations. There is still a need, however, to verify that genuine disabilities exist and that issues of language and culture are considered throughout the entire special education process. In addition, there is a need to verify that students with disabilities have equitable opportunities to achieve and are not left out of school improvement initiatives. Using the Individuals with Disabilities Education Act (1990) (IDEA) as the basis for protecting the rights of CLD students, educators should evaluate their policies relative to prereferral intervention, selection of the multidisciplinary evaluation and IEP teams, selection of evaluation procedures, design of the IEP, and involvement of parents:

- *Prereferral intervention:* Has prereferral intervention taken place? Have the strategies used taken differences of language and culture into consideration? What do the results of the interventions tell us about the instructional environment and the learning and behavior of the student?

- *Selection of the multidisciplinary teams:* Do members of the team possess the language skills and cultural expertise to communicate effectively with the student and family? Can members of the team represent the best interests of the student across issues of general, bilingual, and special education and across issues of home and community? Do members of the team have adequate knowledge and experience to make decisions about the lives of CLD students?
- *Selection of evaluation procedures:* Does the assessment protocol involve a combination of standardized, norm-referenced measures in addition to measures such as observation, analysis of work samples, dynamic assessment strategies, and curriculum-based assessment? Is the language proficiency of the student examined for skills in basic interpersonal communication and cognitive/academic language proficiency? Do the measures selected discriminate against the student on the basis of language, culture, or suspected disability?
- *Design of the IEP:* How will the language and cultural needs of students be addressed in the special education services provided? Do the IEP forms specify the language to be used during instruction and who will deliver the instruction? What opportunities will the student have to interact with members of her language and cultural peer group? How will the IEP facilitate meeting the goals set by the school for all students?
- *Involvement of parents:* How well do the parents understand the nature of disability and the special education services provided in this country? Is the input of the parents extensively solicited, including their perceptions of the child's functioning, their goals for the child, and their concerns about her educational program? Are there opportunities for the parents to consult with outside advocates?

5. Does the school have models for providing instruction in inclusive settings?

There are a number of models that schools may use to deliver services to CLD students with or at-risk of learning problems without removing them from the general education environment. We should remember, however, that the selection of a service delivery model depends upon the individual needs of students and not upon the organizational structure that the school happens to have in place. For example, it is not acceptable for a CLD student to receive pull-out learning disability services because that is the only type of delivery system available in the school if the student would clearly benefit from remaining in the bilingual classroom with direct and/or consultative service by the learning disabilities teacher. Schools may have one primary model in place for delivering services, such as full inclusion, but create variations to that model as needed. Schools may also have several models in place simultaneously, such as resource room services in addition to team-teaching and/or consultative services, each of which can be utilized with only minor adjustments to fit individual needs.

The following examples describe several full-inclusion models for students with disabilities who also require specialized language services:

Model 1: Team Teaching in the Bilingual Classroom

In the team-teaching model, two fully certified teachers, one a bilingual teacher and one a bilingual special education teacher, work together in the general education classroom, providing services to bilingual students with and without disabilities. In addition to the obvious benefits of a smaller teacher-student ratio, this option is especially attractive when there is a sufficient number of students with disabilities and/or students at-risk who are at or near the same grade level. For example, a first- and second-grade bilingual classroom might have a total of thirty students, including seven students with identified disabilities and seven others who are below grade levels in their academic progress. This option is also attractive when students with severe disabilities are included in the classroom because of the full-time special education support. Organizational approaches in such a classroom include: (1) a model in which the bilingual teacher presents the typical curriculum while the bilingual special education teacher adapts instruction to students with disabilities and provides intensive instruction to students at-risk; and (2) a model in which the two teachers trade roles and responsibilities according to subject matter and/or student groupings.

Model 2: Consultative Special Education Services to the Bilingual Classroom Teacher

In the consultative model, the bilingual teacher provides an adapted program of instruction to students with disabilities in the general education classroom with the consultative support of the special education teacher, who may be bilingual or monolingual. The role of the special education teacher is not to provide direct instruction but to monitor students' progress and assist the bilingual teacher in various aspects of the curriculum, including revising grading procedures, adaptating test taking, prioritizing instructional goals, and developing specialized instructional strategies. The special education teacher may also consult with the bilingual teacher about students at-risk. Bilingual teacher assistants may be utilized to provide individual instruction as needed. This model is especially feasible in situations where students have mild disabilities and/or in classrooms where the number of total students is small.

Model 3: Direct Service in the Bilingual Classroom

In this direct service model, bilingual special education teachers provide direct instruction to students with disabilities on a regular part-time basis in the general education bilingual classroom. These teachers, who have been assigned to specific bilingual classrooms or to specific students with disabilities across the bilingual program, travel from room to room, providing individual or small-group instruction to students at selected times and/or for specific academic areas. For example, a special education teacher with three students with learning disabilities in one classroom may join that class daily for math and reading instruction, while he may visit a student with behavior disorders in another classroom at the beginning, middle, and end of the day to monitor her behavior management program. This model also allows for students at-risk to be served by the special education teacher and may include instructional roles for bilingual teacher assistants.

Model 4: Direct Service in the English-Only Classroom

In one variation of this direct service model, special education teachers who are bilingual or who have expertise in ESL provide service to students with disabilities in general education English-only classrooms. In another variation of this model, special education teachers and bilingual or ESL teachers provide service to students with disabilities in general education English-only classrooms. In both cases, teachers travel from setting to setting, are highly engaged in collaborative planning with the classroom teacher, and may also provide services to students at-risk. This model may be considered for use in schools where the small number of CLD students inhibits the establishment of independent bilingual and ESL programs. This model may also be considered for students who have developed sufficient academic proficiency in English to be successful in an English-only setting. Bilingual or monolingual teacher assistants may be used to provide instructional support in both variations.

6. Does the school have a program to involve the parents of CLD students with or at-risk of learning problems?

Ideal programs for families of CLD students with or at-risk of learning problems result in parent empowerment. Although the word "empowerment" has suffered from overuse in the current literature, its meaning conveys precisely the type of outcome that programs should achieve: the enhanced ability of parents to assume authority and control over issues related to their children's education. Many of us fear parent empowerment because it lessens the authority we wield as professionals. We cannot work with parents in a true partnership, however, unless power is equally distributed and respect is mutual. According to a review by Harry (1992, p. 100), CLD parents whose children receive special education services differ from their counterparts in the traditional mainstream by displaying less involvement in the schools, less awareness of the special education process, a heightened sense of isolation and helplessness, lower self-confidence in interactions with school professionals, greater life stresses, greater need for supports such as transportation and child care, culturally based attitudes of noninterference with school issues, and the implicit or explicit discouragement of parent participation in the special education process. These findings tell us that successful empowerment programs must address the needs of both parents and educators. Program content should be evaluated in terms of how well it promotes parental understanding of disability and involvement in the school and professional knowledge of and sensitivity to cultural issues.

Using "involvement" rather than "training" as the operative term in program planning, school personnel should consider the following components as part of the process toward empowerment: (1) inclusion of CLD parents with children in bilingual and in special education programs on existing parent advisory groups; (2) establishment of new parent advisory groups on bilingual special education issues; (3) employment of professional and paraprofessional staff who have bilingual and bicultural skills; (4) staff development on cross-cultural communication skills and the impact of cultural concepts of disability on the special education process; (5) establishment of family literacy programs; and (6) establishment of programs in which parents assist parents in becoming critical consumers of services and advocates for their children.

7. Does the school have a plan for personnel development?

Schools typically face two problems related to personnel and meeting the needs of CLD students with disabilities. One problem is a shortage of educators with appropriate bilingual abilities or ESL training in addition to expertise in special education. The second problem involves the lack of knowledge and negative attitudes about cultural diversity and disability among currently employed staff. Both issues involve long-term planning and the support of financial and human resources.

Addressing the shortage issue requires knowledge of the population demographics of the state or community in which the school is located in addition to knowledge of state certification requirements and the availability of appropriate course work at the university level. In states where large populations of same-language groups reside, there are several options to pursue. High school graduates, particularly those working as teaching assistants, may be recruited for teacher preparation programs in special education at the bachelor's level, while college graduates with degrees in areas other than teaching may be recruited for teacher certification programs at the master's level. Bilingual teachers who are already certified and employed may also be recruited for programs offering additional certification and/or advanced degrees. These options are not as feasible, however, when language groups are small. In these cases, preparing special educators in techniques of ESL is a more viable option. All of these options require that schools collaborate with universities to provide the course work and that financial support is available from the district or from an outside source such as a community grant. This process is facilitated if the state has certification requirements for bilingual special educators. Illinois, for example, provides such a vehicle with a state "approval" in bilingual special education, which may be obtained by teachers and support staff with a minimal amount of course work. Limited scholarship funds are available through the state on a yearly basis, and universities are beginning to establish related programs.

Addressing the lack of knowledge and poor attitudes about diversity issues in the school system requires a comprehensive staff development plan and individuals who can provide the needed expertise. For schools that have not developed a philosophy of service delivery to CLD students with disabilities, this plan should begin with an intensive exploration of values and the establishment of initial policy at a system level in addition to, and preferably prior to, development activities related to specific content areas or to changes in staff roles and responsibilities. Administrators beginning at this step may need to assemble a team of individuals who can be called upon at different stages in the process. Experts on multicultural education may be best at dealing with attitude changes, while experts on assessment and instruction may provide technical assistance. In some cases, administrators may only need to provide staff with the time and support necessary to collaborate in-house. SEAs may also provide support by supplying the locations of model programs, by responding to requests for out-of-state experts, or, as suggested in the objectives of Goal 8, by establishing formal plans with LEAs for recruitment, retention, and professional development activities.

8. Does the school engage in continuous program evaluation?

If services to CLD students with or at-risk of learning problems are to improve and maintain a high level of quality, four critical questions must be continuously addressed by school evaluation programs: Are CLD students equitably represented in special education programs? Are CLD students, including those with disabilities, exiting the school program with well-developed skills in L1, L2, and other academic areas? Are the families of

CLD students satisfied with school services, including special education services? Are CLD students, including those with disabilities, able to obtain employment and adjust to community expectations upon graduation and throughout their lives? In our fast-paced society, however, keeping up with day-to-day school affairs is often so demanding that we neglect these serious issues and the related long-term planning necessary for successful outcomes. Braden and Fradd (1987) contend that successful outcomes for CLD students are more likely when educators adopt a proactive school organization model in which potential sources of difficulty are identified and addressed in advance. These authors show how a basic four-step cyclical process can be utilized when administrators, school staff, and the community work collaboratively with the needs of CLD students in mind. The process requires collaborators to (1) collect data; (2) hypothesize and prioritize needs; (3) develop interventions; and (4) evaluate outcomes.

- *Collect data:* The first step in the model is the collection of descriptive data, which Braden and Fradd (1987) refer to as the building blocks of the proactive educational process. This descriptive data collection process has the potential for answering some of the basic questions related to meeting the National Education Goals, including:
  —What are the demographic characteristics of students and families being served by the school?
  —What are the academic strengths and weaknesses of various student groups?
  —What are the value systems of families served by the school?
  —What does the community think about the effectiveness of the school?
  —What are its attendance and graduation rates?
  —What connections has the school made with business and community agencies?

- *Hypothesize and prioritize needs:* The second step is to use these data to formulate priorities for intervention. Priorities should always be stated in terms of the intrinsic needs of students so that there is a direct match between needs and interventions and so as not to be limited by school politics (e.g., a principal not wanting to disagree with a powerful teacher) or by organizational structures (e.g., a student being considered for special education because no supportive services for students at-risk exist). If descriptive data show a fundamental lack of respect by teachers for the cultural mores of the community, for example, the scheduling of required professional development activities will take precedence over other areas of need, even though this move may be unpopular among the staff.

- *Develop interventions:* The third step calls for the collaborative development of interventions that may be directed to the entire student body, to a specific population of students, or to school personnel. This collaboration may be conducted between various community agencies and the school, schools within the district, administrators and students, and administrators and staff. For example, the CLD community that the school serves or potential employers of students in the district may offer viable suggestions and resources for reducing the dropout rate, involving parents, and increasing school safety, especially for students with disabilities, that administrators might not otherwise consider.

- *Evaluate outcomes:* The fourth step is an evaluation of outcomes that flows back to the first step of data collection. This continuous process of self-monitoring and self-adjustment is the essence of the proactive approach. When outcomes are less than adequate, Braden and Fradd (1987) suggest that "what if" questions, rather than "who's to blame" questions, be asked so that the school remains engaged in the problem-solving process. In essence, the quality of services that we provide to CLD students depends on our willingness and ability to engage in critical self-examination. Being able to complete the feedback loop, even when the input "smarts," is essential to the long-term evaluation process.

In summary, this chapter has offered a framework for analyzing our actions and progress in support of diverse student groups against the background of national efforts to improve schools for all students. This chapter has also stressed the concept of providing supportive services to CLD students with learning problems, whether or not they have disabilities, in the context of the general education system. We believe that the success of CLD students with or at-risk of learning problems is highly dependent on our ability to be strong advocates, to work on preventing potential situations for school failure, and to help establish the base for a student-centered, all-one-system approach. Now is the opportunity to make dramatic changes in our schools that will positively affect the quality of our students' lives. We may make mistakes, as we have done in other educational ventures. Nevertheless, we will accept the responsibility and attempt to do the right things.

REFERENCES

Bilingual Education Act of 1994 (Title VII of Improving America's Schools Act, P.L. 103-382), 108 Stat. 3716.

Braden, J. P., & Fradd, S. H. (1987). Proactive school organization: Identifying and meeting special population needs. In S. H. Fradd & W. J. Tikunoff (Eds.), *Bilingual education and bilingual special education* (pp. 211–230). Boston: College Hill.

Chalfant, J. C., & Pysh, M. V. (1981, November). Teacher assistance teams—A model for within-building problem solving. *Counterpoint*, pp. 16–21.

Cloud, N. (1990). Planning and implementing English as a second language program. In A. L. Carrequillo & R. E. Baecher (Eds.), *Teaching the bilingual special education student* (pp. 106–131). New Jersey: Ablex.

Garcia, E. E. (1994). Education 2000 and beyond: The challenge of our culturally diverse students. In *The National Education Goals: Implications for counselors and teachers of language-minority students.* pp. 7–14. Des Plaines, IL: InterAmerica Midwest Multifunctional Resource Center.

Garcia, E. E. (1995). Letter from OBEMLA. *NABE News, 18*(4), 7–8.

Garcia, S. B., & Ortiz, A. A. (1988, June). Preventing inappropriate referrals of language-minority students to special education. *Focus,* pp. 1–12.

Goals 2000: Educate America Act of 1994, P.L. 103-227, 108 Stat. 125.

Greico Jones, T. (1993). The connection between urban school reform and urban student populations: How are urban reform efforts addressing the needs of language-minority students? *The Journal of Educational Issues for Language-Minority Students, 12,* 61–75.

Harry, B. (1992). *Cultural diversity, families, and the special education system.* New York: Teachers College Press.

Helping Disadvantaged Children Meet High Standards Act of 1994 (Title I of Improving America's School Act, P.L. 103-382), 108 Stat. 3519.

Hodgkinson, H. (1985). *All one system.* Washington, DC: Institute for Educational Leadership.

Hodgkinson, H. (1991). Reform vs. reality. *Phi Delta Kappan, 73,* 8–16.

Improving America's Schools Act of 1994, P.L. 103–382, 108 Stat. 3518.

Individuals with Disabilities Education Act of 1990, P.L. 101–467, 104 Stat. 1103.

Lipsky, D. K., & Gartner, A. (1989). *Beyond separate education.* Baltimore: Paul H. Brooks.

Lyons, J. J. (1995). The view from Washington. *NABE News, 18*(4), 5–6.

10

A DIALOGUE ON FUTURISTIC VIEWS IN BILINGUAL SPECIAL EDUCATION

In this last chapter, we want to present a dialogue on our futuristic views on the assessment and instruction of culturally and linguistically diverse (CLD) students, with a particular emphasis on the bilingual/multicultural and bilingual special education perspectives. The three of us will engage in a panel discussion of our perceptions, beliefs, ideas, and visions of the major theoretical, educational, and methodological problems and applied dilemmas affecting educators serving CLD students that have been reviewed throughout the book. It is our intent to promote in the reader a realization of the importance of assuming an advocacy role when assessing, placing, and instructing CLD students. Thus, this dialogue will give closure to the ideas proposed in this book, and at the same time will open a new vision and offer a new resolution of contemporary issues affecting the field of the assessment and instruction of CLD students.

Our dialogue will take the form of a round-table discussion of five questions that synthesize the dilemmas discussed in this book:

1. What are some of the most serious current problems that we are facing when assessing and instructing CLD students?
2. What research provides evidence that can help us assess more appropriately CLD students?
3. What recommended instructional practices, based on this research, can we suggest for CLD students?

4. How has the situation of assessing CLD students changed in the last twenty to thirty years, and what changes can we expect in the next twenty to thirty years?

5. What is our vision for the future of the fields of bilingual/multicultural education and bilingual special education?

We want to give closure to our book by opening these questions because, as pointed out in the vision statement, the state of the fields of bilingual/ multicultural education and bilingual special education can be enlightened by exploring openly new ideas stemming from the "ethnic educator" paradigm. Then, we believe that panaceas, the "magic" solutions for improving the assessment and instruction of CLD students, do not exist, because tests and educational programs are not the most important tools for assessment and instruction. Rather, we believe that the most important tools for developing a valid and reliable assessment and diagnostic process and appropriate educational programs are the attitudes, values, beliefs, and personal cultural and linguistic identities of the evaluators and educators working with CLD students.

Thus, we are calling for a shift of paradigms from a focus on internal processes in the medical model to a focus on the interaction between internal and external developmental factors endorsed by the "ethnic educator" model, from the measurement of products and knowledge acquired to the assessment of processes of thinking and potential for learning, from quantitative to qualitative assessment approaches that merge assessment with instruction, and in general from the devaluation of the experience of bilingual/bicultural students to the endorsement of a multicultural/bilingual education philosophy that values the richness of cultural diversity.

In summary, in this last chapter we want to stimulate our readers to think creatively and critically about their professional needs, problems encountered in their daily professional activities with CLD students, the status quo of the institutional realities in which they work, and ways in which they can develop a commitment for accepting the challenge of becoming mentors and advocates for CLD students. In general we want our dialogue in this last chapter to serve as a support group for our readers, because all of us, as educators, are facing the same challenges represented by the five questions discussed here. Thus, we have chosen to end our book by opening questions and not pretending to provide answers for every challenge that professionals serving CLD students are facing today, because we believe that the process of thinking critically about our own intrinsic and idiosyncratic needs is the most important one. Throughout the book we have tried to use research findings to shed some light on our current assessment and instructional practices with CLD students. However, we also have acknowledged that professionals have the responsibility to evaluate critically their attitudes, values, and beliefs toward the assessment and instruction of CLD students for a genuine change in practice to occur. Finally, we pose this challenge because we believe it is possible for educators to undergo this attitudinal change—¡¡Sí, se puede!! (Yes, we can make it!!). Thus, we hope that the five questions below offer educators the opportunity to think critically with us about our vision for the future.

1. What are some of the most serious current problems that we are facing when assessing and instructing CLD students?

Dr. Virginia Gonzalez: I think that until now we educators have been looking for the panacea, the magic valid and reliable instrument that could solve what is still considered to be the most serious psychometric problem: the lack of valid and reliable instruments for accurately measuring abilities and potential in CLD students. This idea about the presence of external solutions, such as the panacea, for what was supposed to be the most serious problem, is a misconception that prevents us from solving this problem.

I think that the *most important tool for assessment is our own personality.* Thus, I think that the core of the assessment problem is formed by the effect of educators' attitudes toward minority languages and cultures, and their knowledge regarding the influence of living in a bilingual and bicultural environment on the diagnosis of minority children's cognitive, linguistic, and socioemotional development. By changing our conceptualization of the problem from an emphasis on the internal learning problems of CLD students to the external problems of institutions, such as the school system, and by changing educators' attitudes and lack of knowledge regarding CLD students' backgrounds, we can generate new solutions and real changes.

Moreover, by considering the influence of educators' attitudes and knowledge on the assessment and instruction of CLD students as central to the issue, we make educators responsible for the social consequences of their educational decisions regarding CLD students. Thus, a change in our view of the problem also challenges educators to become advocates, committed mentors, and role models for CLD students.

Dr. Thomas D. Yawkey: I think we currently have the technology for both qualitative monitoring and quantitative assessment. In addition, we currently understand the "loop" between assessment and instruction of CLD students. Here, understanding means having taken courses in methods and at the minimum having been exposed to the interactive concepts of assessing and instructing. Given that we have the technology and at least exposure at some degree to meaningful understanding of the interrelations between assessment and instruction, we as professionals still need practice in apply-

ing these concepts, especially with CLD students. Perhaps we need courses
that directly focus on these topics. Perhaps we need additional practice with
tailored experiences in applying these concepts with CLD students. These
practice might be part of in-service staff development programs of local educational agencies. These courses and/or practice might be part of a partnership between an institution of higher education and a local education agency.
Regardless of the delivery system or multiple delivery systems used to
implement these concepts practically, we professionals must take the step of
utilizing honestly, genuinely, and professionally the interrelations between
assessment and instruction and focusing them on the CLD students.

Dr. Rita Brusca-Vega: In terms of practicing good assessment and instruction
at the local school level, one major obstacle is educators' lack of knowledge
about the relationship of language and culture to learning. I believe that
while most educators want to provide the best possible programs for CLD
students, their attitudes and behavior have been limited by inadequate
attention to issues of human diversity in their general educational background and in their teacher preparation programs. This situation creates a
self-defeating pattern in which uninformed educators make poor decisions
about policies and procedures for CLD students that then become the model
for new uninformed educators entering the system. Since old habits are hard
to break, even well-informed educators who put themselves in advocacy
roles have difficulty enacting change.

   If we go beyond local schools and examine assessment and instruction
at the state and district levels, the greatest obstacle we face is the lack of policy and enforcement regarding the adequate delivery of services to CLD students. Discussing the relative merits of particular strategies for assessment
and instruction seems almost esoteric when in many districts across the
country the needs of these students are simply ignored. Legal battles may
have to be waged with districts in order to put delivery systems in place
before the specific content of instructional services can be addressed.

   I also believe that Local Education Agencies (LEAs) and State Education
Agencies (SEAs) are hampered in the steps they do take to provide improved
assessment and instruction to CLD students and students with disabilities
because we lack a student-centered, inclusive, and "all-one-system" philosophy of service delivery. We use our assessment data to label and segregate
rather than to prevent learning problems and guide instruction in the typical
setting of the student. We also often work at cross-purposes, representing
our various isolated disciplines to the detriment of what is best for the student and his or her family over the long run. We would have an easier time
implementing what we acknowledge to be best practices in the field if we
adopted a more holistic educational approach.

Dr. Gonzalez: As Dr. Brusca-Vega said, the major battle that practitioners "in
the trenches" need to overcome when trying to assume advocacy roles is the

absence of supporting policy for introducing change in the misdiagnosis and inappropriate education that do a disservice to CLD students. She also mentioned the need to break the cycle of misinformation and lack of knowledge that leads to the myths that still exist in teacher and other professional preparation programs in higher education. This problem that we are facing currently when assessing and instructing CLD students is related to the fact that teacher and other professional programs still endorse mainstream theories. For instance, most school psychologists-to-be, who will be evaluating CLD students, are trained only in mainstream intelligence and developmental theories and their corresponding assessment models and standardized tests, which discriminate against CLD students. These mainstream theories explain external cultural and linguistic differences as if they are genetically innate and thus racially dysfunctional. Thus, if we want to change the teacher and other professional education programs, we need to create our own ethnic developmental theories that can explain the differences found in children who grow up in more complex bilingual/multilingual and bicultural/multicultural environments.

Moreover, educators also need to be knowledgeable about philosophical assumptions and theories underlying different assessment models. In this manner, educators can understand that following standardized administration and scoring procedures does not assure an "objective" assessment with the resulting avoidance of personal responsibility and "subjective" biases. On the contrary, assuming that the use of standardized instruments makes the assessment of CLD students an "objective" process is the origin of discriminatory procedures in education.

Dr. Yawkey: These are excellent points. Spending a great deal of time in schools in staff development, we must move beyond the sacredness of the intelligence quotient (IQ). We as professionals are still very heavily influenced by what was once—that is, by how we were taught and how we were thought to learn. Jumping over the IQ hurdle and breaking the mold of the past teaching and learning ideas that we hold internally are going to take time! In fact, the more I think about us knowing the philosophies and assumptions of various theories of learning and development, the more I am convinced that this approach to teacher development may help break the IQ and "teach-as-we-have-been-taught" molds. However, we do have some distance to travel, or retravel, in order to construct and reconstruct our old conceptualizations, as the case may be. In returning to the philosophies of learning as the basis for teaching and assessing, we begin to use a pluralistic approach to the learning and growth of CLD students. This pluralistic approach, I am hoping, will replace our current eclectic approach of intuitively doing what is necessary at the time or doing whatever works. The notion of "doing whatever works" is professionally irritating, because "whatever works" is based on individual experiences that are changeable moment to moment and on intuition. Accordingly, "whatever works" bypasses all of the philosophies of development and much needed pluralism.

2. What research provides evidence that can help us more appropriately assess CLD students?

Dr. Gonzalez: We have learned several lessons from research regarding the best assessment practices with CLD students. First, we have learned that we need to use a battery of instruments that includes quantitative and qualitative methods that assess verbal and nonverbal performance. Second, this assessment battery needs to include appropriate linguistic and cultural contents and problem-solving novel tasks. Third, this battery needs to differentiate potential for learning from acquired knowledge. Fourth, it must reflect performance across different real-life and academic contexts, including different informants in the real world (e.g., parents, siblings, peers, teachers) and different testing situations (e.g., evaluators with different cultural and linguistic backgrounds and those who defend different schools of thought and assessment models). Finally, the last but not least important characteristic of this assessment battery is to encompass different developmental stages and domains (i.e., physical, motor, perceptual, cognitive, linguistic, emotional, and social). Thus, we have learned that the assessment of CLD students needs to be a multidimensional problem-solving process that uses collaborative and consultation models between interdisciplinary professionals and the community. Moreover, we have also learned that the assessment process needs to be linked with instruction by including qualitative and performance instruments that give the classroom teacher the role of an informant and evaluator of CLD students.

Dr. Brusca-Vega: I find the most exciting research on assessment to be from descriptive studies in which the behavior of students is documented across various natural environments. Then, this evidence is evaluated qualitatively and/or quantitatively in terms of the relationship between adequacy of performance and characteristics of the particular setting. One remarkable study conducted along these lines, by Commins and Miramontes (1989), examined the perceived and actual linguistic competence of CLD students' home and school settings. The findings not only showed how teachers can be misled about student performance because of limiting characteristics of the instructional environment but also provided a rich look at the capabilities of students in real-life situations. This type of ecobehavioral approach to assessment has a number of implications for diagnosis and instruction, including differentiating perceived from actual weaknesses or disabilities, establishing criteria for performance in particular settings or for particular tasks, and determining how to maximize the goodness of fit between students and their environments. The approach is especially appropriate for CLD students because their learning environments are often at odds with their language and cultural characteristics.

Dr. Yawkey: I think that what we are saying is that many roads are better than one road of quantitative assessment. I remember so clearly that not so long ago one point on a single quantitative battery separated those who passed from those who flunked, or those who were labeled "gifted" from those who were "average," or those who were "smart" from those who were "stupid," or those who were in special education from those who were in regular education. Think of the damage to self-esteem and the stigmatization process that were created by one single quantitative point criterion. Using more assessment instruments than one and blending qualitative with quantitative instrumentation are viable and highly recommended for our CLD students for several reasons. First, the results of multiple assessments provide a more accurate picture of the student. "Accurate picture" here means more reliable as well as monitoring the whole student, and not just her written knowledge of nouns, verbs, and so forth. Written knowledge of nouns, for example, is just one small skill within the infinite set of concepts comprising the intellectual, emotional, social, and physical being we call the student.

Second, and from the perspective of a program's impact on a student, multiple measurements provide tremendous insight into whether the program has validity. From a P.I.A.G.E.T. Program perspective, we monitor formatively and summatively and with both qualitative (e.g., interview and observation) and quantitative (e.g., Peabody Picture Vocabulary Test) instruments. The number of assessments we gather monthly on the P.I.A.G.E.T. student is quite substantial. These data then are viewed from an activities' perspective—that is, they suggest this activity or learning center or that experience. Within P.I.A.G.E.T. Programs as well as any other good bilingual program, multiple assessments are used. Here, multiple assessments are better for our CLD students.

3. What recommended instructional practices, based on this research, can we suggest for CLD students?

Dr. Gonzalez: Evidence derived from research supports developmental bilingual programs in which both languages and cultures are used as methods for instruction. Moreover, we have come to realize that the future citizens of the world need to be multilingual and multicultural in order to promote mutual understanding, peaceful relationships, and prosperity at the international level.

We also have come to understand that development is a holistic process in which valuing CLD students' culture and language also stimulates assertiveness, intrinsic motivation for learning, a higher self-esteem and self-concept, a secure identity, and higher achievement and performance levels in academia. By using a more holistic view of instruction, we have also realized the tremendous impact of educators' attitudes on the achievement and performance levels of CLD students. Now, we are trying to move away from the label of "difficult-to-teach" children, which focuses on internal learning problems, and instead to assume an advocacy role and responsibility for external factors that can be modified by educators.

Evidence from research has also shed light on our understanding of the value of collaborative learning models, such as peer tutoring and heterogeneous grouping, for increasing developmental growth and learning in CLD students. Our knowledge base of learning styles and individual differences has also increased, leading us to become aware of the danger of stereotyping children from minority groups if we forget about individuality in the developmental process of CLD students.

Research results also support the importance of stimulating CLD students to develop critical thinking skills and problem-solving abilities, and to generate creative ideas and new knowledge in order to be successful in our contemporary technological society. We have come to realize that we need to move away from the basic curriculum that stimulates primarily rote memorization of information and to advocate for a thinking curriculum that develops in CLD students the inquisitive mind and intrinsic motivation for learning they need to become responsible and productive adults who can make decisions within a democratic society and take a stand when evaluating complex academic and social problems.

Dr. Yawkey: Research-based instructional practices are keys to nurturing continued development and learning of CLD students. The outcomes of using instructional practices that work with CLD students include learning at their potential, improved self-esteem, and ultimately bilingualism—that is, proficiency in English as well as other languages. Several examples of these instructional practices bounce into mind. Within P.I.A.G.E.T. Programs, we stress, train for, and monitor classroom- and family-based program liaisons for a total of twenty-five instructional strategies. When we began the P.I.A.G.E.T. Programs in the early 1980s, we began with a set of eighty major instructional practices, which we have reduced through statistics and adult logic to twenty-five strategies for both classroom and family staff. One of our research-based instructional strategies is diagnosing the student's level of language. Here, we use levels of language in the more common, general sense of monitoring for index, symbol, and sign. Another instructional strategy is having the CLD student use elaboration or extended forms of communication in oral and written language. In native languages and English, this means the use of adjectives or name descriptors such as "the black, quick, and shiney rabbit," or "pretty, blue hat with a feather on top!" A third example of a sound instructional strategy is the use of choices. Giving the students multiple options they can handle and process at their developmental and language levels helps nurture decision-making and problem-solving. Deciding among options whose choices are honored and acted upon also leads to meeting individual needs. Professionals obtain added insight into students' learning, development, and individuality while observing them in decision-making.

Dr. Brusca-Vega: While I agree with Dr. Gonzalez and Dr. Yawkey about the potential of the methods they mention, I think that we should be careful not to overdramatize the benefits of any particular approach. Assuring that CLD students graduate from high school and college at the same rate as students from the traditional mainstream and that their academic achievement in the arts and sciences is comparable to the achievement of others is an exceedingly complex undertaking. Making curricular and instructional changes in response to research findings is certainly one part of the picture, but we must also deal with the many factors that put CLD students at-risk in the schools. In the 1960s, for example, we studied African Americans in order to "fix" their problems when we ought to have been studying the cause of those problems, namely white racism. In the 1990s, we are studying how to improve the welfare system when we should be addressing the poverty that compels people to go on welfare. Improving the quality of education for CLD students requires systemic change that reaches beyond the classroom. We need to examine how the social, political, and economic structures of American life, including our own attitudes and beliefs, contribute to the difficulties that CLD students experience in our schools and work to influence these factors.

4. How has the situation of assessing CLD students changed in the last twenty to thirty years, and what changes can we expect in the next twenty to thirty years?

Dr. Gonzalez: I consider that it is important for us educators to look back and evaluate the tremendous progress that we have made in the last twenty to thirty years in the field of assessing and instructing CLD students, and particularly in the areas of bilingual/multicultural education and bilingual special education. It is important to say that our interest and professional work developed basically by necessity, given the growing number of CLD students who were placed in bilingual or bilingual special education classrooms due to correct or incorrect diagnoses. Nowadays the challenge is still present; we are still fighting against an overrepresentation of CLD students in special education due to false positive diagnoses, and we are still fighting for the right of CLD students with genuine disabilities to receive an appropriate education. Even though the challenge is still present, research evidence and advocates of CLD students have made possible the passage of many pieces of legislation that intend to protect the rights of CLD students to receive appropriate educational services and that prevent discriminatory practices.

Another major achievement has been the large and growing number of researchers and other professionals in the field of bilingual/multicultural education and bilingual special education who come from a multidisciplinary background, and who are also members of various minority and majority groups in this country and around the world. We can say proudly that we preach for diversity in education, and that we are also a diverse group of professionals and researchers whose attitudes and behaviors merge in our advocacy role for CLD students.

We can also say proudly that the basic groundwork has been accomplished by major leaders and founders of the field of bilingual special education. However, major work is still needed in continuing our efforts to expand our horizons and solve our major dilemmas for better serving CLD students. I think that the future belongs to a new generation of "ethnic researchers" who have as their major responsibilities to merge the new interdisciplinary fields of bilingual/multicultural education and bilingual special education with more traditional fields, such as cognitive developmental psychology or psycholinguistics; and to develop unique assessment and instructional procedures that depart from the mainstream perspective, and that can do justice to the potential abilities present in our CLD students. I think that my colleagues, Dr. Brusca-Vega and Dr. Yawkey, bring a different perspective to this book that enriches our vision of the field of bilingual/multicultural education and bilingual special education, as they have personal and professional backgrounds that are different from mine.

Dr. Brusca-Vega: As a special educator who graduated college in the 1970s, I was explicitly instructed on the sanctity of multidisciplinary staffing and nondiscriminatory assessment procedures, while at the same time I was implicitly trained to honor the diagnostic decisions of school psychologists and remember my "place" as a classroom teacher in the assessment process. When I began to work in the schools, I was uncomfortable with a number of the common assessment practices but was unable to articulate these concerns in a meaningful way to myself or others. My reaction was to "turn off" to traditional, standardized measures. It is from this perspective that I make the following comments.

Over two decades ago we began to experience an explosion of standardized instruments designed to reveal complex problems of cognitive and academic functioning. Questions like, "Does it make sense to administer these instruments to certain populations?" and "How should results of testing be interpreted in light of language and cultural differences?" were disregarded in the quest for what Dr. Gonzalez has referred to as the "panacea" and in the zeal to use what was then the new technology. Since psychologists were the masters of this new technology, they wielded great influence in spite of guidelines calling for shared decision-making. In addition, since many of us were still operating under the medical model (i.e., the student as carrier of the problem), it was easy to simply label students and move along.

Currently, the manufacture, sale, and application of assessment instruments is a large industry in special education and, to an increasing extent, in the education of CLD students. What we gain for students by supporting this industry is questionable. Concerning special education, much of the information contained in psychological reports focuses on the selection of a diagnostic category while shedding almost no light on how best to instruct students in the classroom. If we are looking at a future in which the vast majority of students with disabilities will be educated in the context of general education settings, the need to verify diagnostic categories in assessments is clearly secondary to the need to obtain information about how these students learn. In the case of CLD students, much of the assessment information we collect actually works to harm them because of the way we chose to use the information, and also because typically used instruments provide superficial information on language and cognition.

In the future, I hope that assessment will be valued only in relation to how it can directly benefit instruction. I would especially like to see the deconstruction of the assessment industry in favor of an investment of our resources in instructional personnel who would operate within a diagnostic teaching model.

Dr. Yawkey: Over the past twenty to thirty years, the assessment of CLD students has changed. For me, one of the biggest changes is the realization that assessment can be done in native languages—that is, by "using a foreign language," in the lingo of the 1960s and 1970s. Relatedly, under many conditions native-language concepts can transfer into English-language concepts. Although the days of speaking only English to show that we are 100 percent American are still with us in many ways and in many areas of the United States, this maxim is lessening in quality and quantity. It is becoming acceptable to speak, read, and write other languages in addition to English. Students are even permitted to speak with each other in languages other than English in many areas.

Finally, there is an increasingly healthy regard for diverse cultures, ethnic customs, and native languages. This growing awareness of cultural and linguistic diversity and sharing diversities among communities, especially in Title VII programs, for me becomes a celebration of diversities. I often think that the growing healthy regard for diversities is contrary to previous immigrant groups who wanted to become more American by giving up their native languages, religions, and cultural customs. In addition, perhaps we have learned that acculturation works only at the expense of diminishing our self-esteem, giving up ourselves to a common criterion that we really do not fully and meaningfully understand, and throwing away a generation of immigrants' lives so their sons and daughters could "become American" and lead American lives.

In looking through the crystal ball into the future of some twenty to thirty years, we can have some challenges and interesting speculations on changes in assessing CLD students. Assuming the paradigm shifts in education have taken hold and are implemented, we should see a completely different educational system. These new paradigm shifts suggest students developing and using processes to develop products and having longer periods of time to accomplish their objectives. This should also mean that the responsibilities for students should increase given the focus on products as outcomes of committee work. The responsibilities include committee deliberation, decision-making, division of task assignments into workable units, and meeting of due dates established by the committee.

Relatedly, teacher education at preservice levels will have changed. For example, we know that in twenty to thirty years we will be living with the projected increases in immigration demographics. Instead of trying to infuse teacher education with a "diversities course," our entire teacher preparation will focus on meeting individual needs of all students—including CLD students. Said differently, all methods courses will focus (from varying content areas) on diversities and meeting CLD students' needs.

Lastly, being a very strong proponent of family involvement and development in schooling processes, I am willing to predict that in twenty to thirty years families will play significantly greater roles in education than they do now. There must be greater partnerships between family members and school professionals if we are to succeed in our efforts in educating our students. I am hoping that these partnerships will provide greater, more stringent criteria to local educational agencies, especially when these criteria concern CLD students. Like the others, I am hoping that future changes will truly benefit our CLD students.

5. What is our vision for the future of the fields of bilingual/multicultural education and bilingual special education?

Dr. Gonzalez: I really think, as Dr. Yawkey asserted earlier in our dialogue, that we have already improved the technology that has helped us to develop alternative assessments and new educational models for better assessing and instructing CLD students. "Ethnic researchers" have demonstrated in a series of studies that when we assess with appropriate cultural and linguistic content and tasks, we can prove that bilingualism can enhance intelligence, provided that both languages are used for instruction within developmental programs.

So far we have seen progress made in legislation as a result of research but that progress is still slow, because attitudes are difficult to change. Our future needs are primarily to realize that legal requirements, such as dual-language testing for CLD students, can be fulfilled for the benefit or harm of CLD students, depending on who uses what assessment procedures, in what manner, and for what purposes.

Thus, progress has already been made by changing the focus of the problem from the lack of valid and reliable instruments and theories for CLD students to the influence of the attitudes and knowledge of educators on assessment and instructional decisions for CLD students. Given the state of assessment instruments derived from different assessment models and theories, contradictory results can be obtained that can then be used by educators for defending different diagnostic, placement, and instructional decisions. Thus, this major realization that the "panacea," the magic "objective" psychometric test, does and cannot exist is a major shift in our conceptualization of how to assess and educate CLD students better.

We are already entering a new era in which our research focuses on how to change higher education to prepare future professionals serving CLD students to better educate the "new mainstream" student who comes from multiple cultural and linguistic backgrounds. In these new higher educational programs, educators will be encouraged to think and to pose significant questions, to criticize theories, and to develop their own philosophical and theoretical positions. When educators realize the power and the freedom they will gain by developing their own critical thinking skills and generating new questions of their own, they will engage in a meaningful personal search for knowledge with intrinsic motivation for forming a new attitude toward knowledge generation and thus teaching and learning processes. Moreover, teachers who can think critically can become better role models, committed mentors, and advocates for CLD students.

Then, in this new educational era of future professionals, we may realize that our quest for finding "true" answers is in vain and that we first need to discover meaningful questions. Thus, this new era in bilingual/multicultural education and in bilingual special education puts back on educators the responsibility regarding the long-lasting ethical, social, and educational consequences of decisions they make regarding CLD students. This new era also includes the community in the assessment and instructional process, calling for the participation of parents and multidisciplinary professionals in a collaborative problem-solving effort that encompasses real-world performance assessment.

Dr. Brusca-Vega: In the schools of the future, I see bilingual/multicultural education and bilingual special education as one of several specialized services that will be provided within the context of the general education setting. As developmental bilingual education and two-way bilingual programs grow in the schools, there will be increased opportunities for CLD students with disabilities to develop socially among their bilingual and monolingual peers and to be challenged academically by the general education curriculum. There will not be bilingual special education programs per se but rather educators with expertise in serving CLD students with behavior and learning difficulties. These educators will consult with classroom teachers and provide direct service to these students in general education settings. There will also be increased opportunities for CLD students to obtain services at earlier ages and have these services provided with the needs of the family in mind.

The job of educators in this scenario will be to put this approach into practice at the university and local school levels by using collaboration across disciplines. For educators to operate effectively in the schools of the future, they will need a combined knowledge base from general education, special education, and bilingual/ESL education as well as practical experience in collaborative learning and working situations. Currently, few programs offer the opportunity for such multidimensional preparation, so we have much left to accomplish.

I also believe that computer technology will do much to improve teaching and learning in the bilingual classrooms of the future, especially in the case of students with learning problems. There are now technologies on the market capable of "reading" complex printed material to the listener and "writing" the oral output of the speaker in languages including English, Spanish, and French. These technologies will most likely be introduced into the schools as a way of supporting monolingual English-speaking students with learning, visual, and physical disabilities in the general education classroom, but the capabilities of these technologies to function across languages and to enhance language learning for all students will be quickly discovered and put into use.

Dr. Yawkey: The vision for the future of the field of bilingual special education is varied. Yes, I agree that alternative, more qualitative assessments will be used. They will be utilized within more constructivist rather than behaviorist settings. Additionally, both languages are necessary requirements for the continued growth and meaningful development of our CLD students. These items and understandings are the future. Further, I am hoping that we educators will become more knowledgeable and more professional in our assessing and instructing of CLD students. Although this idea has been stated previously, we professionals need an attitude change and attitude shift toward more pluralism rather than eclecticism or behaviorism when implementing assumptions of theoretical views regarding the learning and development of our CLD students. I am also interested in preparing professionals to have greater understandings of cultures and ethnic perspectives. This will come to reality given our previous notes, comments, and justifications.

Further, we now see various forms of collaboration increasing in our local education agencies. Collaboration here means, for example, cooperative learning at the student's level and collegiality at the professional's level. This collaboration must also expand to decision-making in the learning lives of students. Here, I am referring to the tremendous current need and increased future need for multidisciplinary planning teams to review data, deliberate, and arrive at sound decisions from these various perspectives.

In summary, the three of us think that the future of bilingual special education is *now!* Let us professionals do our best daily to educate our CLD students to the best of our abilities. Best wishes and successes!

INDEX